BY STEVEN LEVITSKY AND DANIEL ZIBLATT

Tyranny of the Minority

How Democracies Die

TYRANNY OF THE MINORITY

TYRANNY OF THE MINORITY

WHY AMERICAN DEMOCRACY
REACHED THE BREAKING POINT

STEVEN LEVITSKY & DANIEL ZIBLATT

CROWN
NEW YORK

Published in the United States by Crown, an imprint of Crown Publishing Group,
a division of Penguin Random House LLC, New York.

CROWN and the Crown colophon are registered trademarks of Penguin Random House LLC.

Library of Congress Cataloging-in-Publication Data
Names: Levitsky, Steven, author. | Ziblatt, Daniel, author.
Title: Tyranny of the minority / Steven Levitsky and Daniel Ziblatt.
Description: First edition. | New York: Crown, 2023. | Includes index.
Identifiers: LCCN 2023020872 (print) | LCCN 2023020873 (ebook) |
ISBN 9780593443071 (hardcover) | ISBN 9780593728161 | ISBN 9780593443088 (ebook)
Subjects: LCSH: Republican Party (U.S. : 1854-) | Representative government and representation—
United States. | Social change—Political aspects—United States. | Democracy—Social
aspects—United States. | United States—Politics and government—21st century.
Classification: LCC JK1021 .L48 2023 (print) | LCC JK1021 (ebook) |
DDC 320.47309/05—dc23/eng/20230519
LC record available at https://lccn.loc.gov/2023020872
LC ebook record available at https://lccn.loc.gov/2023020873

Printed in the United States of America on acid-free paper

crownpublishing.com

2 4 6 8 9 7 5 3 1

First Edition

Book design by Debbie Glasserman

In memory of
Jill Kneerim and David Ziblatt

Somehow we've weathered and witnessed
A nation that isn't broken
But simply unfinished.

—Amanda Gorman, *The Hill We Climb*

CONTENTS

TYRANNY OF THE MINORITY

INTRODUCTION

O n January 5, 2021, an extraordinary event took place in Georgia. In a state where politics had long been stained by white supremacy, voters turned out in record numbers to elect their first African American senator, the Reverend Raphael Warnock, and their first Jewish American senator. Warnock was only the second Black senator to be elected in the South since Reconstruction, joining the Republican Tim Scott of South Carolina. That night, he introduced supporters to his mother, a former sharecropper, noting that "the 82-year-old hands that used to pick somebody else's cotton picked her youngest son to be a United States senator." For many, the election presaged a brighter, more democratic future. "There's a new South rising," declared LaTosha Brown, co-founder of Black Voters Matter. "It's younger, it's more diverse . . . and it's more inclusive." This was the democratic future that generations of civil rights activists had been working to build.

The next day, January 6, Americans witnessed something that seemed unimaginable: a violent insurrection, incited by the president of the United States. Four years of democratic decline had culminated in an attempted coup. The fear, confusion, and indignation that many Americans felt as they watched these events unfold echo the way people in other countries have described feeling as their own democracies unraveled. What we had just lived through—a surge in politically motivated violence; threats against election workers; efforts to make it harder for people to vote; a campaign by the president to overturn the results of an election— was democratic backsliding. The republic did not collapse between 2016 and 2021, but it became undeniably less democratic.

In a span of twenty-four hours on January 5 and January 6, 2021, the full promise and peril of American democracy were on vivid display: a glimpse of a possible multiracial democratic future, followed by an almost unthinkable assault on our constitutional system.

Multiracial democracy is hard to achieve. Few societies have ever done it. A multiracial democracy is a political system with regular, free, and fair elections in which adult citizens of all ethnic groups possess the right to vote and basic civil liberties such as freedom of speech, the press, assembly, and association. It is not enough for these rights to exist on paper: individuals of all ethnic backgrounds must enjoy equal protection of democratic and civil rights under the law. The 1964 Civil Rights Act and the 1965 Voting Rights Act finally established a legal foundation for multiracial democracy in America. But even today, we have not fully achieved it.

Access to the ballot remains unequal, for example. A 2018 survey by the Public Religion Research Institute (PRRI) found that African American and Latino citizens were three times as likely as whites to be told they lacked the proper identification to vote and twice as likely to be told—incorrectly—that their names were not listed on voter rolls. Laws barring convicted felons from voting disproportionately affect African Americans. And nonwhite citizens still do not receive equal protection under the law. Black men are more than twice as likely to be killed by police during their lifetime as are white men (even though Black victims of police killing are about half as likely to be armed); they are more likely than white men to be stopped and searched by police; and they are more likely to be arrested and convicted—with longer sentences—for similar crimes. If you have any doubt that Black citizens do not enjoy the same rights under the law as white citizens, apply the Kyle Rittenhouse test: Could a young Black man cross state lines with a semiautomatic rifle, walk unmolested by police into a protest, fire into a crowd, kill two people, and go free?

But if America is not yet a truly multiracial democracy, it is becoming one. In the half century between the passage of the Voting Rights Act and Donald Trump's rise to the presidency, American society changed in fundamental ways. A massive wave of immigration transformed what had been a predominantly white Christian society into a diverse and multiethnic one. And at the same time, the growing political, economic, legal, and cultural power of nonwhite Americans challenged—and began to level— long-entrenched racial hierarchies. Public opinion research shows that for the first time in U.S. history a majority of Americans now embrace ethnic diversity and racial equality—the two key pillars of multiracial democracy. By 2016, then, America was on the brink of a genuinely multiracial democracy—one that could serve as a model for diverse societies across the world.

But just as this new democratic experiment was beginning to take root, America experienced an authoritarian backlash so fierce that it shook the foundations of the republic, leaving our allies across the world worried about whether the country had any democratic future at all. Meaningful steps toward democratic inclusion often trigger intense—even authoritarian—reactions. But the assault on American democracy was worse than anything we anticipated in 2017, when we were writing our first book, *How Democracies Die.* We have studied violent insurrections and efforts to overturn elections all over the world, from France and Spain to Ukraine and Russia to the Philippines, Peru, and Venezuela. But we never imagined we'd see them here. Nor did we ever imagine that one of America's two major parties would turn away from democracy in the twenty-first century.

The scale of America's democratic retreat was sobering. Organizations that track the health of democracies around the world captured it in numerical terms. Freedom House's Global Freedom Index gives countries a score between 0 and 100 each year, with 100 being the most democratic. In 2015, the United States received a score of 90, which was roughly in line with countries like Canada, Italy, France, Germany, Japan, Spain, and the U.K. But after that, America's score declined steadily, reaching 83 in 2021. Not only was that score lower than every established democracy in western Europe, but it was lower than new or historically troubled democracies like Argentina, the Czech Republic, Lithuania, and Taiwan.

This was an extraordinary turn of events. According to nearly every major social scientific account of what makes democracies thrive, America should have been immune to backsliding. Scholars have discovered two virtually law-like patterns regarding modern political systems: rich democracies never die, and old democracies never die. In a well-known study, the political scientists Adam Przeworski and Fernando Limongi found that no democracy richer than Argentina in 1976—its per capita GDP, in today's dollars, was about $16,000—had ever broken down. Democracy subsequently eroded in Hungary, which had a per capita GDP of about $18,000 (in today's dollars). The United States' per capita GDP was about $63,000 in 2020—nearly *four times* that of the richest country ever to suffer a democratic breakdown. Likewise, no democracy over fifty years old has ever died. Even if we take the passage of the 1965 Voting Rights Act as the moment of America's democratization (that is, after all, when the country achieved full adult suffrage), our democracy was still over fifty when Trump ascended to the presidency. So both history and decades of social science research tell us that American democracy should have been safe. And yet it wasn't.

America is not alone, of course, in its growing diversity. Nor is it alone in experiencing an extremist right-wing reaction to that demographic shift. The number of foreign-born residents has increased in most of the world's oldest democracies, especially in western Europe. Immigrants and their children now constitute a growing segment of even historically homogeneous societies like Norway, Sweden, and Germany. Cities like Amsterdam, Berlin, Paris, and Zurich look nearly as diverse as America's great cities. And the 2015 refugee crisis brought millions of North African and Middle Eastern newcomers to Europe, turning immigration

and ethnic diversity into issues of great political salience. Together with the fallout from the 2008 financial crisis, these changes
triggered a radical backlash. In nearly every western European
country, between about 10 and 30 percent of the electorate—
disproportionately white and less educated voters who live in declining regions or outside urban centers—is open to xenophobic
appeals. And everywhere from the U.K. and France to Italy, Germany, and Sweden, these voters have boosted the electoral for-
tunes of far-right parties and movements.

And yet America stands apart in two ways. First, the reaction to
growing diversity has been unusually *authoritarian*. Rarely in western Europe has the rise of xenophobic and antiestablishment parties taken on the overtly antidemocratic form that we have seen in
the United States. There are many features of western Europe's far-
right parties that give cause for concern, including their racism,
xenophobia, disregard for minority rights, and, in some cases, sym-
pathies for Russia's president, Vladimir Putin. But so far, nearly all
of them have played by democratic rules, accepting election results
and eschewing political violence. America also differs in another
way: extremist forces actually ascended to national power, whereas
in Europe they have been largely confined to the opposition or, in
a few cases, coalition governments.

So we must confront an uncomfortable fact: Societal diversity,
cultural backlash, and extreme right parties are ubiquitous across
established Western democracies. But only in America did such
extremists actually win control of the national government and
assault democratic institutions. Why did America, alone among
rich established democracies, come to the brink? This is the question that should haunt us in the wake of January 5 and 6.

It is tempting to turn the page on the Trump era. After all, President Trump lost his reelection bid, and his effort to overturn the results of that election failed. The most dangerous election deniers in key swing states also were defeated in the congressional 2022 midterm elections. It appears as if we successfully dodged the bullet—that at the end of the day the system worked. And now, as Trump's hold over the Republican Party is contested, maybe we can finally stop worrying so much about the fate of our democracy. Maybe the crisis wasn't as bad as we initially feared. Maybe democracy *wasn't* dying after all.

Such thinking is understandable. For those of us who were left worn down by the seemingly incessant crises of the Trump era, the (dodged) single bullet theory is reassuring. Unfortunately, it is misguided. The threat facing American democracy was never simply a strongman with a cultlike following. The problems are more endemic than that. In fact, they are deeply rooted in our politics. Until we address those underlying problems, our democracy will remain vulnerable.

To fully reverse America's democratic retreat—and crucially, to prevent it from happening again—we must understand what caused it. What are the forces that drive a mainstream political party to turn away from democracy? This doesn't happen often, but when it does, it can destroy even a well-established political system. We can draw lessons from other countries' experiences, but also from episodes in our own history—including the southern Democratic Party's authoritarian reaction to the post–Civil War Reconstruction.

We must also understand why America proved so exceptionally prone to backsliding. This question compels us to look hard at the core institutions of our own democracy. Reactionary voters are a minority in the United States, just as they are in Europe. This is an important—and often neglected—point. The Trump-led Republican Party, like radical right movements in European countries, has *always* represented a political minority. But unlike far-right parties in Europe, it was able to win national office.

That leads us to another unsettling truth. Part of the problem we face today lies in something many of us venerate: our Constitution. America has the world's oldest written constitution. A brilliant work of political craftsmanship, it has provided a foundation for stability and prosperity. And for more than two centuries it has succeeded in checking the power of ambitious and overreaching presidents. But flaws in our Constitution now imperil our democracy.

Designed in a pre-democratic era, the U.S. Constitution allows partisan minorities to routinely thwart majorities, and sometimes even *govern* them. Institutions that empower partisan minorities can become instruments of minority rule. And they are *especially* dangerous when they are in the hands of extremist or antidemocratic partisan minorities.

Prominent eighteenth- and nineteenth-century thinkers, from Edmund Burke to John Adams to John Stuart Mill and Alexis de Tocqueville, worried that democracy risked becoming a "tyranny of the majority"—that such a system would allow the will of the many to trample on the rights of the few. This can be a real problem: Governing majorities undermined democracy in twenty-first-century Venezuela and Hungary and are threatening to do so in Israel. But the American political system has always reliably checked the power of majorities. What ails American democracy today is closer to the opposite problem: Electoral majorities often cannot win power, and when they win, they often cannot govern. The more imminent threat facing us today, then, is minority rule. By steering the republic so sharply away from the Scylla of majority tyranny, America's founders left it vulnerable to the Charybdis of minority rule.

Why are the threats to American democracy emerging *now,* in the early twenty-first century? After all, the Constitution is centuries old. Understanding how we got here is a principal task of this book. The more urgent question, however, is how to get out. One thing is clear: Our institutions will not save our democracy. We will have to save it ourselves.

CHAPTER 1

FEAR OF LOSING

On the evening of October 30, 1983, as the votes were being counted in Argentina's first democratic election in a decade, Peronists who gathered in their Buenos Aires campaign bunker were in a state of shock. "When do the votes from the industrial belt come in?" party leaders asked nervously. But the votes were already in. For the first time ever, the Peronists—Argentina's working-class party—had lost a free election.

"We didn't see it coming," recalls Mario Wainfeld, then a young lawyer and Peronist activist. The Peronists had been Argentina's dominant party since Juan Perón, a former military officer, first won the presidency back in 1946. Perón was a talented populist figure who built Argentina's welfare state and quadrupled the size of its labor movement, earning the deep loyalty of the working class. Those loyalties persisted even after he was overthrown in a military coup in 1955 and exiled from the country for eighteen years. Even though Peronism was banned for much of the next two decades, the movement not only survived but remained a force at the polls—winning every national election in which it was allowed to compete. And when an aging Perón was allowed to return and run for president in 1973, he won easily, with 62 percent of the vote. He died a year later, however, and in 1976, Argentina fell prey to another coup and descended into a seven-year military dictatorship.

Still, when democracy returned in 1983, just about everybody expected the Peronist candidate, Italo Luder, to prevail.

But much had changed in Argentina. Perón was gone, and industrial decline had destroyed hundreds of thousands of blue-collar jobs, decimating Peronism's working-class base. At the same time, younger and middle-class voters were turned off by Peronism's old guard union bosses, and as Argentina emerged from a brutal military dictatorship, most of them preferred Raúl Alfonsín, the human-rights-oriented candidate of the rival Radical Civic Union. Peronist leaders had lost touch with Argentine voters. They made the problem worse by choosing some thuggish and out-of-touch candidates. Their gubernatorial candidate in the all-important province of Buenos Aires, Herminio Iglesias, was known for his shoot-outs with rival Peronist factions during the violent 1970s. At the Peronists' final campaign rally two days before the election, Iglesias stood prominently on center stage, on live national television, and burned a casket with the symbol of Alfonsín's Radical Civic Union—a violent act that most Argentines, having just suffered through a decade of terrifying repression, found appalling.

When early results showed Alfonsín ahead in the 1983 race, Peronist leaders, searching desperately for explanations, briefly fell into a state of denial. "They still haven't counted the votes from La Matanza" (a working-class Peronist bastion outside Buenos Aires), party boss Lorenzo Miguel insisted. The Peronist vice presidential candidate, Deolindo Bittel, even accused the election authorities of withholding the results from working-class neighborhoods. By midnight, however, it was clear that these hidden votes simply didn't exist. Peronists have a saying: "The only truth is reality." And the reality was that they had lost.

Defeat was hard to swallow. Party leaders, licking their wounds, initially hid from the press. But none of them considered rejecting the results. The next day, the losing Peronist candidate Luder joined President-elect Alfonsín in a press conference and congratulated him. When reporters asked Luder about Peronism's historic defeat, he replied, "All politicians have to live with the fact that elections can produce . . . unexpected results."

After the election, Peronists plunged into a heated internal debate over the party's future. A new faction, known as the *Renovación* (Renewal), called for the resignation of the established party leadership, arguing that Peronism would have to adapt to changes in Argentine society if it wanted to win again. The party needed to broaden its base and find a way to reach middle-class voters who had been repulsed by the casket-burning Peronism of 1983. Though derided by internal critics as "jacket-and-tie Peronists," the Renewal leaders eventually succeeded in sidelining Peronism's rough-edged old guard, jettisoning many of its backward-looking ideas, and improving the party's image among middle-class voters. Peronism won the next two presidential elections handily.

This is how democracy should work. As the political scientist Adam Przeworski memorably put it, "Democracy is a system in which parties lose elections." Losing hurts, but in a democracy it is inevitable. And when it happens, parties must do what the Peronists did: accept defeat, go home, and then figure out how to win a majority in the next election.

The norm of accepting defeat and peacefully relinquishing power is the foundation of modern democracy. On March 4, 1801, the United States became the first republic in history to experience an electoral transfer of power from one political party to another. On that day, the incumbent president, John Adams, a leader of America's founding Federalist Party, quietly left Washington, D.C., by carriage before dawn. President-elect Thomas Jefferson of the rival Democratic-Republican Party, the man who had defeated Adams in the 1800 election, was inaugurated in the U.S. Senate chambers several hours later.

This transition was indispensable to the new republic's survival. But it was neither inevitable nor easy. In 1800, the norm of accepting defeat and handing power to one's opponent had not yet taken hold. The very existence of partisan opposition was regarded as illegitimate. Politicians, including many of the founders, equated it with sedition and even treason. And since no transfer of power had ever taken place before, it was hard to imagine that the opposition would reciprocate in future elections. Handing over power was a "plunge into the unknown."

The transition was especially difficult for the Federalists, who suffered from what might be called the "founders' dilemma": in order for a new political system to take hold, its founders must accept the fact that they don't get to call the shots forever. As designers of the Constitution and inheritors of George Washington's legacy, Federalist leaders like Adams and Alexander Hamilton considered themselves the rightful stewards of the new republic. They viewed their own interests and the nation's interests as one and the same, and they recoiled at the thought of yielding power to untested challengers.

The emergence of the Democratic-Republicans, America's first opposition party, thus challenged the stability of the new nation. Democratic-Republican societies had originally sprung up in Pennsylvania and other states in 1793. The movement soon morphed into a genuine opposition, under the leadership of Jefferson and James Madison. The Democratic-Republicans broke with the Federalists on many leading issues of the day, including economic policy, public debt, and above all matters of war and peace. They regarded the Federalists as quasi-monarchists ("monocrats") and worried that Adams's diplomatic overtures to Great Britain constituted a covert effort to restore British rule to America.

Many Federalists viewed the Democratic-Republicans, in turn, as nothing less than traitors. They suspected them of being sympathetic to France's revolutionary government—at a time when mounting U.S.–French hostilities posed a real threat of war. The Federalists feared that Republican "domestic enemies" would aid a French invasion. These fears were reinforced by slave revolts in the South. Federalists charged that slave rebellions—such as Gabriel's Rebellion in Virginia in mid-1800—were inspired by Republicans and their ideology as part of what Federalist newspapers called the "true French plan."

At first, the Federalists tried to destroy their opponents. In 1798, Congress passed the Alien and Sedition Acts, which were used to jail Democratic-Republican politicians and newspaper editors who criticized the federal government. The acts further polarized the country. Virginia and Kentucky declared them null and void in their territories, which the Federalists viewed as sedition. Seeing Virginia's behavior as part of a "conspiracy" to aid France, Hamilton called on the Adams administration to raise a "sound military force" that could be "drawn towards Virginia." In response, Virginia's state legislature began to arm its own militia.

The specter of violence—even civil war—hung over the young republic on the eve of the 1800 election. Mutual distrust, fueled by partisan animosity, imperiled prospects for a peaceful transfer of power. As the historian James Sharp put it, "Federalists and Republicans were willing to believe that their opponents were capable of virtually any action, no matter how treacherous, or violent, in order to gain or retain power."

Indeed, Federalist leaders explored ways of subverting the electoral process. In the Senate, they passed a bill to establish a committee consisting of six members from each house of Congress (which were dominated by Federalists) and the chief justice of the Supreme Court to "decide which votes to count and which ones to disallow." Hamilton urged New York's governor, John Jay, to call a special session of the lame-duck (Federalist-dominated) state legislature so that it could pass a law transferring the authority to appoint electors from the incoming (Democratic-Republican–dominated) leg-

islature to Governor Jay, who was a Federalist. In a letter seething
with animosity toward his rivals, Hamilton embraced the kind of
hardball politics that, as we showed in *How Democracies Die,* can
wreck a democracy. Hamilton wrote,

> In times like these in which we live it will not do to be over-
> scrupulous. It is easy to sacrifice the substantial interests of
> society by a strict adherence to ordinary rules. . . . [But]
> [t]hey ought not to hinder the taking of a *legal* and *constitu-
> tional* step to prevent an *atheist* in religion and a *fanatic* in
> politics from getting possession of the helm of the state.

The Federalists never actually enacted these plans, but their
very willingness to consider them shows just how difficult it was
for America's first incumbent party to accept defeat.

The 1800 contest was also nearly derailed by a flawed electoral
system. In December, after the votes were tallied, the Electoral
College delivered a vexing result: while Adams had clearly lost,
the two Democratic-Republican candidates, Jefferson (the party's
presumed presidential candidate) and Aaron Burr (the presumed
vice presidential candidate), found themselves in an unexpected
tie, with seventy-three electoral votes each. That sent the election
to the lame-duck House of Representatives, where the Federalists
still maintained a majority.

Although Adams grudgingly accepted defeat and prepared to
return home to Quincy, Massachusetts, many Federalists saw an
opportunity to use hardball tactics to stay in power. Some floated
the idea of a new election. Others wanted to elect Burr, presum-
ably in exchange for a Federalist role in a future Burr administra-

tion. Such a move was entirely legal, but because the victorious Democratic-Republicans had clearly intended for Jefferson to be president and Burr to be vice president, it would have, in the words of one newspaper at the time, violated "the spirit of the Constitution [which] requires the will of the people be executed." An even more controversial idea emerged in Federalist circles that December: extending the debate past the March 4, 1801, inauguration deadline, which would, in the words of Senator Gouverneur Morris, "throw the Government into the Hands of a President [pro tem] of the Senate"—a Federalist. Such a move, which Jefferson decried as "stretching the Constitution," would almost certainly have triggered a constitutional crisis.

Federalist leaders' consideration of these hardball tactics reinforced Democratic-Republican fears that the Federalists were planning to illegally "usurp" power. This led Jefferson and his allies to contemplate, in Jefferson's own words, "resistance by force." The governors of Pennsylvania and Virginia mobilized their militias and threatened to secede if Jefferson's election was blocked.

On the snowy morning of February 11, 1801, the House of Representatives met to resolve the Electoral College tie. The Constitution stipulated that each of the sixteen state delegations had a single vote, and a majority of nine votes was required for victory. For six painful days, over the course of thirty-five ballots, the results remained unchanged: over and over, eight states voted for Jefferson, six for Burr, and two states were unable to reach a consensus within their delegations and thus abstained. At least one Federalist would have to vote for Jefferson to break the deadlock. Finally, on day six, the Federalist congressman James Bayard of Delaware (the state's only representative) announced he was withdrawing his support for Burr, eliciting shouts of "Deserter!" from the floor of the chamber. Delaware, which had backed Burr, would now abstain. Soon Maryland and Vermont, which had been abstaining, cast their votes in favor of Jefferson, giving him a solid ten-state majority. Two weeks later, Jefferson was sworn in as president.

Why did the Federalists relent? In a letter to a friend, Bayard explained that he changed his vote because he feared that the alternative to Jefferson was constitutional breakdown or even civil war. He wrote,

> Some of our [Federalist] Gentlem[e]n from an intemperate hatred to Jefferson were disposed to proceed to the most desperate extremities. Being perfectly resolved not to risk the constitution or a civil war, I found the moment arrived at which it was necessary to take a decided Step.

Grudgingly, then, the Adams administration oversaw America's first transfer of power. It was neither entirely peaceful (the threat of violence loomed throughout) nor inevitable. But in accepting defeat and leaving office, the Federalists took a major step toward solidifying the constitutional system that would eventually become American democracy.

Once parties learn to lose, democracy can take root. And once democracy takes root, alternation in power becomes so routine that people take it for granted. In December 2021, seventy years after German democracy was reestablished following World War II, the country's long-serving chancellor, Angela Merkel, retired from office. That fall, her Christian Democratic Party had been defeated by the opposition Social Democrats. The simple swearing-in ceremony of the new Social Democratic chancellor felt more like a marriage ceremony at the county clerk's office, marked by the signing of papers and handing over of documents. Observers were more worried about catching the latest COVID variant than the possibility of violence or an illegal seizure of power. When the new chancellor, Olaf Scholz, met his vanquished opponent, the Christian Democrat Armin Laschet, on the floor of the Reichstag building, they greeted each other with a friendly fist bump.

How does a democracy get to where Germany is today, where the transfer of power is drama-free? What enables the norm of accepting defeat to take hold?

Two conditions help. First, parties are most likely to accept defeat when they believe they stand a reasonable chance of winning again in the future.

The Peronists might have been shocked by their 1983 electoral defeat, but they remained Argentina's largest party, with more members than all other parties combined. Confident that they could win again, many leading Peronists quickly set about doing just that. Carlos Menem, who had just been elected governor of the small northwestern province of La Rioja, started preparing his presidential bid soon after his party's 1983 defeat. Menem would go on to win the presidency in 1989, and the Peronists would win four of the five presidential elections that followed.

Although Federalist leaders' uncertainty about the future made America's 1801 transition more difficult, many of them ultimately exhibited confidence that they would soon regain power. "We are not dead yet," one Federalist declared three days after Jefferson's inauguration. Fisher Ames advised his fellow Federalists to embrace their new opposition status, because they "should soon stand on high ground, and be ready to resume the reins of government with advantage." Likewise, Oliver Wolcott Jr., Adams's Treasury secretary, expected the Federalists to "remain a party, and in short time regain our influence." Indeed, a New Jersey Federalist who had recently begun work on a new house declared he would suspend construction until the Federalists returned to power. (That proved to be a mistake.)

A second condition that helps parties accept defeat is the belief that losing power will not bring catastrophe—that a change of government will not threaten the lives, livelihoods, or most cherished principles of the outgoing party and its constituents. Elections often feel like high-stakes battles, but if the stakes are *too* high, and losing parties fear they will lose *everything,* they will be reluctant to relinquish power. In other words, it is an outsized fear of losing that turns parties against democracy.

The lowering of stakes was critical to the 1801 transition in the United States. Amid the polarized campaign, many Federalists cast the Republicans as an existential threat, associating a Jefferson victory with a Jacobin-style revolution that would condemn Federalists to poverty and exile, or worse, cause them to "wade in blood," in the words of the Federalist U.S. senator Uriah Tracy. Ultimately, however, Hamilton and other founding leaders recognized that Jefferson was a pragmatist who would work within the existing system. As Rufus King wrote to a Federalist friend during the campaign, "I have no notion that our Government or the security of our property can or will be, in any material degree, affected" by a Jefferson victory. Backroom negotiations appear to have convinced key Federalists that their most cherished priorities—such as the navy, the Bank of the United States, and the national debt—would be protected under Jefferson. For good measure, the outgoing Federalists packed the courts, creating sixteen new federal judgeships and filling them with allies. The Federalists thus left power believing that a Jefferson presidency would not be calamitous. Upon hearing Jefferson's conciliatory inaugural address, Hamilton concluded that "the new president will not lend himself to dangerous innovations, but in essential points will tread in the steps of his predecessors."

Accepting defeat gets harder when parties are fearful—fearful that they won't be able to win again in the future or, more fundamentally, that they will lose more than just an election. When defeat feels like an existential threat to politicians or their constituents, they grow desperate to avoid it.

Such fears often arise during periods of far-reaching social change.

Research in political psychology teaches us that social status—where one stands in relation to others—can powerfully shape political attitudes. We often gauge our social status in terms of the status of the groups we identify with. Those groups may be based on social class, religion, geographic region, or race or ethnicity, and where they sit in the larger societal pecking order greatly affects our own individual sense of self-worth. Economic, demographic, cultural, and political change may challenge existing social hierarchies, raising the status of some groups and, inevitably, lowering the relative status of others. What the writer Barbara Ehrenreich called the "fear of falling" can be a powerful force. When a political party represents a group that perceives itself to be losing ground, it often radicalizes. With their constituents' way of life seemingly at stake, party leaders feel pressure to win at any cost. Losing is no longer acceptable.

Existential fear thwarted the emergence of democracy in early twentieth-century Germany. On the eve of World War I, imperial Germany was only a partial democracy, still dominated by a small circle of high-status aristocrats, industrialists, and bureaucrats. There were national elections, but real power lay with Prussia, whose highly restrictive suffrage rules heavily favored the rich: a tiered voting system effectively gave wealthy people more votes. Prior to 1903, there was no secret ballot; voting in the open allowed local elites and government officials to keep close tabs on how their communities voted. Even after 1903, landowners and industrialists pressured government officials to tamper with the vote.

There was a great deal of public demand for political reform. Germany was an industrial economy with a big middle class and a robust civil society. Yet democratic reformers confronted a reactionary, shrinking, and thus increasingly terrified conservative elite. Long dependent on a rigged electoral system, German conservatives and their landowner allies were convinced that any tinkering with voting rules would dilute their power and bring electoral defeat. And electoral defeat, they believed, would hasten the demise of the entire aristocratic order. Democracy thus constituted a threat to everything they stood for. Big landowners feared they would lose their grip over cheap labor in the countryside. They feared they would lose the protectionist tariffs that sustained their outmoded agricultural system. Factory owners in the booming industrial heartlands feared they would lose control over workers who were becoming emboldened by the growing labor movement.

In short, Prussian conservatives feared more than losing elections. They feared losing their dominant position in society. In May 1912, during a final prewar effort to reform Prussia's voting system, the Prussian Conservative leader Ernst von Heydebrand took to the floor of the parliament and passionately defended the old order, insisting that "rule by the undifferentiated masses . . . is an attack against the basic laws of nature!" During World War I, General Erich Ludendorff, a prominent government official, embodied the most extreme form of German conservatism. Writing to a friend, Ludendorff described democracy as "a terror without end." "With the equal franchise we cannot live," he wrote. "It would be worse than a lost war!"

So German conservatives voted again and again (a total of sixteen times) to block political reform. Driven by a deep-seated fear of the working class and socialism, they resisted democratization until the final days of World War I.

German conservatives never really learned how to lose until after World War II. But on occasion even established democratic parties lose the ability to lose. To see how and why, consider a very different setting: twenty-first-century Thailand. The country has had a rocky political history, with more than a dozen military coups since the 1930s. In the 1990s, however, democracy seemed to be consolidating. Popular protests had brought an end to military rule, and the middle-class-based Democrat Party, a longtime opponent of the military, triumphed in the 1992 elections. A new constitution, a decade of double-digit economic growth, and an expanding and increasingly self-confident middle class all left Thailand's democratic future looking bright. Some observers even surmised that Thailand was on track to join the ranks of other wealthy East Asian democracies, like Japan, South Korea, and Taiwan.

But things went awry in the early twenty-first century. A succession of military coups destroyed Thailand's embryonic democracy and restored the army to a position of dominance. And surprisingly, the Democrat Party, which had led the fight for democracy in the 1990s, embraced these coups. What happened?

A telling moment came on the first Sunday of February 2014. It was Election Day. In Bangkok, a massive city of ten million, getting to the polls had always been difficult. But on this day, it was harder than usual. Protesters, drawn mainly from Thailand's educated middle classes, clogged the streets. For months, the protesters had been organizing carnival-like gatherings in Bangkok's central squares, shopping malls, and major intersections. Political speeches were mixed with live music and public large-screen TV viewings. University students and professionals returning home from their office jobs gathered in the streets with Thai flags painted on their faces, posing for selfies to post on their Facebook pages. Actors, pop stars, and scions of some of Thailand's wealthiest and most famous families were there. In a high-profile moment of radical chic, Chitpas Bhirombhakdi, the twenty-eight-year-old heiress to the $2.6 billion Singha beer family fortune, rode a bulldozer through police barricades. When officers began to use tear gas, she posted Instagram pictures of herself washing out the eyes of her compatriots. "People you would normally see in the society pages were out there," the editor of Bangkok's fashion magazine the *Thailand Tatler* told a Reuters journalist. "All the people from big families used to be called the silent minority. Well, they're not silent anymore."

Despite the festive atmosphere, the gatherings had a serious purpose: protesters were calling for the resignation of the elected prime minister, Yingluck Shinawatra, whom they attacked as corrupt. And now that Prime Minister Yingluck had called an election, the protesters had taken to the streets to *oppose* it. Many of the movement's organizers, surprisingly, came from the Democrat Party. Led by the former Democrat Party general secretary, Suthep Thaugsuban, a group called the People's Democratic Reform Committee (PDRC) had organized an elaborate campaign to prevent the election from happening at all. PDRC and Democrat Party activists physically blocked candidates from registering, and protest leaders called for a boycott of the election. The Democrats— apparently in coordination with the protesters—ultimately decided to stay out of the election in protest, and two days before the polls opened, a team of lawyers working for the Democrats petitioned the Constitutional Court to have the election declared invalid. On Election Day, protesters interfered with the distribution of ballots, pressured election officials to close polling stations, and intimidated voters. Voting was disrupted in nearly one out of every five districts. In many instances, election officials simply couldn't reach polling stations through the crowds of protesters. Frustrated voters stood in line, voter registration cards in hand, chanting, "Election! Election! We want to vote today!" But the mostly middle-class Bangkok protesters had given up on elections. One of their slogans, proposed by the real estate magnate Srivara

Issara as she threw herself into the protest movement, was "Moral righteousness comes above democracy!"

The protesters succeeded in disrupting the February 2014 election, and the Constitutional Court eventually annulled it. In May, Prime Minister Yingluck was impeached on a technicality. Two weeks later, the military, with the blessing of the king, declared martial law, scrapped the constitution, and established a junta called the National Council for Peace and Order, putting an end to Thai democracy. PDRC activists celebrated, handing out roses to the soldiers and thanking them for their service. "This is a victory day," said the protest leader Samdin Lertbutr. "The military has done its job. And we have done our job." The Democrats later joined the military-led government, thereby de facto endorsing the coup.

How did a mainstream middle-class party like the Thai Democrats, which had long considered itself a champion of democracy, come to reject elections and embrace a military coup?

The Democrats were a party of professionals, university students, and urban middle-class voters—the kind who showed up at the PDRC's protests. Their base was concentrated in Bangkok and in parts of Thailand's south. But Bangkok is only a small island in a country of seventy million people, and the Democrats never made a serious effort to appeal to the poor rice farmers, agricultural workers, taxicab drivers, small shopkeepers, and other rural and small-town voters who populated the country's heartland, to the north of Bangkok. For many years, this didn't matter much. The millions of voters in Thailand's provincial heartland had no stable allegiances to the multiplicity of national parties in faraway Bangkok, and their votes were often purchased by local political brokers. This fragmentation allowed the Democrats to stay competitive even as they remained mostly confined to Bangkok and the south. But things changed in the late 1990s. The 1997 Asian financial crisis eroded public support for mainstream parties, especially the Democrats, allowing the outsider business tycoon Thaksin Shinawatra and his newly formed Thai Rak Thai (Thais Love Thais) party to sweep to victory in the 2001 elections.

Thaksin was a controversial prime minister whose government faced numerous corruption allegations. But he was also an astute politician who grasped that policies aimed at the poorer rural regions of the north could be electorally rewarding. In 2001, Thaksin campaigned on a new "social contract" that included a three-year moratorium on farmer debt, grants to help villages diversify their economies beyond rice farming, and an ambitious universal health-care program. And he delivered. His government spent billions of dollars on public policies aimed at poorer voters, turning Thailand into one of the first middle-income countries in the world with universal health care. Poverty rates fell dramatically, especially in rural areas, and for the first time in decades levels of inequality also declined.

Thaksin's social policies paid off at the polls. In the 2005 elections, his Thai Rak Thai won an astounding 60 percent of the vote, nearly tripling that of the second-place Democrats. Suddenly the Democrats could not compete. When Thaksin, facing mounting criticism over his financial dealings, called new parliamentary elections in 2006, the Democrats began to wobble in their commitment to democratic norms. They boycotted the election (Thaksin again won in a landslide), and shortly afterward the election was invalidated by the Constitutional Court. A few months

later, the military seized power in a coup, forcing Thaksin to flee
into exile to escape arrest. Although the military scheduled new
elections for 2007, it banned Thaksin's Thai Rak Thai party.

The ban didn't work. The 2007 elections were won by the People's Power Party, a new party serving as a stand-in for Thai Rak
Thai and the exiled Thaksin. When that party was also dissolved,
Thaksin supporters regrouped in a third party, Pheu Thai. Under
the leadership of Thaksin's sister, Yingluck Shinawatra, they won
the 2011 parliamentary elections, gaining nearly twice as many
seats as the Democrats.

The Democrats now seemed unable to win free and fair elections. Despite their close ties to the monarchy and the backing of
the Thai establishment, they lost five straight times between 2001
and 2011.

But it wasn't just the Democrats' electoral futility that brought
their educated, professional, and middle-class supporters into the
streets in 2013 and 2014. Nor was it merely their voters' anger over
alleged corruption in the Yingluck government or a proposed am-
nesty bill that would allow the exiled Thaksin to return to Thailand. The anger had deeper roots: The Bangkok elite was
increasingly resentful of the shifting balance of power, wealth, and
status in Thai society. They had long sat atop Thailand's political,
economic, and cultural hierarchies. The most prestigious universities were in Bangkok. The well-to-do sent their children there or to
universities in Great Britain or the United States. These elite institutions were, in turn, the main pathway to prestigious positions in
the private sector and the government. Although governments
came and went with remarkable frequency in the twentieth century, the circle of high-status elites remained stable—and closed.

This began to change under Thaksin. Since 2001, the poor's share of national income had been rising, reducing inequality but squeezing the urban middle classes. Thaksin and Yingluck had mobilized the poor in the countryside like no one before them, flouting the cozy Bangkok-centered world that had dominated Thai politics for decades. Even though Thaksin's reputation was marred by accusations of corruption, tax evasion, and abuse of power, his movement's continued electoral success left no doubt of his enduring popular appeal.

What really shook the Bangkok social and political elite about Thaksin's victories, then, was *who* was winning on the other side. The Bangkok Singha beer heiress, Chitpas Bhirombhakdi, the glamorous foot soldier in the 2014 protests, captured this sentiment when she declared, in an interview with *The Japan Times*, that Thais lacked a "true understanding" of democracy, "especially in the rural areas." Another high-profile protester, Petch Osathanugrah, a well-known cultural figure and CEO of a Thai energy drink company, told a reporter, "I'm not really for democracy. . . . I don't think we're ready for it. We need a strong government like China's or Singapore's—almost like a dictatorship, but for the good of the country." Most protesters shared this view. In a 2014 survey, 350 protesters were asked whether they agreed with the statement "Thais are not yet ready for equal voting rights." Only 30 percent of respondents said the statement "seriously offends the principles of democracy," while 70 percent either agreed with the statement or said, "We have to accept its reality."

For many higher-status Thais, this resistance to democracy was driven by a fear of being displaced. Whereas the urban middle classes had once been the protectors of democratic norms in Thai-

land, by the first decade of the twenty-first century, the writer
Marc Saxer observed, they soon

> found themselves to be the . . . minority. Mobilized by
> clever political entrepreneurs, it was now the periphery
> who handily won every election. Ignorant of the rise of a
> rural middle class demanding full participation in social and
> political life, the middle class in the center interpreted de-
> mands for equal rights and public goods as "the poor get-
> ting greedy."

This was the sentiment fueling the protesters in 2013–14.
Their principal goal, according to the political scientist Duncan
McCargo, was to return to "an imagined pre-Thaksin era in which
the ruling network and its supporters [could] still call the shots,
and provincial voters [could] be marginalized."

Many of the middle-class groups that had pushed for democracy in the 1990s had now grown frightened of its consequences.
So that's why when Prime Minister Yingluck tried to defuse the
protests by calling new elections for 2014, the Democrats repudi-
ated her call and boycotted the election. In fact, there was nothing
the protesters and their Thai Democrat allies feared *more* than free
and fair elections. That's also why the Democrats, who had once
fiercely opposed coups and absolutist royal power, quietly supported the 2014 coup and later joined the military-led government. When democracy gave rise to a movement that challenged
the social, cultural, and political dominance of the Bangkok elite,
the Democrats turned against democracy.

Fear is often what drives the turn to authoritarianism. Fear of losing political power and, perhaps more important, fear of losing one's dominant status in society. But if fear can drive mainstream parties to turn against democracy, what exactly does it drive them to do? In Thailand, democracy's assailants were easy to identify: for the twelfth time in the country's history, military leaders seized power. But in more established democracies, the methods are often harder to see and harder to stop.

CHAPTER 2

THE BANALITY
OF AUTHORITARIANISM

I n late January 1934, Parisians were jittery. A little over a decade earlier, France had emerged victorious from World War I. Most of its citizens had grown accustomed to thinking of their country, Europe's oldest democracy, as a model for the rest of the continent. By 1934, though, the world felt unhinged. The Great Depression, a series of prominent corruption scandals, mounting unrest in the streets, and a period of governmental instability—thirteen prime ministers in five years—left a growing segment of the population feeling angry and disaffected.

On the afternoon of February 6, 1934, tens of thousands of angry young men, mostly members of veterans' associations and right-wing militias (or "leagues") with names like Young Patriots, French Action, and Croix de Feu (Cross of Fire) gathered in or near the prominent Place de la Concorde, across the river from France's national parliament building. Although the groups diverged in their ideologies and goals, they were united in their hostility toward parliamentary democracy. Some of them were quasi-fascist, emulating Mussolini's Blackshirts. The Young Patriots, for example, admired Italian fascism and often marched in the streets with berets and blue jackets. A few groups sought to shut down parliament and replace it with a "ministry of public safety" or even a restored Bonapartist government. Others merely aimed to block the official tallying of votes inside the parliament building, with the hope of installing a right-leaning government. But all the groups regarded themselves as patriots—adopting slogans like "France for the French"—and cast their liberal and socialist rivals as weak and even traitorous.

That night events took a nasty turn. A surging mob headed toward the parliament and its occupants. A bus was set on fire. Tens of thousands of rioters threw chairs, metal grates, and rocks. Armed with long poles with razor blades at the end, they shouted and marched across the square toward the parliament building. Police on horseback arrived, pushing them back. The protesters used their long poles to slash at the legs of the horses. Within the parliamentary chambers, gunshots could be heard from outside. "They are firing!" one member of parliament cried. From inside, members of parliament were haunted by chants of "Hang the Deputies!" which had been heard outside the parliament only days earlier. Some scrambled for cover as one deputy yelled, "They are storming the doors of the chambers!" Journalists inside the building evacuated to the press gallery, hanging a handwritten sign on the outside saying, "Notice to the Demonstrators: No Deputies in Here!" One journalist from the Manchester *Guardian,* holed away in the press gallery, telephoned his editors to file his story as the events unfolded. His frantic words appeared on the front page of *The Guardian* the next day:

> I am telephoning you from a besieged fortress. No one can leave the Chamber of Deputies. The whole district on the south side of the river adjoining the Chamber is cordoned off by police and as I speak thousands of rioters are attempting to break through the barricade of police vans [to get into the chamber].

More police arrived. Eventually, by 10:30 P.M., police had repelled efforts to breach the doors of parliament. By then, several people were dead. Hundreds of others were injured. Members of parliament had to sneak out the back door, frightened for their lives. One minister attempted to escape but was discovered by protesters, who dragged him to the river, chanting, "Throw him in the Seine!" (He was saved by police officers who happened to be nearby.)

France's democracy survived the February 6, 1934, assault. But it was badly weakened. Prime Minister Édouard Daladier immediately resigned. He was replaced by Gaston Doumergue, a right-wing politician who was considered acceptable to the leagues. The goal of some of the insurrectionists had been achieved: the center-left Daladier government had been brought down by street pressure. Right-wing extremists were emboldened and mobilized.

Many French politicians responded to these tumultuous events with outrage. President Albert Lebrun, a moderate conservative, denounced the riot as an "assault against republican institutions."

Parties of the left (socialists and communists) and the liberal center (the Radicals) jointly condemned the attack. Although these parties had been sharply divided over a range of issues before February 6, they now reached a rapprochement, worried that the riot could be a harbinger of fascism. Even the far-left communists, some of whom had marched against the republic on February 6, now closed ranks with the socialists and liberals.

Yet France's leading conservative party, the Republican Federation, took a remarkably tolerant stance toward these extremist groups. Founded in 1903, the Federation had been led for many years by Louis Marin, a man with solid democratic credentials. But in the early 1930s, the party drifted to the right, first flirting with, and then openly embracing, the Young Patriot activists in its midst. Long considered a party of the elite, the Federation grew dependent on the Young Patriots and other far-right leagues as a source of activism and energy. Because the same individuals appeared in both groups, the boundary between the official "party" and the violent activists of the leagues grew harder to discern.

At least thirty-five Federation members of parliament belonged to the Young Patriots, and three members of the Young Patriots leadership were simultaneously leaders of the Federation's parliamentary party. The Young Patriots, dressed in military garb, provided security at Republican Federation party meetings and helped deliver votes on Election Day. Philippe Henriot, a prominent Federation member of parliament (who would later remake himself as minister of propaganda in the Nazi-allied Vichy government), described the Young Patriots as his party's "shock troops."

The violent assault of February 6, 1934, did not serve as a wake-up call for most French conservatives. To the contrary, Federation leaders, fueled by their hatred of the left, doubled down on their support for the leagues.

Mainstream conservatives' sympathy for the antidemocratic extremists was a major factor in the February 6 attack. Eyewitnesses to the attack later reported that the insurrectionists had accomplices inside parliament itself, including Federation and other right-wing politicians. On February 6, the center of the action was Paris's city hall, the Hôtel de Ville, which the historian Serge Berstein described as "a sort of political headquarters for the day's events." On the morning of the assault, a group of seemingly respectable conservative politicians, including city council members and members of parliament, gathered in the Hôtel de Ville, well aware of the events as they unfolded. A few of them would march alongside the rioters later that afternoon. This group of politicians had signed their names to flyers that would be distributed and hung on city walls ahead of time to encourage action on the streets: "This is a decisive moment: the whole of France is waiting for the capital to speak; Paris will make its voice heard!"

In the aftermath of the assault, other prominent conservatives downplayed it or even tried to justify it. Constructing the "meaning of February 6" became a high-stakes political battle. Some conservative newspapers and politicians dismissed the importance of the attack, calling it a legitimate protest by apolitical veterans and denying the existence of a plot to overthrow the government.

But most mainstream conservative politicians and press outlets offered a different account altogether. The insurrectionists, they claimed, were heroic patriots who had tried to save the republic from corruption, communism, and political dysfunction. It was the police who should be condemned for their brutality. A vice

president of the Republican Federation described the insurrectionists as "martyrs who can never be sufficiently praised or honored,
[they] have paid with their lives. . . . The blood poured out on
February 6, 1934 will be a seed of a great national awakening."
The city councillor Charles des Isnards, who has been described as
"the brains behind February 6," later responded to questions about
having supported a violent effort to change the government by
saying, "There are moments when insurrection is the most sacred
of duties."

Having aided and then publicly defended the February 6
assault, French conservatives then tried to thwart an official investigation into the incident. In the wake of the assault, a forty-four-
member parliamentary committee of investigation (*commission
d'enquête*) produced thousands of pages of evidence, based on interviews, testimony, police files, and other documents. Because the
committee aimed to be representative of the partisan makeup of
the parliament, it included right-wing parliamentary members.

By most accounts, the committee chairman, Laurent Bonne-
vay, a centrist, tried to lead an impartial investigation. But from
the beginning, right-leaning committee members worked to undermine it from within. Informed by rumors and accusations in
the press, they repeatedly tried to impede the committee's fact-
finding mission. They sought to include language in the report
that vindicated the insurrectionists and cast them as victims while
placing the bulk of the blame on the parliament and the police.
Seeking to forge a consensus, the committee reached a watered-
down set of conclusions that focused mainly on the police response.

Even these cautious conclusions were too much for the committee's right-wing members. So when the chairman released the committee's findings, one leading Federation committee member led an effort to torpedo it, formally rejecting the findings and proposing an alternative narrative of events in which the insurrectionists were "noble," the government and the police were at fault, and all arrests of those attempting to breach the parliament were unjustified. The Republican Federation representatives ultimately withdrew from the committee.

The resulting committee report was virtually toothless. In the absence of accountability for the events of February 6, French democracy was badly weakened. Within six years, it would be dead.

February 6, 1934, was a consequential day for French democracy. But what made the day's events so important was less the actions of the rioters in the streets themselves than the reaction of mainstream conservative politicians. Their response eventually played a subtle but decisive role in killing democracy itself.

Politicians who are committed to democracy, or what the political scientist Juan Linz called loyal democrats, must always do three basic things. First, they must respect the outcome of free and fair elections, win or lose. This means consistently and unhesitatingly accepting defeat. Second, democrats must unambiguously reject violence (or the threat of violence) as a means of achieving political goals. Politicians who support military coups, organize putsches, incite insurrections, plot bombings, assassinations, and other terrorist acts, or deploy militias or thugs to beat up opponents or intimidate voters are not democrats. Indeed, any party or politician that violates *either of these two basic rules* should be considered a threat to democracy.

But there is a third, more subtle action required of loyal democrats: they must always break with antidemocratic forces. Democracy's assassins always have accomplices—political insiders who appear to abide by democracy's rules but quietly assault them. These are what Linz called "semi-loyal" democrats.

From a distance, semi-loyal democrats may look like loyal democrats. They are mainstream politicians, often in suits and ties, who ostensibly play by the rules and indeed even thrive under them. They never engage in visibly antidemocratic acts. So when democracies die, their fingerprints are rarely found on the murder weapon. But make no mistake: semi-loyal politicians play a vital, if hidden, role in democratic collapse.

Whereas loyal democrats clearly and consistently reject antidemocratic behavior, semi-loyal democrats act in a more ambiguous manner. They try to have it both ways, claiming to support democracy while at the same time turning a blind eye to violence or antidemocratic extremism. It is this ambiguity that makes them so dangerous. Openly authoritarian figures—like coup conspirators or armed insurrectionists—are visible for all to see. By themselves, they often lack the public support or legitimacy to destroy a democracy. But when semi-loyalists—tucked away in the hallways of power—lend a hand, openly authoritarian forces become much more dangerous. Democracies get into trouble when mainstream parties tolerate, condone, or protect authoritarian extremists— when they become authoritarian enablers. Indeed, throughout history, cooperation between authoritarians and seemingly respectable semi-loyal democrats has been a recipe for democratic breakdown.

How can we tell a loyal democrat from a semi-loyal one? A litmus test is how politicians respond to violent or antidemocratic behavior *on their own flank*. It's easy to oppose authoritarians on the other side of the political spectrum. Progressives are quick to denounce and oppose fascists. Conservatives reliably denounce and oppose violent radical leftists. But what about antidemocratic elements that arise within one's own party—a radical youth wing, an emergent faction, a newly arrived political outsider, or an allied group that many party leaders and activists belong to or sympathize with? Or perhaps a new political movement that excites much of the party base?

When faced with these challenges, loyal democrats follow four basic rules. First, they *expel antidemocratic extremists from their own ranks,* even at the cost of antagonizing the party base. In the 1930s, for example, Sweden's largest conservative party expelled its forty-thousand-member youth wing, the Swedish National Youth Organization, which embraced fascism and Hitler. By contrast, semi-loyalists tolerate and even accommodate antidemocratic extremists. Although they may privately disapprove of the extremists, they remain silent, out of political expediency: they fear dividing the party, and ultimately losing votes.

Second, loyal democrats *sever all ties—public and private—with allied groups that engage in antidemocratic behavior.* They not only eschew alliances with them but also refuse endorsements from them, avoid public appearances with them, and abstain from secret or closed-door conversations with them. Semi-loyal democrats, on the other hand, continue to cooperate with extremists. They may form political alliances with them, as when Spain's center-left Republicans forged a coalition with leftists who had participated in an armed uprising in 1934. More often, though, cooperation is loose and unofficial. Semi-loyalists may keep their distance from extremists in public but still quietly work with them or accept their support.

Third, loyal democrats *unambiguously condemn political violence and other antidemocratic behavior,* even when it is committed by allies or ideologically proximate groups. During periods of extreme polarization or crisis, antidemocratic positions may enjoy considerable rank-and-file support. Even then, loyal democrats resist the temptation to condone, justify, or accommodate these positions. Instead, they publicly and unequivocally condemn them. When supporters of the losing Brazilian presidential candidate Jair Bolsonaro stormed the Congress in January 2023, seeking to overturn the results of the recent presidential election, the leader of Bolsonaro's own party immediately and forcefully condemned their actions. And when ideological allies are responsible for violent or antidemocratic acts, loyal democrats take steps to hold them accountable before the law.

Semi-loyal democrats, by contrast, deny or downplay their allies' violent or antidemocratic acts. They may blame violence on "false flag" operations. They may minimize the importance of antidemocratic behavior, deflect criticism by drawing attention to similar (or worse) behavior by the other side, or otherwise justify or condone the acts. Semi-loyalists frequently try to have it both ways: expressing disapproval of the perpetrators' methods while sympathizing with their goals. Or they may simply remain silent in the face of violent attacks on democracy.

Finally, when necessary, *loyal democrats join forces with rival pro-democratic parties to isolate and defeat antidemocratic extremists*. This is not easy. Forging broad coalitions to defend democracy often requires that loyal democrats (temporarily) set aside cherished principles and policy goals and work with politicians from the opposite end of the ideological spectrum to defeat groups that are ideologically closer to them. Semi-loyal democrats, by contrast, refuse to work with ideological rivals even when democracy is on the line.

These principles of loyal democratic politics may appear simple and straightforward, but they are not. When much of a party's base sympathizes with antidemocratic extremists, leaders of that party who denounce or break ties with those extremists often run a substantial political risk. Loyal democrats do it anyway. And they help preserve democracy in the process.

A good example of a loyal democratic response to an authoritarian assault comes from Spain in the early 1980s. Spain's first democracy (1931–36) had collapsed amid polarization and civil war. The semi-loyal behavior of both the major center-left and center-right parties contributed to that collapse. In 1934, socialists and communists—fearing fascism—had launched an armed insurrection to prevent conservatives from joining the government. Nevertheless, mainstream center-left politicians tolerated and later forged an electoral coalition with them. And likewise, when military officials—fearing communism—plotted to overthrow the Republican government in 1936, mainstream conservative politicians backed them, plunging Spain into civil war and dictatorship.

Spanish democracy was finally restored in 1976 after four decades of authoritarianism under Francisco Franco. Early in the transition, economic growth was slow, inflation raged, and the country suffered a wave of terrorist attacks by Basque separatists. Prime Minister Adolfo Suárez grew unpopular. Suárez had already angered his old allies on the *franquista* (pro-Franco) right when he legalized the Communist Party in 1977. Now, it seemed, he had fallen out of favor with King Juan Carlos, who remained highly influential, especially with the military. The socialists, long a bête noire of the right, were poised to win the next elections.

In late January 1981, Suárez announced his resignation. Parliament was scheduled to vote on his successor, the centrist Leopoldo Calvo-Sotelo, on February 23. But at 6:23 in the evening, as the votes were being counted, two hundred civil guardsmen, led by Lieutenant Colonel Antonio Tejero, stormed into the chambers wielding pistols and submachine guns. Claiming falsely that they were acting under orders from the king, the soldiers seized control of the parliament building. The coup plotters aimed to prevent Calvo-Sotelo's election and force parliament to elect General Alfonso Armada prime minister. General Armada was a longtime aide to King Juan Carlos who aspired to be Spain's de Gaulle. His close ties to Juan Carlos led the coup leaders to believe that the king would back them.

Lieutenant Colonel Tejero climbed the speaker's rostrum with gun held high, shouting, "Hit the floor! Hit the floor!" Soldiers fired shots into the ceiling, causing panicked members of parliament to duck under their seats for cover. Only three men refused to hide: Prime Minister Suárez; Deputy Prime Minister Manuel Gutiérrez Mellado, an old *franquista* general who indignantly confronted Tejero and had to be forcibly restrained; and Santiago Carrillo, an old communist who had spent a lifetime combating the *franquistas* and now sat calmly, smoking a cigarette. Both Gutiérrez

Mellado, who joined Franco's coup in the 1930s, and Carrillo, a lifelong revolutionary, were latecomers to democracy. But now each put his body on the line to defend it.

The prime minister and 350 members of parliament were held hostage overnight. Tanks rolled through the streets in neighboring Valencia. Soldiers occupied state television and radio stations. National radio played military music. Outside the parliament building, rightist supporters of the coup sang the Spanish fascist song "Face to the Sun."

The coup ultimately failed because the king refused to go along with it. Shortly after midnight, he appeared on television—dressed in military garb—and delivered a speech defending the democratic order.

Nearly as important, though, was the reaction of Spain's politicians. The entire spectrum of parties, from the left-wing communists to the right-wing ex-*franquistas,* denounced the coup. Inside the parliament building, Manuel Fraga, a prominent Franco government official and now leader of the right-wing Popular Alliance, leaped to his feet and shouted, "This is an attack on democracy!" His parliamentary allies responded by shouting, "Long live Spain! Long live democracy!" Four days later, more than a million people marched in the streets of Madrid in what the Spanish newspaper *El País* described at the time as the "biggest demonstration in Spain's history." At its head, leaders of all the parties—the communist Carrillo, the rightist Fraga, the socialist leader Felipe González, and leaders of the incumbent Union of the Democratic Center—marched side by side. Politically isolated, the coup leaders were arrested, tried, and eventually sentenced to thirty years in prison. After that, coups became unthinkable in Spain, and democracy took root.

This is how democracy is defended. In Spain, the date of February 23 is celebrated publicly as a moment of triumph. In 2006, on the event's twenty-fifth anniversary, the parliament issued a statement, endorsed by all parties, that described the coup as "the gravest attempt to forcefully violate freedoms and to abort the democratic process in Spain." No one excused the attempted coup. No one downplayed it.

Semi-loyal behavior often appears benign. After all, it's usually carried out by respectable politicians who have not participated directly in violent attacks on democracy. But this is a deeply misleading perception. History teaches us that when mainstream politicians take the more expedient path of semi-loyalty, tolerating or condoning antidemocratic extremists, the extremists are often strengthened, and a seemingly solid democracy can collapse upon itself.

For one, semi-loyalty protects antidemocratic forces. When violent extremists enjoy the tacit support of a mainstream party, they are more likely to be shielded from legal prosecution or expulsion from public office. Consider again the French experience. Many of the mainstream conservatives who condoned the February 6 insurrectionists went on to have successful political careers. On the day of the assaults, the parliamentarian Pierre Laval spoke on the phone with Lieutenant Colonel François de La Rocque of the Croix de Feu, advising him on tactics. Never held to account for his role in the attack, the ambitious Laval continued his rapid political ascent. He ended up serving as vice president and then head of government in the Nazi-aligned Vichy regime formed in 1940.

It wasn't just prominent members of the political elite who were protected. In the aftermath of the attack, some right-wing demonstrators who had been wounded that day formed a group they called the Victims of February 6. Rather than being prosecuted, expelled from public life, or banned from future office, the "victims" were treated as heroes in influential conservative circles. Louis Darquier de Pellepoix, a notorious anti-Semite, became the president of the group. The thrill of violence and his own injury on that day gave him a new mission in life—according to his biographer. Darquier felt he had a "winning ticket in the lottery." After the German invasion in 1940, Darquier and many of his fellow "victims" enthusiastically joined the Vichy regime. He became French commissioner for Jewish affairs, overseeing the deportation of Jews to concentration camps. Another member of the group became president of the Paris city council in 1941. Yet another February 6 participant—the notorious nationalist poet and writer Philippe Henriot—became the Vichy government's leading radio spokesman. As the historian Robert Paxton puts it, February 6 veterans "were a kind of fraternity, and one finds job seekers during Vichy being recommended as 'good 6 February men.'"

In addition to protecting antidemocratic extremists, semi-loyal behavior legitimizes their ideas. In a healthy democracy, antidemocratic extremists are treated as pariahs. They are shunned by the media. Politicians, businesspeople, and other members of the establishment, fearing for their reputations, avoid contact with them. But a tacit endorsement from prominent politicians can change all that, helping to normalize extremists and their ideology. Mainstream media begin to cover them as they would any other politician, inviting them for interviews and debates. Business leaders may now choose to contribute money to their campaigns. Political consultants who once avoided them now begin to return their calls. And the many politicians and activists who privately sympathized with them but dared not support them publicly may now decide it is safe to do so.

Again, the French case is instructive. At the core of the Young Patriots' agenda in 1934 was an idea that had for decades been utterly anathema to most of the political establishment: the dismantling of parliament—and even of France's Third Republic democracy. As a growing number of conservatives came to view French democracy as corrupt, dysfunctional, and infiltrated by communists and Jews, authoritarian "constitutional reform" became a mainstream idea on the right. Radicalized right-wing forces spoke about the reformist Popular Front government, which took office in 1936 and was led by Léon Blum, a Jewish socialist, in apocalyptic terms, describing it as Stalinist. The slogan "Better Hitler than Blum" became popular on the right. French conservatives had traditionally defined themselves as nationalists, and many of them loathed Germany. But by 1940, their fear of communism, Soviet infiltration, and social change at home had led them to acquiesce to the Nazis.

When politicians from across the spectrum repudiate violent or antidemocratic behavior, it often isolates extremists, blunting their momentum and deterring others. In the United States in the 1950s, the anticommunist extremist Joseph McCarthy became a pariah after he was censured by the U.S. Senate, in a bipartisan vote, in 1954. Other U.S. senators would "drift off the floor" when he rose to speak, and "nobody would stir" when he called a press conference. But when mainstream parties tolerate, condone, or tacitly support antidemocratic extremists, it sends a powerful message that the cost of antidemocratic behavior has been lowered. The deterrent effect evaporates. Semi-loyalty doesn't just normalize antidemocratic forces; it encourages—and may even radicalize—them.

This is the banality of authoritarianism. Many of the politicians who preside over a democracy's collapse are just ambitious careerists trying to stay in office or perhaps win a higher one. They do not oppose democracy out of deep-seated principle but are merely indifferent to it. They tolerate or condone antidemocratic extremism because it is the path of least resistance. These politicians often tell themselves they are just doing what's necessary to get ahead. But, ultimately, they become indispensable partners in democracy's demise.

Mainstream politicians can help kill a democracy by enabling antidemocratic extremism. But they can also undermine it another way: through constitutional hardball—behavior that broadly conforms to the letter of the law but deliberately undermines its spirit. We are not talking about bare-knuckle politics, which exists in all democracies, but rather the use of law as political weapon. Any constitution, no matter how brilliantly designed, can be used to break democracy—in ways that are technically legal. Indeed, that's precisely what makes constitutional hardball so dangerous: politicians do not openly violate the law; their hands remain clean.

It is vitally important, then, that citizens be able to recognize constitutional hardball when they see it. Even well-designed constitutions and laws inevitably contain ambiguities and potential loopholes, are open to multiple interpretations, and may be enforced in different ways (and to different degrees). Politicians may exploit these ambiguities in ways that distort or subvert the very purpose for which the laws were written. There are four ways this can happen.

1. EXPLOITING GAPS

No rule or set of rules covers all contingencies. There are always circumstances that are not explicitly covered by existing laws and procedures. If a behavior is not explicitly prohibited, that behavior—no matter how inappropriate—often becomes permissible. We see this in our daily lives: for example, when children remind their parents that they "never said we couldn't" do something that, in the parents' minds, was obviously out of bounds. Whenever the rules do not specify that something must be done in a certain way, opportunities for exploitation emerge. Societies often develop norms—or unwritten rules—to fill in the gaps in the rules. Norms help encourage behavior that is not legally required (tipping, covering your mouth when you cough) and discourage behavior that is not legally forbidden ("running up the score" in a little league baseball game or taking up two seats on a crowded bus or train). But norms can't be legally enforced. While their violation may elicit criticism, finger wagging, and even ostracism, individuals who are willing to bear those costs can violate norms with impunity.

Politicians routinely exploit gaps in the rules, often in ways that weaken democracy. One example is the U.S. Senate's 2016 refusal to allow President Barack Obama to appoint a new Supreme Court justice in the wake of Justice Antonin Scalia's death. According to the Constitution, presidential nominees to the Supreme Court must have the consent of the Senate. Historically, the Senate used its power of "advice and consent" with forbearance. Most qualified nominees were promptly approved, even when the president's party did not control the Senate. Indeed, in the 150-year span between 1866 and 2016, the Senate never once prevented an elected president from filling a Supreme Court vacancy. Every president who attempted to fill a court vacancy before the election of his successor was eventually able to do so (though not always on the first try). In March 2016, however, when President Obama nominated Merrick Garland—a highly qualified and moderate judge—for the court, Senate Republicans refused to hold hearings on the grounds that it was an election year. Denying the president's ability to fill a Supreme Court vacancy clearly violated the spirit of the Constitution. It allowed Senate Republicans to steal a Supreme Court seat (Donald Trump filled the seat with Neil Gorsuch in 2017). But because the Constitution does not specify *when* the Senate must take up presidential court nominees, the theft was entirely legal.

2. EXCESSIVE OR UNDUE USE OF THE LAW

Some rules are designed to be used sparingly, or only under exceptional circumstances. These are rules that require forbearance, or self-restraint, in the exercise of legal prerogatives. Take presidential pardons. If U.S. presidents used their constitutional pardon

authority to the full extent, they could not only systematically
pardon friends, relatives, and donors but also legally pardon political aides and allies who commit crimes on their behalf, in the
knowledge that if caught, they will be pardoned. The result would
be a mockery of the rule of law.

Or consider impeachment. In presidential democracies, constitutions usually empower legislatures to remove elected presidents,
with the understanding that such measures should be undertaken
only *under exceptional circumstances*. Impeaching a president involves
overturning the will of voters, which is a momentous event for
any democracy. So impeachment should be rare—used only when
presidents egregiously or dangerously abuse their power. This has
been the case in the world's two oldest presidential democracies:
the United States and Costa Rica. The United States averaged one
presidential impeachment *per century* during its first 230 years.
Never in Costa Rica's seventy-four-year democratic history has a
president been removed before the end of their term.

But the power to remove presidents may be used excessively.
Consider Peru. According to Article 113 of the Peruvian constitution, the presidency becomes "vacated" if the president dies, re-
signs, or is deemed by two-thirds of Congress to be in a state of
"permanent physical or moral incapacity." The constitution does
not define "moral incapacity." Historically, it was understood narrowly, to mean "mental incapacitation." In recent years, however,
amid escalating conflict between presidents and Congress, Peruvian legislators began to use "moral incapacity" to cover anything
they deemed "ethically objectionable." Suddenly two-thirds of
Congress could remove the president on virtually any grounds,
ushering in what one journalist called "presidential hunting sea-

son." In 2018, President Pedro Pablo Kuczynski resigned in the face of an imminent congressional vote to remove him. In November 2020, Congress voted to "vacate" Kuczynski's successor, Martín Vizcarra, again on grounds of "moral incapacity." Peruvians elected Pedro Castillo president in 2021, but Castillo's opponents in Congress launched efforts to "vacate" him almost immediately after he took office. They succeeded in December 2022, after Castillo tried to illegally close Congress. So Congress "vacated" three presidents in a span of four years. As the journalist Diego Salazar put it, things have reached the point where anytime the opposition can muster the votes to remove the president, it does so. It's simply "a question of arithmetic."

An egregious example of undue use of the law to remove an elected leader comes from Thailand, where the prime minister, Samak Sundaravej, an ally of the exiled former prime minister Thaksin Shinawatra, was removed from office on a technicality in 2008. Widely known for his culinary passions, Samak had hosted a popular television cooking show, *Tasting, Grumbling,* for eight years prior to becoming prime minister, stepping down from the show soon after coming to office. But early in his premiership, Samak appeared four times on *Tasting, Grumbling,* where he prepared his favorite dishes such as Samak's Fried Rice and Pork Leg in Coca-Cola. He received an honorarium of around $500 for each show, which he insisted was used to pay for ingredients and transportation. But in a polarized country in which thousands of anti-government protesters were occupying the grounds of his official residence, Thailand's Constitutional Court ruled that Samak had violated Article 267 of the constitution, which bars government ministers from engaging in outside business while in office. Samak was forced to resign, and the pro-Thaksin government collapsed soon thereafter.

Undue use of constitutional provisions can kill a democracy. Most democratic constitutions, for example, allow governments to declare a state of emergency, during which basic rights are suspended. In healthy democracies, such provisions are governed by norms of forbearance: Politicians share a commitment to using them only in the rarest of circumstances, such as major wars or large-scale national disasters. They agree to break the glass only in a true emergency. Were this not the case, and governments routinely declared emergencies, stripping citizens of basic rights, democracy would be seriously imperiled.

But autocratic-minded leaders are sometimes tempted to abuse the emergency powers afforded to them by the constitution. The Indian prime minister, Indira Gandhi, fell prey to such temptation in 1975. Gandhi's Congress Party had spearheaded the struggle for Indian independence. Her father, independence hero Jawaharlal Nehru, had become the country's first prime minister in 1947. The Congress Party had won every parliamentary election since.

But the 1970s were a challenging decade. After sweeping to reelection in 1971, Gandhi faced rising public discontent and a wave of protests. Jayaprakash Narayan, a widely respected figure, came out of retirement and emerged as the face of the opposition. By 1975, Narayan's anticorruption drive had snowballed into a mass movement. Gandhi's problems were compounded by legal threats. In 1971, a political opponent had accused her of using government resources to boost her campaign (a government official apparently worked on her campaign for six days, and her reelection campaign used government vehicles). The Allahabad High

Court ruled in favor of her opponent, which disqualified Gandhi from public office for six years. The Supreme Court granted a stay, allowing Gandhi to appeal the ruling, but the stunned prime minister suddenly found herself fighting for her political life. Narayan launched a series of mass rallies calling for her resignation.

Gandhi and her aides had been contemplating some kind of power grab for months, but they were unsure of how to pull it off. Summoned to the prime minister's residence on June 24, Gandhi's trusted aide, Siddhartha Shankar Ray, ordered a copy of the Indian constitution delivered from the Parliament Library and spent the evening "perusing it with hermeneutical rigor." Ray settled on Article 352, which allowed governments to declare a state of emergency suspending basic constitutional rights if India were threatened by "war or external aggression or internal disturbance." A legacy of colonial rule, the clause had lain "dormant" since independence. Although national emergencies had been declared during wars in 1962 and 1971, it would take what the historians Jaffrelot and Anil called a "pretzeled interpretation of the law" to declare an "internal emergency"; indeed, Article 352 had never been used for such a purpose.

But on the evening of June 25, 1975, Gandhi persuaded India's ceremonial president, Fakhruddin Ali Ahmed, to sign a declaration of emergency, suspending constitutional rights. Within hours, police were knocking on opposition leaders' doors and arresting them. By dawn, 676 politicians—including Narayan and the leaders of all major opposition parties—were in jail. Dusting off laws such as the Maintenance of Internal Security Act, which had previously been used against smugglers, the government arrested more than 110,000 critics in 1975 and 1976. It also imposed strict media censorship. With the stroke of a pen, Prime Minister Gandhi snuffed out nearly three decades of democracy and established an autocracy "cloaked in constitutional dress."

3. SELECTIVE ENFORCEMENT

Governments can punish their rivals not only by skirting the law but also by *applying it*. Wherever nonenforcement of the law is the norm—where people routinely cheat on their taxes, businesses routinely flout health, safety, or environmental regulations, and well-placed public officials routinely use their influence to do favors for friends and family members—enforcement can be a form of constitutional hardball. Governments may enforce the law selectively, targeting their rivals. The government may be acting legally (after all, it is *enforcing the law*), but it is also acting unfairly because enforcement is directed at political opponents. In other words, the law is weaponized. As the Peruvian dictator Óscar Benavides (1933–39) reportedly once said, "For my friends, everything. For my enemies, the law."

Vladimir Putin is a master at selective enforcement. When he came to power in 2000, Russian businessmen, or "oligarchs," had been enriching themselves for a decade, gobbling up assets as the government privatized large sectors of the economy and raking in cash as the new market economy took off without effective regulation or oversight. Bribery, fraud, and tax and regulatory evasion were standard operating procedure for Russian businesses, which meant that just about every oligarch had broken the law en route to getting rich. Under President Boris Yeltsin, the government largely turned a blind eye to this lawbreaking—by friend and foe

alike. Putin was different. In July 2000, just two months after taking office, he summoned twenty-one of Russia's leading oligarchs
to a meeting at the Kremlin. He told them that if they stayed out
of politics, he would not question how they had amassed their for-
tunes. Implicit, of course, was the threat that he would apply the
law to those who remained politically active. Most of the oligarchs
got the message. Those who did not, like Boris Berezovsky, whose
television station aired critical coverage of the government, were
punished. Berezovsky was stripped of his media assets and forced
into exile to avoid charges of fraud and embezzlement. When
Mikhail Khodorkovsky, owner of the Yukos oil company and
Russia's richest man, continued to criticize Putin and finance opposition parties, he was arrested and charged with tax evasion,
fraud, embezzlement, money laundering, and other crimes. He
spent a decade in prison. Berezovsky and Khodorkovsky were
hardly innocent; they had almost certainly violated the law. But
unlike the many oligarchs who broke similar laws but cooperated
with Putin, they were penalized.

4. LAWFARE

Finally, politicians may design *new* laws that, while seemingly impartial, are crafted to target opponents. This is a form of what is
often called lawfare. Lawfare was prominently used in Zambia following that country's 1991 democratic transition. The longtime
autocrat Kenneth Kaunda had lost a multiparty election to Frederick Chiluba of the Movement for Multiparty Democracy (MMD),
but when Chiluba prepared to seek reelection five years later, he
worried about opposition from Kaunda and the former ruling

United National Independence Party. So six months before the 1996 election, the now-ruling MMD passed a constitutional amendment establishing new requirements for those seeking to hold the presidency. Not only would all candidates have to be Zambian by birth, but both of their *parents* would have to be Zambian by birth. And they could not be tribal chiefs. Why these new requirements? One of Kaunda's parents was Malawian by birth, and his vice presidential candidate was a tribal chief. As Human Rights Watch put it, the constitutional reform was "precisely tailored to disqualify specific opposition leaders from running for president." As if to vanquish any remaining doubts about the amendment's purpose, MMD legislators chanted *Kaunda yamana!* (Kaunda is finished!) after they voted it into law.

Most twenty-first-century autocracies are built via constitutional hardball. Democratic backsliding occurs gradually, through a series of reasonable-looking measures: new laws that are ostensibly designed to clean up elections, combat corruption, or create a more efficient judiciary; court rulings that reinterpret existing laws; long-dormant laws that are conveniently rediscovered. Because the measures are couched in legality, it may appear as if little has changed. No blood has been shed. No one has been arrested or sent into exile. Parliament remains open. So criticism of the government's measures is dismissed as alarmism or partisan bellyaching. But gradually, and sometimes almost imperceptibly, the playing field tilts. The cumulative effect of these seemingly innocuous measures is to make it harder for opponents of the government to compete—and thereby entrench the incumbents in power.

The model for building an autocracy via constitutional hardball is Viktor Orbán's Hungary. When he came to power in 2010,
Orbán had already been prime minister once before, from 1998
until 2002. A student leader in the anticommunist movement, he
had cast himself first as a "liberal" and then as a Christian Democrat during the heady postcommunist days of the 1990s. Orbán
had governed democratically during his first term, and his Fidesz
party had positioned itself then as mainstream center right. After
losing the 2002 election, however, Fidesz moved in a sharply conservative, ethno-nationalist direction. Orbán, who had studied at
Oxford University on a scholarship funded by the liberal Hungarian American George Soros, now remade himself. He had always
been known as an unusually ambitious, even ruthless, politician.
Few, however, anticipated that he would undermine Hungarian
democracy when Fidesz returned to power in 2010.

But as Orbán once said, "In politics everything is possible."
Fidesz's assault on democracy was made possible by a scandal that
weakened the rival Hungarian Socialist Party: a socialist prime
minister was caught on tape admitting that he had lied to voters
about the state of the economy. The party's subsequent collapse
allowed Fidesz to score a landslide victory in 2010. The size of the
party's victory was inflated by Hungary's "first past the post" election system, which turned 53 percent of the vote into a two-thirds
parliamentary majority. That was enough for Fidesz to single-
handedly rewrite the constitution. Which it did, almost immediately.

Orbán used his party's parliamentary supermajority to build an
unfair advantage over his opponents. One of his first moves was to
purge and pack the courts. Prior to 2010, justices of the Constitu-

tional Court were selected by a parliamentary committee composed of representatives of all the political parties. The new constitution replaced this multiparty mechanism with a procedure allowing Fidesz to use its supermajority to unilaterally appoint justices. Another constitutional amendment expanded the Constitutional Court from eleven to fifteen, which created four vacancies for Fidesz to fill with allies. Then Orbán removed the independent-minded Supreme Court president, András Baka, via a law requiring Supreme Court presidents to have at least five years of judicial experience in Hungary. This was a clear instance of lawfare: the new law obviously targeted Baka, a prestigious judge who had served seventeen years on the European Court of Human Rights but lacked five years of experience in Hungary. Baka was forced to step down. But that wasn't enough. Parliament also passed a law lowering the retirement age for judges from seventy to sixty-two and forcing all judges over the age of sixty-two to retire immediately. A total of 274 judges were forced out. Although the law was later repealed under pressure from the European Union, many of the retired judges did not return to their posts. By 2013, the judiciary had been captured and transformed into a "puppet of the government." As a former Constitutional Court justice put it, Orbán had pulled off "an unconstitutional coup . . . [under] the cover of constitutionality, with constitutional means."

Orbán also used "legal" means to capture the media. In most European democracies, public television is an important—and independent—news source (think of the BBC, for example). This was the spirit of the law in Hungary prior to 2010, even if public television was never quite as independent as the BBC. Under Orbán, however, public television became the government's propaganda arm. As part of a "restructuring" process, Fidesz officials sacked more than a thousand public media employees, including dozens of respected professional journalists and editors. The positions were filled by political loyalists, and public media coverage grew nakedly partisan.

Orbán also legally captured the *private media*. The Fidesz government worked behind the scenes to help Orbán's friends in the business community buy major media outlets or gain controlling shares in parent companies that owned independent media outlets. The new Orbán-friendly ownership would then pressure independent media to self-censor or, in a few cases, would simply shut them down. In 2016, the newspaper *Népszabadság,* Hungary's largest opposition newspaper, was suddenly closed, not by the government, but by its own corporate owners.

The few remaining independent media outlets were targeted in several ways. A 2010 law prohibited reporting that was "imbalanced," "insulting," or against "public morality." Violators of the new law would face fines of up to $900,000. A Media Council, packed with Fidesz loyalists, was created to enforce the law. Although comparable laws exist in other countries, democratic governments almost never enforce them. They use forbearance. But the Orbán government played hardball with its new media law. Dozens of media organizations were slapped with hundreds of thousands of dollars of fines. The Media Council also denied licenses to independent media on narrow technical grounds. In 2020, for example, it declined to renew the license of Klubrádió, a progressive-liberal radio station with 500,000 daily listeners, citing "regulatory offenses." According to Klubrádió's director, András Arató, violations included failing to fill out a form correctly and reporting the length of one of its programs as forty-five minutes when, in reality, it was fifty minutes.

These hardball measures dramatically altered the media landscape. One study found that 90 percent of Hungarian media was in the hands of the Orbán government or its private sector allies by 2017. Some 80 percent of Hungarian television viewers and radio listeners received only information provided by the government or its supporters.

Finally, the Orbán government used constitutional hardball to tilt the electoral playing field. First, it packed the Electoral Commission, which prior to 2010 was appointed via multiparty consensus. Five of the ten seats were filled by delegates of each of the five largest parties in parliament, while the other five were filled by mutual agreement between the government and the opposition. This ensured that no single party controlled the electoral process. Fidesz abandoned this practice and filled all five nondelegate seats with loyalists, thereby giving itself a controlling majority on the Electoral Commission.

The politicized Electoral Commission then egregiously gerrymandered parliamentary election districts to overrepresent Fidesz's rural strongholds and underrepresent the opposition's urban strongholds. One think tank calculated that the opposition needed to win 300,000 more votes than Fidesz to capture a parliamentary majority. The former prime minister Gordon Bajnai complained that the new rules gave Fidesz "a good 30-yard advantage . . . in a 100-yard sprint."

In another act of lawfare, the government banned the use of campaign advertisements in commercial media. The law ostensibly affected all parties equally, but because both public and private media were heavily biased toward Fidesz, a ban on campaign ads severely limited the opposition's ability to reach voters. So the electoral system was "neither fair nor free."

All these efforts paid off. In the 2014 election, Fidesz lost 600,000 votes relative to 2010; its share of the popular vote fell from 53 percent to 45 percent. And yet it captured the same number of seats as in 2010, retaining control of two-thirds of parliament despite failing to win a majority of the vote. Fidesz repeated the trick in 2018, winning two-thirds of parliament with less than half the popular vote. In 2022, the ruling party defeated a broad opposition coalition, reinforcing the emerging conventional wisdom that Orbán "cannot be defeated under 'normal' circumstances."

Viktor Orbán thus pulled off an extraordinary feat: not only did he wreck a full-fledged democracy, but he did so by almost entirely legal means. There was no bloodshed, no mass arrests, no political prisoners or exiles. And yet, as Bajnai put it, "the spine of Hungarian democracy has systematically been broken, one vertebra after another."

Although some of Orbán's methods feel new, he was actually following a playbook that is centuries old. Indeed, the practice of constitutional hardball was perfected in one of the world's oldest republics: the United States. And its effect there was equally devastating.

CHAPTER 3

IT HAS HAPPENED HERE.

Wilmington, North Carolina, was booming in the late 1890s. Founded on the coastal edge of the eighteenth-century slave economy, the port city became the home of an innovative industrialized system of cotton production in the years after the Civil War. New railroad lines brought cotton from inland cotton-growing regions to Wilmington's brick warehouses, where modern compressors produced bales of cotton more efficiently than ever before. The city's largest employer, Alexander Sprunt & Son, had become the biggest cotton exporter in the United States. And in its warehouses, docks, and busy lumberyards, white and Black laborers worked alongside one another as loaders, haulers, and stevedores.

The largest city in North Carolina, Wilmington was majority Black. And as its post–Civil War economy expanded, numerous

Black-owned businesses had sprung up—barbershops, grocery stores, restaurants, butcher shops, and soon doctor's offices and a law firm. Black Wilmington became wealthier, which gave rise to a vibrant civic life of literary societies, public libraries, baseball leagues, and a Black-owned newspaper. At the center of the community were several churches, including St. Stephen A.M.E. Church, with its large congregation, and St. Mark's Episcopal Church, which was attended by the most affluent Black families.

Although the federal government's post–Civil War project of Reconstruction had waned by the late 1870s and the Democratic Party, the self-proclaimed defender of white supremacy, had used violence and election fraud to reclaim most state and local governments across the South, many Blacks bravely continued to vote. And in the last decade of the nineteenth century, their votes gave rise to a new politics in Wilmington and across North Carolina.

The catalyst was the emergence of the Populist Party, which appealed to disaffected poor white tenant farmers and sharecroppers who felt neglected by the wealthy merchant class that dominated the Democratic Party. In 1893, as the country slid into an economic depression, the Populists in North Carolina forged an alliance with the Republican Party, which retained strong African American support. The Fusion, as the alliance was called, brought Black and poor rural white voters together in an ambitious biracial coalition. It aimed to expand public education, regulate powerful business monopolies, and shore up voting rights that had been weakened since the demise of Reconstruction.

This improbable coalition upended North Carolina politics. And it struck fear in the Democratic Party establishment. The Fusion ticket won a sweeping majority in the North Carolina state legislature in 1894, and in 1896 it captured the governorship and elected to the House of Representatives George Henry White, who at the time was America's only African American congressman. The Fusion-dominated state legislature restored direct elections for local offices and adopted what has been called "probably the fairest and most democratic election law in the post-Reconstruction South." As a result, Black Republicans and white populists won public offices across the state. In Wilmington, three Black aldermen were elected to the city council. Ten of twenty-one city policemen and four deputy sheriffs were Black. Black magistrates sat in the courthouses. The county treasurer, the county jailer, and the county coroner were Black. There were Black health inspectors, Black registrars of deeds, and a Black superintendent of streets. Black postal workers delivered mail to Black and white homes alike. The highest-paid official in the state was an African American, John Dancy, who served as head of Wilmington's federal customs office.

For a moment, one could see in Wilmington the stirrings of a multiracial democracy. Although deep racial antipathies and inequalities persisted, Black citizens were voting, and politicians *needed them* to win elections. This seemed to open the door to a more inclusive democracy as America entered a new century.

But the moment of democratic promise proved fleeting. The rise of multiracial politics triggered a fierce reaction. For many whites, steeped in norms of white supremacy, these changes were intolerable. And the Democratic Party establishment, which had dominated state politics since the end of Reconstruction, launched a counterrevolution. In 1898, a group of prominent Democrats, including the state party chairman, Furnifold Simmons, the gubernatorial hopeful Charles Brantley Aycock, and the Raleigh

News & Observer publisher, Josephus Daniels, launched what became a violent crusade to restore white rule. The upcoming November midterm election would determine the composition of the state legislature, now controlled by the Fusionists. Together these leading figures of North Carolina politics plotted a relentless media campaign of lies and hate waged by *The News & Observer,* while Democratic politicians stoked whites' fears of "Negro domination." Alfred Moore Waddell, a charismatic Civil War veteran who would help lead a violent movement against these political changes in Wilmington, declared that "the white people who settled this country . . . should alone govern it."

Backed by the Democratic Party, more than eight hundred White Government Union clubs were formed across North Carolina. Because more than 56 percent of Wilmington's population was Black, and the city's Black citizens voted and voted Republican, it was clear that "white government" would not be restored by democratic means. As one Democratic leader acknowledged at a rally, "We cannot outnumber the negroes. And so we must either outcheat, outcount, or outshoot them."

And that's what they did. White Wilmington residents began to stockpile weapons, leading a Washington, D.C., journalist to observe that the city seemed to be "preparing for a siege instead of an election." Whites formed militias called Red Shirts, which patrolled the streets with Winchester rifles, beating, whipping, and intimidating local Blacks and warning them not to vote. The city, located on the Cape Fear River, became a place of terror. The militias were backed by the Democratic Party (which supplied them with red shirts and food and drink) and cheered on by *The News & Observer.* Democratic politicians whipped whites into a violent frenzy. At an October 1898 preelection rally with "sixty of Wilmington's most prominent citizens" onstage behind him, Waddell declared,

> Shall we surrender to a ragged rabble of Negroes? . . . A thousand times no! . . . We will have no more of the intolerable conditions under which we live. We resolve to change them [even] if we have to choke the Cape Fear with carcasses.

As Election Day approached, an atmosphere of intimidation and violence haunted the city. Red Shirts terrorized Black neighborhoods and threatened local officials, while Wilmington's Democrats demanded that the Fusionists withdraw all their candidates for county office. Fearing violence, Governor Daniel Lindsay Russell agreed, and the entire county slate of Republican candidates withdrew. On the eve of the election, Waddell told a crowd of Red Shirts:

> You must do your duty. This city, county and state shall be rid of negro domination, once and forever. . . . You are the sons of noble ancestry. You are Anglo-Saxons. . . . Go to the polls tomorrow and if you find a negro out voting, tell him to leave the polls and if he refuses, kill him! Shoot him down in his tracks. We shall win tomorrow if we have to do it with guns.

On Election Day, White Government Unions deployed election "observers" at local polling places, local newspapers advised

Blacks not to vote, and Red Shirts patrolled the streets on horse-back. Few Blacks ventured out, and many of those who did were turned away at gunpoint. In predominantly Black precincts, after the polls closed, Democratic thugs entered polling stations, threatened poll workers, and directly stuffed the ballot boxes. Not surprisingly, the Democrats swept to victory, capturing 98 of 118 seats in the state legislature.

But since Wilmington city officials were not up for reelection until 1899, leaving Blacks in positions of power, the Democrats did not limit themselves to stealing an election. On November 10, they launched a violent coup. In one of the most brutal domestic terrorist attacks in American history, a mob of at least five hundred white supremacists, armed and dressed in their paramilitary red shirts, marched through the streets of Wilmington, shooting bystanders, attacking Black churches, and burning the city's only Black-owned newspaper to the ground. As David Zucchino vividly describes in his book *Wilmington's Lie,* Black men were gunned down on the street and in their homes. At least twenty-two (and as many as sixty) Black residents were killed, and more than two thousand had to flee the city. The mob entered Wilmington's city hall and, with guns in hand, forced all members of the biracial city government—including the mayor, the police chief, and eight elected aldermen—to resign. They, along with other Fusionist politicians and many of Wilmington's most influential Black citizens, were run out of town at gunpoint and banished permanently. Waddell, the coup's leader, became the new mayor.

Days earlier, North Carolina's African American congressman, George Henry White, had visited President William McKinley, a fellow Republican, at the White House, warning him of the impending coup and imploring him to send federal marshals to protect Wilmington's government. McKinley chose not to intervene.

After reclaiming statewide power in North Carolina, the Democrats quickly amended the state constitution to impose a series of suffrage restrictions, including a poll tax, literacy tests, and property requirements. The number of registered Black voters in the state plummeted from 126,000 in 1896 to 6,100 in 1902, and Black turnout fell from 87 percent in the 1896 gubernatorial election to near zero in 1904. In Wilmington, after three Black aldermen were forcibly removed from office in 1898, no African Americans would serve on the city council again until 1972.

The Wilmington coup occurred toward the end of an ambitious, but ultimately failed, experiment with democratization across the U.S. South. The conclusion of the Civil War had prompted a series of constitutional and legislative reforms that transformed the American political system. The historian Eric Foner describes the Reconstruction era as America's "Second Founding," a moment when the constitutional order was broken and then remade, leading to a "stunning and unprecedented experiment in interracial democracy." Neither equal rights nor the right to vote—two basic components of modern democracy—was enshrined in the original Constitution. By establishing these rights, and by granting the federal government the authority to enforce them, the second founding represented a major step toward America's democratization—on paper, at least.

The legal foundation for multiracial democracy was built in the decade between 1865 and 1875. It was accomplished primarily through three constitutional amendments. The Thirteenth Amendment (1865) abolished slavery. The Fourteenth Amendment (1868) established birthright citizenship and formal equality before the law, giving rise to contemporary rights of due process and equal protection. And the Fifteenth Amendment (1870) prohibited restrictions on the right to vote on the basis of race. At a celebration of the Fifteenth Amendment's passage, Frederick Douglass declared, "Never was a revolution more complete."

The Reconstruction Amendments were accompanied by the Reconstruction Acts of 1867, which placed former Confederate states under federal military rule and made readmission to the Union conditional on passage of the Fourteenth Amendment and the writing of a new state constitution guaranteeing Black suffrage. Federal authorities launched a massive campaign to register newly enfranchised Black voters.

Then the 1875 Civil Rights Act extended the Fourteenth Amendment's guarantee of equal treatment to everyday "public" places, such as streetcars, restaurants, theaters, and hotels. The act's preamble recognized "the equality of all men before the law" and declared it "the duty of government in all its dealings with the people to mete out equal and exact justice to all, of whatever nativity, race, color, or persuasion."

The Reconstruction reforms were the work of one party alone: the Republicans. The Democrats opposed the Thirteenth Amendment as a violation of property rights. (As one Kentucky Democrat put it, "Give up our right to have slavery, and in what rights are we secure?") They opposed the Fourteenth Amendment, insisting that America's government was "made for white men" and that citizenship should be reserved for the "Caucasian race." And they opposed the Fifteenth Amendment, mainly on the grounds that Blacks were inferior. In the U.S. Congress, no Democrat—from the North or South—voted for the Fourteenth or Fifteenth Amendments or any of the subsequent voting and civil rights bills of the Reconstruction era. All were passed exclusively with Republican votes. America's post–Civil War democratization was a strictly partisan affair.

Although nearly the entire Republican Party backed early Reconstruction, the energy—and the vision of a multiracial democracy—came from the so-called Radical Republican faction. The two leading Radicals were Senator Charles Sumner of Massachusetts and Congressman Thaddeus Stevens of Pennsylvania. Stevens and Sumner were, by all accounts, genuine racial egalitarians. Indeed, it is for this very reason their opponents called them Radicals. Their vision of democracy, in which civil and voting rights were extended to all men (and in some of their aspirations, all *women*), regardless of race, reflected deeply held moral beliefs, rooted in the religious revival of the pre–Civil War Great Awakening. In a gripping Senate speech in February 1866, Sumner explained his support of the Fourteenth Amendment this way:

> Show me a creature, with erect countenance, looking to heaven, made in the image of God, and I will show you a man, who, of whatever country or race, whether darkened by equatorial sun or blanched by northern cold, is with you, a child of the Heavenly Father, and equal with you in

title to all the rights of Human Nature. You cannot deny
these rights without impiety.

Sumner insisted on equal political rights for all people, whether
(in the jarring terminology of that era) those individuals were
"Caucasian, Mongolian, Malay, African, and American," because
they were all "made in the image of God."

But the Radical Republicans did not invent the ideas under-
pinning America's first experiment with multiracial democracy.
Rather, they inherited a tradition, forged by a generation of Black
activists and writers from the pre–Civil War era. As early as the
1820s, Black abolitionists, mostly in and around Boston, began to
employ, as Sandra Gustafson writes, a "prophetic rhetoric to advance a *multiracial* ideal of the modern republic" based on full citizenship rights and equality before the law.

Among the leaders of this movement were writers like David
Walker, a freeborn Black man, living in Boston but originally from
Wilmington, and Maria Stewart, the first American woman of any
race to give a political speech to a mixed audience of men and
women. Walker's 1829 work *Appeal to Colored Citizens of the World*
centered on the hypocrisies of an exclusively white "Christian" republic. Walker, Stewart, and other activists were part of the small
but vibrant free Black community that had sprung up in the narrow colonial-era streets of Boston's Beacon Hill, which was also
the location of Boston's African Meeting House. During the 1820s
and 1830s, they argued not just against slavery but for a new notion: the "colored citizen." They rejected proposals—endorsed by
many prominent opponents of slavery—to return freed slaves to
Africa. Instead, they broke new ground by calling for full rights of

citizenship in America, inspired by the promise of equality contained in "the most sacred of all American political scriptures," the Declaration of Independence. The movement gradually became biracial. The prominent abolitionist William Lloyd Garrison was influenced by Walker's ideas, and his antislavery newspaper, *The Liberator,* published Stewart's writings. And in the 1840s, a young Charles Sumner, often seen in conversation with Black Bostonians, worked with the Beacon Hill Black community, arguing as a lawyer for the desegregation of Massachusetts public schools.

Genuine multiracial democracy, as Walker and his fellow activists knew, required universal legal protections. This turned out to be a high bar even for some Republicans. For example, a proposal guaranteeing the right to vote to *all* adult men was on the table in the debate over the Fifteenth Amendment, but some northern Republicans found it too sweeping. Although nearly all Republicans favored suffrage protections for Blacks in the South, many of them were less inclined to grant similar protections to immigrants in their own states: Irish Catholic immigrants in the case of northeastern Republicans; Chinese immigrants for western Republicans. Senator Henry W. Corbett of Oregon argued that extending the right to vote to Black men was "blessed" by the "Great Ruler of the universe," but that the same did not apply to Chinese immigrants. In short, the coalition for a genuinely multiracial democracy was fragile.

Ultimately, universal voting rights lost out to a narrower proposal that barred restrictions on the basis of race or "previous servitude." The aim was clearly to protect Black voters in the South. Other forms of exclusion, including in the North, remained legal. This loophole was critical, because it allowed for the possibility of suffrage restrictions on bases other than race, such as literacy and property ownership. Poll taxes, registration fees, and "tests" to discard "unwanted" voters were also fair game. Thus, the incompleteness of the Fifteenth Amendment was due not only to southern resistance but also to northern Republicans' own ambivalence about voters who were not white Protestant men.

Notwithstanding these limitations, Reconstruction transformed southern politics. Within one year, the percentage of Black men in America who were eligible to vote rose from 0.5 percent to 80.5 percent, with the entire increase coming from the former Confederacy. By 1867, at least 85 percent of African American men were registered to vote in Alabama, Florida, Georgia, Louisiana, Mississippi, and North and South Carolina.

Black suffrage had far-reaching consequences. African Americans were a majority of the population in Louisiana, Mississippi, and South Carolina and a near majority in Alabama, Florida, and Georgia and made up around 40 percent of the population in North Carolina and Virginia. By 1867, registered Black voters outnumbered registered whites across much of the Deep South. African Americans began to ascend to public office across the entire South, in some places in large numbers. A majority of delegates in Louisiana's and South Carolina's Reconstruction-era constitutional conventions were Black. African Americans won a majority of seats in the South Carolina legislature and a near majority in Louisiana; state legislatures in Mississippi and South Carolina elected Black speakers in 1872. There were Black lieutenant governors in Louisiana, Mississippi, and South Carolina and Black secretaries of state in Florida, Mississippi, and South Carolina. Across the Deep South, African Americans filled important local offices, including justices of the peace, county supervisors, school commissioners, election commissioners, and even sheriffs.

More than thirteen hundred Black Americans held public office during the Reconstruction era. Sixteen Black Americans were elected to the U.S. House and Senate during Reconstruction, and more than six hundred were elected to state legislatures. James Pike, a northern journalist visiting the South Carolina state legislature in the late 1860s, critically observed, "The body is almost literally a black parliament. . . . The speaker is black, the Clerk is black, the door-keepers are black, the little pages are black, the chairman of the Ways and Means is black, and the chaplain is coal black." It was, Pike concluded, a "society suddenly turned bottomside up."

Less than two years removed from the era of slavery, southern white communities were accustomed to a rigid racial hierarchy. Norms of white supremacy were nearly universal. But now, suddenly, racial equality and Black suffrage—enforced by federal troops—had become a reality.

The prospect of multiracial democracy threatened southern whites in several ways. On the economic front, the former slaveholding elite feared losing its unfettered control over Black labor. On the political front, Black suffrage jeopardized the political power of the Democratic Party, especially in states where African Americans were now a majority or near majority of the electorate.

Finally, and perhaps most importantly, democracy promised to upend long-established social and racial hierarchies. In the midst of the 1898 white supremacy campaign, Josephus Daniels, the publisher of the Raleigh *News & Observer,* wrote that life during Reconstruction "was just as bad as could be. There were negro sheriffs, negro clerks, a negro State Senator—negroes were in complete control of everything until it grew intolerable." Many whites came to harbor fears of "Negro rule." These fears were fanned by Democratic politicians and newspaper publishers, who used editorials, racist cartoons, and sensationalized press reports to establish a false narrative of Black violence and political corruption. In particular, the prospect of democratized *social relations*— white women interacting freely with Black men—produced a "hysteria" of unfounded accusations of "black-on-white" rape. According to the historian Glenda Gilmore, the widespread diffusion of the myth of sexual danger posed by Black men was the clearest embodiment of the raw fear associated with the overturning of an entire social order.

Many southern whites thus viewed Reconstruction and multiracial democracy as existential threats. As Ben Tillman, a white supremacist governor and senator from South Carolina, later recalled in a 1907 speech on the Senate floor,

> We felt the very foundations of our civilization crumbling beneath our feet, that we were sure to be engulfed by the black flood of barbarians who were surrounding us and had been put over us by the Army under the Reconstruction acts.

For Congressman Hernando Money of Mississippi, living under "the offensive theory of majority rule" was like "placing our necks beneath the foot of a veneered savage."

White reactionaries responded to the emergence of multiracial democracy by waging a terrorist campaign unparalleled in American history. Since Black citizens were either majorities or near majorities in most southern states, white supremacists' return to power would require, in W.E.B. Du Bois's words, "brute force." Backed by the Democratic Party, white supremacists organized paramilitary groups with names like the Whitecaps, the White Brotherhood, Jayhawkers, Pale Faces, and the Knights of the White Camellia. The largest of these, the Ku Klux Klan, emerged in Tennessee in early 1866 and quickly spread throughout the South. The Klan carried out a wave of violent terror in which countless Black homes, businesses, churches, and schools were attacked; thousands of Black Americans were killed; and many more were beaten, whipped, raped, and forced to flee. Republican politicians—Black and white—were physically assaulted and even assassinated.

Klan terror crippled Republican organizations and kept Black voters from the polls, making a mockery of elections and allowing the Democrats to unconstitutionally seize power across the South—a process they euphemistically called "Redemption." In Louisiana, a "civil war of secret assassination and open intimidation and murder" left at least five hundred African Americans dead. In Georgia, Klan terror so decimated Black turnout in the 1868 presidential election that eleven counties with Black majorities registered no Republican votes. In 1871, Klan pressure allowed Democrats to retake the state legislature and force the Republican governor, Rufus Bullock, to resign and flee the state. In North Carolina, Klan violence weakened the Republicans and enabled the Democrats to win a veto-proof majority in the state legislature, which they used to impeach and remove the Republican governor.

In response to this wave of terrorism, President Ulysses S. Grant and the Republican-dominated Congress passed a series of Enforcement Acts that empowered the federal government to oversee local elections and combat political violence. These included an 1870 law authorizing the president to appoint federal election supervisors with the power to press federal charges against anyone who engaged in electoral fraud, intimidation, or race-based voter suppression, as well as the 1871 Ku Klux Klan Act, which allowed for federal prosecution and even military intervention to combat efforts to deprive citizens of basic rights. These laws were unprecedented in that they gave the federal government the authority to intervene in states to protect basic civil and voting rights—an essential component of multiracial democracy.

Initially, these enforcement mechanisms worked. With the help of federal troops, hundreds of Klan members were arrested and prosecuted in 1871 and 1872, especially in Florida, Mississippi, and South Carolina. By 1872, federal authorities had "broken the Klan's back and produced a dramatic decline in violence throughout the South." According to the historian James McPherson, the 1872 election was "the fairest and most democratic election in the South until 1968."

Reconstruction proved politically hard to sustain, however. Eventually, the Republican Party divided. A faction known as the Liberal Republicans grew critical of the costs of enforcement. Prioritizing issues such as free trade and civil service reform, and skeptical of Black suffrage, the liberals began to question the wisdom of the Reconstruction project, preferring a more politically expedient "let alone" policy in the South. The multiracial democratic coalition was further undermined by the 1873 depression, which led to a sweeping Democratic takeover of the House of Representatives in 1874. Public opinion turned against federal intervention in the South, and civil rights activism faded to such a degree that *The New York Times* declared the "era of moral politics" to be over. In this new political climate, federal troops began to be withdrawn.

The turn away from federal protection permitted a second wave of Redemption. In 1875 the Mississippi Democrats launched a violent campaign—known as the Mississippi Plan—aimed at regaining the state legislature. As Foner notes, terrorist acts were "committed in broad daylight by undisguised men," severely depressing the Black vote in the 1875 elections and giving Democrats control of the state legislature. They then impeached the African American lieutenant governor and forced the Republican governor, Adelbert Ames, to resign and flee the state. In South Carolina, the 1876 election was marred by Red Shirt terror and outright fraud. In what one observer described as "one of the grandest farces ever seen," the Democrat Wade Hampton, a former Confederate officer, claimed the governorship.

By the time Grant's successor, Rutherford B. Hayes, withdrew most of the remaining federal troops overseeing the South in 1877 (as part of a negotiated settlement of the disputed 1876 presidential election), Reconstruction had effectively ended. Democrats had seized power in every southern state except Florida and Louisiana. Overall, nearly two thousand Black Americans had been murdered in acts of terror during the ten years that followed the end of the Civil War, a rate of killing roughly equivalent to that of Pinochet's Chile in the 1970s.

The prospects for multiracial democracy were not yet fully

extinguished, however. After all, much of the legal foundation of Reconstruction—including the Fourteenth and Fifteenth Amendments and, in most southern states, Reconstruction-era constitutions—remained intact. And African Americans continued to vote (though in lower numbers), often gathering in groups on Election Day to thwart violent attacks. Indeed, Black turnout remained remarkably high in most of the South during the early 1880s. According to one estimate, more than two-thirds of adult Black men voted in the 1880 presidential election.

Continued Black voting prevented Democrats from entrenching their rule. Amid the agrarian depression of the 1880s and early 1890s, third-party forces—Independents, Greenbackers, Readjusters, Farmers' Alliances, and, beginning in 1892, the Populist Party—won support among disaffected white farmers and, often working with Republicans, forged biracial coalitions to defy Democratic single-party rule. A biracial Readjusters ticket won the Virginia governorship in 1881. Populist or Fusion tickets—backed by many Black voters—nearly won the governorship in Alabama in 1892, Virginia in 1893, Georgia in 1894, and Louisiana and Tennessee in 1896. As we saw, a populist-Republican Fusion ticket won the governorship of North Carolina in 1896.

These biracial coalitions created a renewed sense of threat among the white supremacist Democratic establishment. Once again, the specter of "Negro domination" became a common refrain among Democrats. In Louisiana, the pro-Democratic Baton Rouge *Daily Advocate* warned that Republican government would lead to the "Africanization of the state" and described the Fusionists as "a grave menace to our civilization." Even in South Carolina, where the notorious Eight Box Law (a system in which voters had to deposit ballots in separate boxes for each office and all miscast ballots were disqualified, effectively disenfranchising illiterates) already restricted suffrage, Democrats continued to worry. As Governor John P. Richardson put it, "We now have the rule of a minority of 400,000 [whites] over a majority of 600,000 [Black]. . . . The only thing which stands today between us and their rule is a flimsy statute—the Eight-Box Law."

Indeed, the tactics of terror and fraud that had brought the Democrats back to power in the 1870s were not permanent solutions. And Democratic leaders were concerned that acts of flagrant violence would attract national attention and trigger renewed federal oversight and enforcement. So beginning in the late 1880s, the backlash against multiracial democracy took a new form: Democrats across the South began to undermine democracy through *legal* channels. Between 1888 and 1908, they rewrote state constitutions and voting laws to disenfranchise African Americans. The Democrats could not do away with the Fourteenth and Fifteenth Amendments, but as one southern newspaper put it, "We intend . . . to make them dead letter on the statute-book." And they did, developing what the Republican congressman Jonathan Dolliver described as a "legal machinery . . . which has in a gentlemanly way abolished the republican form of government altogether."

Such "gentlemanly" techniques were pure constitutional hardball. Southern Democrats began by searching for ways to exploit gaps in the law to restrict ballot access. As we have seen, the Fifteenth Amendment contained a grave vulnerability: it only prohibited states from denying the right to vote "on account of race, color, or previous condition of servitude." Seeking to restrict Black suffrage but aware that blatant violations of the Fifteenth

Amendment risked federal intervention, southern whites "carefully avoided open contravention of the amendment," according to the legal historian Michael Klarman, and instead sought to "evade and defeat its admitted purpose."

State by state, southern Democrats did precisely this, crafting "ingenious contrivances," or new restrictions that the Constitution did not explicitly prohibit, including poll taxes, literacy tests, and property and proof of residency requirements that, if vigorously enforced, would make it impossible for most African Americans to register and vote. These laws clearly violated the spirit of the Fifteenth Amendment—and of democracy itself—because they targeted African Americans, who were more likely to be illiterate and less likely to be able to afford a poll tax. Another de facto literacy test came with the hardball introduction of the Australian (or secret) ballot, which required citizens to vote on government-produced ballots—and alone in a voting booth where they could not be assisted by a (literate) friend. Attractive to Democrats because it effectively made it impossible for illiterate people to vote, the secret ballot targeted Black voters who could not understand the ballots without assistance. A form of this ballot was adopted in Tennessee in 1889, and in several other southern states. Though these ballots were justified with laudable-sounding goals of eliminating election "corruption" and fraud, the intent in this context was clear. As the deputy to the Arkansas secretary of state described, the secret ballot

> works smoothly, quietly, satisfactorily, beautifully, and I
> pray God every Southern state may soon have one like it. It

neutralizes to a great extent the curse of the Fifteenth Amendment, the blackest crime of the nineteenth century.

As Democrats in southern state legislatures devised their schemes, they learned from one another (and from many northern states, such as Connecticut and Massachusetts, where literacy tests targeting Irish immigrants were already in place). Mississippi served as an early model: an 1890 constitutional convention adopted a poll tax, the secret ballot, and a literacy test. Over the next decade, such "ingenious contrivances" were adopted in most southern states. As Alabama state legislator Anthony Sayre explained, the laws would "eliminate the Negro from politics, and in a perfectly legal way."

But these "legal" strategies faced a conundrum: they also caught poor, illiterate white voters—most of whom across the South were loyal Democrats—in their disenfranchising net. To circumvent this problem, Democrats often selectively enforced the law. For example, the local registrars who administered literacy tests, and were almost invariably (white) Democratic appointees, judged illiterate Blacks more harshly than whites. Selective enforcement was aided by "understanding clauses," under which registrars would determine whether illiterate prospective voters demonstrated an "understanding" of the Constitution based on sections of the Constitution they read aloud. The laws were designed to give registrars the discretion to apply a higher bar for "understanding" to Black citizens than to white ones. Finally, legislatures in Louisiana, North Carolina, Alabama, and Georgia adopted "grandfather clauses," which allowed (white) illiterate or propertyless voters to register if they had voted before 1867 or were the descendants of pre-1867 voters. Though seemingly neutral, such clauses discriminated against African Americans, who could not vote before 1867.

By 1908, all states of the former Confederacy had adopted poll taxes and seven employed literacy tests. As the pro-Democratic *Memphis Appeal* triumphantly proclaimed following Tennessee's adoption of the poll tax, the new laws provided a "practical, constitutional, and happy solution to the race problem." In one of history's rare cases of a large-scale disenfranchisement, southern Democrats derailed America's embryonic transition to multiracial democracy.

There remained one final check against this "legal" process of disenfranchisement: the federal judiciary. The U.S. Supreme Court might have served as a judicial shield, blocking states' attacks on voting rights. After all, state laws that intentionally restricted Black voting rights clashed with the Fifteenth Amendment's prohibition on racial discrimination.

In the 1890s, civil rights groups began filing lawsuits against state and county governments to protest the multitude of new laws targeting Blacks. Between 1895 and 1905, the Supreme Court heard six challenges to disenfranchisement efforts. The most decisive case was *Giles v. Harris* (1903), which the constitutional law scholar Richard Pildes describes as "one of the most momentous decisions in United States Supreme Court history."

Giles was a voting rights lawsuit against Alabama's Montgomery County Board of Registrars filed by Jackson Giles, a former slave and a janitor by profession who had become a deacon at a Congregational church, a Republican activist, and the president of Alabama's Colored Men's Suffrage Association. Filed on behalf of Giles and 5,000 other Black citizens from Montgomery County, the case was motivated by Alabama's 1901 constitution, which had made registering to vote nearly impossible for Blacks. After passage of the constitution, only 3,000 of the more than 180,000 adult Black men in Alabama were eligible. The chief architect of the new constitution had put his intentions plainly: "What is it that we want to do? Why, it is within the limits imposed by the Federal Constitution to establish white supremacy in this state."

The Supreme Court's majority opinion was written by Oliver Wendell Holmes Jr., a man who was born into a Massachusetts antislavery family, had been wounded three times as a Union soldier in the Civil War, and had been placed on the court at the recommendation of the Massachusetts Republican senator Henry Cabot Lodge, a leading sponsor of voting rights legislation in 1890. But the horrors of Holmes's wartime experience transformed him into a pragmatist who was cynically skeptical of transformative ideas. This skepticism—and a basic lack of commitment to the idea of Black suffrage—led him to abide by a growing body of conservative jurisprudence, such as the 1883 *Civil Rights Cases,* which held that Congress had no constitutional authority to protect Black citizens from discrimination in hotels and theaters, on trains, or in other public spaces. One legal historian has called Holmes's written opinion "the most disingenuous analysis" in the history of the Supreme Court. Holmes argued that since the com-

plaint alleged that Alabama's voter registration system was fraudu-
lent, if the court were to grant relief to Giles and add another voter
to the rolls, it would be complicit in Alabama's fraud. Further-
more, Holmes argued, the court ought not to intervene because
anything the court might mandate was unenforceable given the
absence of federal troops or election supervisors to enforce it.
Holmes, the New England patrician, simply thought the court
should not get its hands dirty. The court thus refused to strike
down Alabama's racial voting restrictions, opting instead to stand
idly by as disenfranchisement proceeded.

The 1903 *Giles v. Harris* decision delivered the deathblow to
America's first experiment with multiracial democracy. After
Democrats won the presidency and both houses of Congress in
1892, they repealed key sections of the Reconstruction-era Enforcement Acts that enforced voting rights. Nearing the end of his
life, the great abolitionist and civil rights activist Frederick Douglass lamented that "principles which we all thought to have been
firmly and permanently settled . . . have been boldly assaulted and
overthrown."

It didn't have to be this way. A brief political opening in the late
1880s had presented an alternative path—one that, if taken, might
have set the country on a different course.

In 1888, Benjamin Harrison, the Republican former senator
from Indiana and a vocal supporter of more robust voting rights
protections, was elected president, and the Republicans regained
control of both houses of Congress. Moreover, Black suffrage and
federal enforcement of voting laws remained in the Republican

Party platform, which called for "effective legislation to secure the integrity and purity of elections."

Two influential Republican leaders, Senator George Frisbie Hoar and Congressman Henry Cabot Lodge (later U.S. senator), began work on a national plan to protect voting rights. Hoar and Lodge were both from Massachusetts, and both men had imbibed their home state's "abolitionist and radical sentiments." The legislators drafted a seventy-five-page bill that protected voting rights in the South and oversaw elections in the North by extending the 1870 Enforcement Act's federal supervision to *all* congressional districts. The bill empowered independent (court-appointed) federal supervisors to scrutinize all stages of the election process, and it allowed citizens in every district in the country to request federal supervision of elections in their district. It was the most ambitious voting rights bill in U.S. history, surpassing even the 1965 Voting Rights Act in its geographic scope, and it would have fundamentally altered the way elections were conducted in America.

In the summer of 1890, solid Republican majorities in both houses of Congress seemed poised to pass the Lodge bill. President Harrison was ready to sign it. The bill passed the House of Representatives in July 1890 with the support of all but two Republicans.

But then things began to unravel.

Nevada's Republican senator William Stewart, a wealthy owner of silver mines, started working behind the scenes with southern Democrats and a handful of Republican senators from sparsely populated western states to sabotage what southerners now called the "Force Bill." On the day the bill passed the House, Senator Stewart was visited in his rooms at Washington, D.C.'s

Shoreham Hotel by the Tennessee congressman Benton McMillin, who had been a supporter of the Confederacy during the Civil War. In his memoirs, Stewart wrote,

> [McMillin] asked me what I thought of the measure, and if I thought it would pass the Senate. I told him I was very much opposed to the bill, but that there was only one chance of defeating it in the Senate, and that was by delay.

In September 1890, two Republican senators from Pennsylvania suggested postponing the Senate vote on the Lodge bill in order to first move on a tariff bill. The Lodge bill was pushed back until after the 1890 midterm elections. But the Republicans' crushing defeat in the midterms—the Democrats won control of the House—weakened the Lodge bill's prospects. Senator Hoar doggedly brought his bill again to the floor of the Senate. But Senator Stewart shocked his Republican colleagues by pushing for another delay, calling for a vote on another measure: abandoning the gold standard for a silver-based currency. Suspicion began to emerge that "silver" Republicans (those, like Stewart, with interests tied to silver mines that would profit from the proposed currency bill) were helping to delay the election bill for the benefit of southern Democrats—in exchange for Democratic support for currency reform. Indeed eight "silver" Republicans voted with the Democrats to put aside the election bill in favor of the silver bill.

When the Lodge bill finally came up for debate in the Senate in January 1891, the minority Democrats turned to their last tool of obstructionism, the U.S. Senate's filibuster—delivering speeches late into the night, issuing impossible amendment proposals, extending debate, and wandering the halls outside the main chamber to prevent a quorum. In a final desperate attempt to pass the bill, Republican leaders proposed a change to Senate rules to allow for the filibuster to be ended with a simple majority vote, thereby allowing the Senate majority to vote in favor of the Lodge bill. But the measure was blocked by a coalition of Democrats and western "silver" Republicans who had voted for currency reform. And so the Lodge bill, which might have preserved fair elections across the country, died by filibuster.

Without federal protection of voting rights, any semblance of democracy in the South was soon extinguished: Black turnout plummeted from 61 percent in 1880 to an unthinkably low 2 percent in 1912. In Louisiana, Mississippi, and South Carolina, states in which *a majority of citizens were African American,* only 1 or 2 percent of Black citizens could vote. Back in 1876, Robert Toombs, a prominent Georgia politician, had declared, "Give us a convention and I will fix it so that the 'people' shall rule, and the Negro shall never be heard from." Within a generation, his wish—shared by white supremacists across the South—had come to pass.

The South succumbed to nearly a century of authoritarianism. Black disenfranchisement undermined political competition and locked in place single-party rule across the South. In every post-Confederate state except Tennessee, the Democratic Party held uninterrupted power for more than seventy years. In five states, the Democrats were in power continuously for *more than a century.* In the words of W.E.B. Du Bois, "Democracy died save in the hearts of black folk."

CHAPTER 4

WHY THE REPUBLICAN PARTY
ABANDONED DEMOCRACY

Nearly a century after the end of Reconstruction, President Lyndon Johnson stood in front of a joint session of Congress in November 1963 and declared, "We have talked long enough in this country about equal rights. We have talked for one hundred years or more. It is time now to write the next chapter, and to write it in the books of law."

In a twist of history, Johnson's Democratic Party, with its liberal wing now ascendant over its southern conservative one, was becoming the champion of civil rights in America. If Reconstruction was America's "second founding," the court decisions and reforms that culminated in the Civil Rights Act (1964) and the Voting Rights Act (1965) constituted a "third founding," establishing a more solid legal foundation for multiracial democracy. This time the reforms were backed by majorities of both parties.

Indeed, because the Jim Crow faction of Johnson's Democratic Party vehemently opposed civil rights, the bills could not have passed without strong Republican support.

One key player was the Ohio Republican congressman William McCulloch, a midwestern conservative and the ranking member of the House Judiciary Committee. A descendant of Ohio abolitionists, McCulloch co-sponsored the 1964 Civil Rights Act. Under his leadership, 80 percent of House Republicans voted for the bill (along with 61 percent of House Democrats). Similarly, in the Senate, which—due to the filibuster—had long been a graveyard for civil rights legislation, the Republican minority leader, Everett Dirksen of Illinois, rallied Republican support for the Civil Rights Act. In the end, more than 80 percent of Republican senators voted for the bill, together with 69 percent of Democrats. According to his biographer, Dirksen viewed it as his most meaningful achievement. The 1965 Voting Rights Act was also backed overwhelmingly by both parties. Senate Republicans voted 30–1 in favor. At a critical moment in the mid-twentieth century, then, the Republican Party played a vital role in passing civil rights and voting rights reforms, aiding America's passage to a more democratic system.

Sixty years later, that Republican Party has become unrecognizable. The same party that was pivotal in passing the Voting Rights Act of 1965 was unanimous in rejecting federal legislation to restore it in 2021. But the Republican Party has done more than walk away from voting rights. It has, in the words of the sober-minded British publication *The Economist,* "walked away from democracy."

Indeed, about a month before Donald Trump's attempt to

overturn the 2020 presidential election, a leading Republican U.S. senator, Mike Lee, questioned the basic principle of democracy itself. "Democracy isn't the objective; liberty, peace, and prosperity are," Senator Lee tweeted. "We want the human condition to flourish. Rank democracy can thwart that."

For decades, the Republicans had been a mainstream center-right party not unlike the British Conservative Party, the Canadian Conservatives, or the German Christian Democrats. Most of its leaders shared a broad commitment to democracy. No longer.

The V-Dem (Varieties of Democracy) Institute, which tracks global democracy, assigns the world's major political parties an annual "illiberalism" score, which measures their deviation from democratic norms such as pluralism and civil rights, tolerance of the opposition, and the rejection of political violence. Most western European conservative parties receive a very low score, suggesting a strong commitment to democracy. So did the U.S. Republican Party—through the late 1990s. But the GOP's illiberalism score soared in the twenty-first century. In 2020, V-Dem concluded that in terms of its commitment to democracy the Republican Party was now "more similar to autocratic ruling parties such as the Turkish AKP and Fidesz in Hungary than to typical center-right governing parties."

Why has the Republican Party gone off the rails? And what does it mean for American democracy?

Paradoxically, the roots of the GOP's transformation lie in its reaction to the very multiracial democracy it helped construct. This transformation did not happen overnight. In the first half of the twentieth century, Republicans were a party of business and the well-to-do, with factions that included northeastern manufacturing interests, midwestern farmers, small-town conservatives, and white Protestant voters outside the South. This coalition allowed the Republicans to dominate national politics in the late nineteenth and early twentieth centuries: between 1890 and 1930, the GOP controlled the presidency for thirty of forty years and the Senate for thirty-two of those years. But things changed in the 1930s as the Great Depression and the New Deal reshaped American politics. Millions of urban working-class voters—Black and white—rejected the Republicans, establishing the New Deal Democrats as the new majority party. The Democrats won five consecutive presidential elections between 1932 and 1948. The Republicans risked becoming a "permanent minority."

The GOP now faced the same "conservative dilemma" that has confronted conservative parties throughout history: How does a party of economic elites appeal to a broader electorate while preserving its main constituencies' interests, power, and way of life?

To break the New Deal majority, the Republican Party did what losing parties are supposed to do in democracies: it cast about for new constituencies. After World War II, Republican leaders looked to the South. As the party of Reconstruction, the GOP had had almost no presence in the Jim Crow South at mid-century. Indeed, as two historians of the South observed, "Republican" was still used as a "cussword" in the region.

But changes taking place within the Democratic Party created an opening. In the late 1930s, the liberal wing of the Democratic Party had forged an alliance with the National Association for the Advancement of Colored People (NAACP) and the Congress of

Industrial Organizations (CIO) to advance civil rights, pushing for anti-lynching laws, abolition of the poll tax, and fair employment law. Gradually, the civil rights coalition gained the upper hand within the party. Whereas Franklin Roosevelt had mostly avoided civil rights, Harry Truman became the first Democratic president to openly embrace them, and for the first time the Democrats included a strong civil rights plank in their 1948 platform. The change did not sit well with southern whites, 98 percent of whom still supported segregation at the outset of World War II. During a 1938 filibuster of anti-lynching legislation, the segregationist senator Josiah Bailey of North Carolina had warned his fellow Democrats that support for civil rights would destroy the party in the South. Bailey reminded them that when the nineteenth-century Republicans had attempted to impose Reconstruction on the South, "we resented it and hated that party with a hatred that has outlasted generations; we hated it beyond measure." The Democrats could not for long embrace both civil rights *and* southern whites.

Cracks in the Democratic coalition emerged in 1948, when the segregationist South Carolina governor, Strom Thurmond, responded to the party's pro-civil-rights platform by bolting and running a third-party presidential bid with the newly formed States' Rights (or "Dixiecrat") Party. The Dixiecrat rebellion made it clear that the Democrats' "solid South" was no longer so solid. Republican leaders saw an opportunity to build a new majority. In 1950 and 1951, the Republican National Committee (RNC) chair, Guy Gabrielson, toured the South, noting in a speech in Little Rock that southern white anger at Truman made the region a "great hunting ground." Initially, GOP leaders differed over how best to make inroads in the region. Whereas conservatives like Ga-brielson sought to align with the Dixiecrats, President Dwight Eisenhower launched Operation Dixie, an organization-building drive that envisioned a GOP as a home for southern urban and suburban moderates.

The conservatives eventually won the day. High-profile events such as the 1954 *Brown v. Board of Education* decision, the 1955–56 Montgomery bus boycott, and the 1957 deployment of federal troops to integrate Little Rock Central High School generated widespread southern white resistance. By the early 1960s, the journalist Robert Novak reported, many right-wing Republican leaders "envisioned substantial political gold to be mined in the racial crisis by becoming . . . the White Man's Party." This is the logic that would drive the "Long Southern Strategy"—a decades-long Republican effort to attract "white southerners who felt alienated from, angry at, and resentful of the policies that granted equality and sought to level the playing field for [minority] groups."

These efforts began in earnest in 1964, the year of the Civil Rights Act. Although most congressional Republicans voted for the act, powerful forces pushed in the other direction. Chief among these was Senator Barry Goldwater, the GOP's 1964 presidential candidate. Following a strategy that he described as "hunting where the ducks are," Goldwater actively pursued the southern white vote. He voted against the Civil Rights Act, championed "states' rights," and campaigned across the South, enthusiastically supported by segregationist Strom Thurmond. Although Goldwater suffered a landslide defeat in 1964, he won the Deep South easily.

The civil rights revolution shook up America's party system. After 1964, the Democrats began to establish themselves as the party of civil rights, attracting a majority of Black voters. The Republicans, by contrast, gradually repositioned themselves as the party of racial conservatism, appealing to voters who resisted the dismantling of traditional racial hierarchies. Eventually, the Republicans would become what the former GOP strategist Stuart Stevens calls America's "de facto White Party." Indeed, the GOP won the largest share of the white vote in *every presidential election after 1964.*

Racial conservatism paid electoral dividends. Nearly 90 percent of the U.S. population was white in the 1960s. And public opinion polls showed considerable white anxiety—in both the North and the South—over civil rights. Although support for formal segregation had declined, most whites in *both* major parties opposed government policies designed to combat segregation, such as busing and affirmative action. White backlash was reinforced by the urban riots of 1965–68. By 1966, polls showed that "social disorder" had displaced civil rights as the biggest problem in voters' minds, and in one late 1966 survey 85 percent of whites said Blacks were moving "too fast" toward racial equality.

Mounting white resentment over civil rights would propel what the strategist Kevin Phillips called the emerging Republican majority. In a society that was both divided over race and still overwhelmingly white, Phillips argued, the GOP could regain its majority status "if the Democrats could be labeled the 'black man's party' and the GOP established [itself] as the defenders of southern racial traditions." The key to the new Republican majority was southern whites. Despite their long-standing ties to the Democrats, Phillips believed they would "desert their party in droves the minute it becomes a black party." Although openly racist appeals were no longer considered acceptable, Republican politicians could attract racially conservative whites via implicit or "coded" language that emphasized "law and order" and opposition to busing and other desegregation measures. This was the essence of Richard Nixon's southern strategy. It worked: four-fifths of southern whites voted for either Nixon or the third-party candidate George Wallace, a longtime segregationist, in 1968. Four years later, Nixon won three-quarters of the Wallace vote en route to a landslide reelection.

Ronald Reagan continued the southern strategy. He had opposed the Civil Rights Act and the Voting Rights Act in the 1960s and continued to embrace "states' rights" into the 1980s. In an act marked by unmistakable symbolism, he launched his 1980 presidential campaign at the Neshoba County Fair in Philadelphia, Mississippi, where three civil rights activists had been brutally murdered in 1964. But Reagan added a new prong—a white *Christian* strategy.

White evangelical Christians, who were concentrated in the South, had no partisan home before 1980. In 1976, they split their vote between Jimmy Carter and Gerald Ford. In the late 1970s, however, evangelical leaders, led by the Reverend Jerry Falwell, entered the partisan fray, founding the Moral Majority. Multiple issues triggered evangelical leaders' entry into politics, including opposition to gay rights, the Equal Rights Amendment, and the 1973 *Roe v. Wade* decision. But as the Christian right activist Paul Weyrich later recognized, a major catalyst was the Carter administration's efforts to desegregate private Christian schools by denying IRS tax exemption status to those that remained segregated. Under Falwell's leadership, the Moral Majority embraced the Republican Party and campaigned hard for Reagan in 1980. Reagan, in turn, championed the evangelical agenda, incorporating much of it into the Republican platform. Reagan succeeded in bringing southern white and evangelical voters into the Republican fold. And he was reelected in 1984 with 72 percent of the southern white vote and 80 percent of white evangelicals.

The "Great White Switch" helped make Phillips's new Republican majority a reality. The Republicans became America's leading party, winning every presidential election between 1968 and 1988 except the 1976 post-Watergate election. In 1994, the Republicans captured the House of Representatives for the first time since 1955. By 1995, they controlled the House, the Senate, and thirty governorships.

But if the Great White Switch created a new Republican majority, it also created a monster. By the turn of the century, surveys showed that a majority of white Republicans scored high on what political scientists call "racial resentment." Racial resentment scores are based on individuals' level of agreement or disagreement with four statements included in the American National Election Study:

1. Irish, Italian, Jewish, and many other minorities overcame prejudice and worked their way up. Blacks should do the same without any special favors.
2. Generations of slavery and discrimination have created conditions that make it difficult for blacks to work their way out of the lower class.

3. Over the past few years, blacks have gotten less than they deserve.

4. It's really a matter of some people not trying hard enough; if blacks would only try harder they could be just as well off as whites.

The GOP's success in winning over southern and other whites who scored high on racial resentment created a problem that is common to parties of conservative elites that attach themselves to a new and energized constituency: it left the GOP vulnerable to capture. In this case, the Republican Party was captured by its *racially conservative* base. This mattered because, although the Republicans remained overwhelmingly white and Christian into the twenty-first century, America did not.

American society grew far more diverse in the late twentieth and early twenty-first centuries. The 1965 Immigration and Nationality Act, which was passed with strong bipartisan support, opened the door to a long wave of immigration, particularly from Latin America and Asia. The percentage of Americans who were non-Hispanic white fell from 88 percent in 1950 to 69 percent in 2000 to just 58 percent in 2020. African Americans, Hispanic Americans, Asian Americans, and Native Americans now constituted 40 percent of the country. Among Americans under the age of eighteen, they were a majority. Across America, neighborhoods and schools became more integrated. According to the U.S. census, the percentage of white Americans living in predominantly white neighborhoods fell from 78 percent in 1990 to 44 percent in 2020. Rates of intermarriage rose dramatically, as did the percentage of Americans identifying as multiracial. Religious diversity also increased as America grew markedly less Christian. Whereas more than 80 percent of Americans identified as white and Christian (Protestant or Catholic) in 1976, only 43 percent did so in 2016.

These transformations changed the face of American politics. Over the last four decades, the number of nonwhite members of Congress has more than quadrupled. The number of African Americans in Congress (House and Senate) increased from seventeen in 1980 to sixty-one in 2021. Over this same period, the number of Hispanic or Latino members of Congress increased from six to forty-six; the number of Asian Americans in Congress increased from six to seventeen; and the number of Native Americans in Congress increased from zero to five. The Supreme Court also looks very different today: whereas all nine justices were white men in 1966, a minority (four of nine) were white men in 2022.

Growing ethnic diversity and movement toward racial equality gave rise to what Jennifer Hochschild, Vesla Weaver, and Traci Burch call a new "racial order." Unlike earlier "racial orders," which were marked by clear boundaries between ethnic groups and established racial hierarchies (with whites on top), the changes of the late twentieth and early twenty-first centuries blurred ethnic and racial boundaries and weakened racial hierarchies. These changes manifested themselves in numerous ways, including growing representation of nonwhites and mixed-raced families on television and movie screens; mounting challenges in classrooms and newsrooms to long-established historical narratives that downplayed or ignored America's racist past; and declining societal tolerance for racist behavior.

Americans also increasingly embraced the core principles of multiracial democracy in the early twenty-first century. Public support for immigration and diversity rose steadily. According to the Pew Research Center, by 2018 about 60 percent of Americans agreed that a "growing number of newcomers strengthens American society" and that ethnic diversity makes America "a better place to live." Americans also exhibited a growing commitment to racial equality. In 1973, only 35 percent of Americans supported laws banning discrimination in home sales, while 64 percent preferred to leave it to homeowners to decide; by 2015, 79 percent of Americans backed a ban on discrimination in home sales. And according to Gallup, the percentage of Americans who believe new civil rights laws are needed to reduce discrimination against Blacks rose from 26 percent in 2003 to 60 percent in 2020.

Changing attitudes toward diversity and racial equality were most pronounced among younger Americans. Young Americans are less white and less Christian than their elders. In a 2014 PRRI survey, only 29 percent of respondents between the ages of eighteen and twenty-nine identified as white and Christian, compared with 67 percent of respondents over the age of sixty-five. Younger generations are also considerably less conservative on issues of race and immigration (as well as gender and sexual orientation). In 2018, Pew found that 52 percent of millennials agreed that discrimination is the "main reason why many black people can't get ahead these days," compared with 36 percent of baby boomers and 28 percent of the so-called Silent Generation.

Unequal legal protection clearly persisted into the twenty-first century, of course, and acts of racial discrimination and other civil rights abuses continued. But rights violations were increasingly contested, both politically and legally. Due to shifting public opinion and the effectiveness of organizations such as the NAACP and the Mexican American Legal Defense and Educational Fund and social movements like Black Lives Matter, acts of racism and discrimination are more likely to trigger public scandals and serious (though not always successful) efforts to prosecute violators.

The rise of multiracial democracy remade America. But it also posed an electoral threat to the Republican Party as it came to be constituted in the late twentieth century. The GOP remained an overwhelmingly white Christian party. In 2012, four out of five Republican voters were white and Christian (that is, Protestant or Catholic). But white Christians were a rapidly diminishing share of the American electorate: they declined from three-quarters of the electorate in the 1990s to barely half the electorate in the 2010s.

Barack Obama's election (2008) and reelection (2012) laid bare the limitations of the GOP's southern strategy. In 1980, Ronald Reagan had won 55 percent of the white vote and translated that into a landslide forty-four-state victory. Thirty-two years later, Mitt Romney won an even more overwhelming 59 percent of the white vote *but still lost the election*.

America's growing diversity did not necessarily spell doom for the Republican Party. Demography is hardly political destiny. Social and political identities are constantly evolving, often in unforeseen ways, shaped by both circumstance and party strategies. Parties can—and frequently do—adapt and find new ways to appeal to broader electorates. But parties that do not adapt to social and demographic change risk electoral disaster.

Consider the fate of the California Republican Party. The recent wave of immigration hit California early, transforming a state that was more than 80 percent white in the 1950s into one that was majority nonwhite by century's end. California leaned Republican during the twentieth century: thirteen of seventeen governors were Republican. But in the early 1990s, with the economy in recession, the Republican governor, Pete Wilson, who aspired to reelection in 1994, found himself trailing badly in the polls.

To regain his standing, Wilson appealed to growing resentment among California's declining white majority. Because whites still constituted 80 percent of the state's electorate at the time, dwarfing the Latino vote (8 percent of the electorate), an anti-immigrant stance seemed like a good political bet. So Wilson turned hard to the right. He embraced Proposition 187, a controversial ballot initiative that would restrict undocumented immigrants' access to education and health care and require teachers, doctors, and nurses to report anyone suspected of being undocumented to the authorities. He also called for a temporary halt on *legal* immigration and an end to America's birthright citizenship policy. Wilson was reelected, thanks to an overwhelming 62 percent of the white vote. Proposition 187 also sailed to victory with 63 percent of the white vote, even though more than three-quarters of Latinos and most Black and Asian American voters opposed it. Republicans also supported ballot initiatives in the 1990s that banned affirmative action in public sector jobs and higher education and restricted bilingual teaching in public schools.

Although the California GOP's anti-immigrant strategy was initially successful at the polls, it ultimately backfired. Not only did California grow increasingly diverse, but soon many first- and

second-generation immigrants were voting. By 2000, a majority
of Californians were nonwhite, and by 2021 about 60 percent of
California *voters* were nonwhite. Having alienated this emerging
majority for short-term electoral gain, Republicans suffered a political collapse of historic proportions. They lost control of the
California legislature in 1996 and never regained it. They lost all
U.S. Senate elections after 1992. And with the exception of Ar-
nold Schwarzenegger, a moderate political outsider who became
governor in a recall referendum in 2003, the Republicans never
again won the governorship. GOP membership declined so pre-
cipitously that in 2016 it dipped to third in the state, behind Democrats and "Other."

The GOP's fate in California was not inevitable. Becoming the
representative of a declining white Christian majority was a *political choice*. Such choices are tempting; they offer considerable short-
term rewards. But as California shows, they can eventually be
disastrous.

National Republican leaders were well aware of these risks by
the early twenty-first century. Reince Priebus, who became chair
of the Republican National Committee in 2011, kept a chart in his
office in the RNC headquarters showing the growth of the Hispanic population and the corresponding level of white support a
Republican presidential candidate would need in order to win future elections. The line crept inexorably higher in 2012, 2016, and
beyond. As the journalist Jeremy Peters observed, "The conclusion
seemed undeniable. There was no way the GOP could survive by
winning a larger and larger share of the white vote in each election." The South Carolina Republican senator Lindsey Graham

put it even more bluntly, noting in 2012, "We're not generating enough angry white guys to stay in business for the long term."

For some national Republican leaders, the solution was clear: if the GOP could no longer win national majorities by appealing to white and conservative Christian voters, it would have to attract new constituencies, especially among nonwhite voters. That meant avoiding the mistake made by California Republicans. In 2005, the RNC chair, Ken Mehlman, acknowledged that the GOP had played the race card in the past and publicly renounced the practice, declaring, "I am here today as the Republican Chairman to tell you we were wrong." Michael Steele, who became the RNC's first African American chair in 2009, declared an end to the southern strategy and created a "coalitions department" to develop strategies for expanding the GOP's voting base.

But the most high-profile effort to broaden the Republican electorate came in the wake of Barack Obama's 2012 reelection, when the RNC chair, Reince Priebus, launched what he proclaimed to be "the most comprehensive election review" ever undertaken after a party's defeat. The review's final report, known as the RNC "autopsy," sharply critiqued the GOP's focus on white voters, warning that the party was "marginalizing itself" by "not working beyond [its] core constituencies." Recognizing that America "looks different" today, the autopsy called on Republicans to be more "welcoming and inclusive" toward nonwhite voters. It worried that many Hispanic voters would perceive that the GOP "does not want them in the United States." If the party did not stop "talking to itself," the report warned, it would be "increasingly difficult for Republicans to win another presidential election in the near future." Among the report's principal recommendations was for the party to support immigration reform that offered undocumented immigrants a pathway to citizenship.

The 2013 autopsy was another example of what losing parties are supposed to do in democracies: adapt to changes in the electorate. Concerned about the GOP's mounting electoral vulnerability in the face of a changing society, national leaders like Mehlman, Steele, and Priebus tried to steer the party off the racialized path it had embarked on in the 1960s. But much of the Republican base—the local leaders, activists, and reliable primary voters who dominate the party's grassroots organization—was radicalizing, and it was pulling the party in another direction.

Indeed, at the same time that RNC leaders were holding press conferences laying out their plans to appeal to nonwhite Americans, state-level Republicans—backed by the same RNC leadership—were working to make it harder for those Americans to vote. Election turnout among Black, Latino, Asian American, and younger voters, or what Ronald Brownstein called the "coalition of the ascendant," increased markedly in 2008 and 2012. In 2012, Black turnout exceeded white turnout for the first time in U.S. history. Whereas most parties change *strategy* in response to electoral defeat, the Republican Party response in many states was to change—indeed, shrink—the electorate.

Following the Republicans' victory in the 2010 midterm election, in which they won control of eleven state legislatures and established supermajorities in several others, the GOP carried out a wave of defensive reforms aimed at restricting access to the ballot. Many of these bills were "voter ID laws," which required voters to provide government-issued photo identification in order to vote. Prior to 2005, no U.S. state required photo identification to vote, and prior to 2011 only Georgia and Indiana did so. But between 2011 and 2016, thirteen states—all Republican led—passed strict photo ID laws. The laws were adopted on seemingly reasonable grounds: combating voter impersonation fraud. But there were two problems. First, election fraud—especially voter impersonation fraud—is virtually nonexistent in the United States. Under President George W. Bush, the Justice Department launched an unprecedented effort to identify and punish cases of voter fraud. They found almost no cases. Out of hundreds of millions of votes cast, only thirty-five voters were convicted of fraud between 2002 and 2005. Most of these cases were simple mistakes or violations of voter registration laws. None would have been prevented by a voter ID law.

So voter ID laws were a solution without a problem, which means that their goal was almost certainly *not* preventing fraud. Rather, their aim was making it harder for certain Americans—particularly Black, Latino, and poorer citizens—to vote. This is the second problem with voter ID laws: they are biased. Requiring identification to vote is not inherently antidemocratic. Most democracies do it. But unlike other democracies, the United States has no national system of IDs, and many citizens lack photo ID the laws required. According to a study by the Brennan Center for Justice, more than 10 percent of voting-age citizens in 2012 lacked a current government-issued photo ID. The problem was most severe among poor and minority voters. For example, when Texas passed a voter ID law in 2011, registered Black voters were more than twice as likely as white voters to lack the necessary ID, and registered Latino voters were three times more likely than white voters to lack valid ID.

Voter suppression was especially severe in swing states. In Florida, for example, Republicans reduced the early voting period from two weeks to eight days, and the last Sunday before Election Day—when many African Americans traditionally voted—was excluded. The move hit Black voters disproportionately hard: whereas African Americans constituted just 13 percent of the Florida electorate, they made up more than a third of the state's early voters. The new legislation placed onerous new requirements on voter registration groups; for example, they had to deliver completed forms within forty-eight hours or risk hefty fines. The law was so extreme that it even led the League of Women Voters to halt their voter registration drives in the state. Finally, in 2011, Governor Rick Scott restored the state's recently repealed felon disenfranchisement law, making Florida one of three states (along with Kentucky and Virginia) that prevented felons from ever voting—even after they had served their time. The move disproportionately affected African Americans. In the wake of Scott's reversal, a stunning 21 percent of the state's African American adults were denied the right to vote.

In North Carolina, early voting laws and same-day registration adopted in the early years of the twenty-first century had brought a substantial increase in turnout: the state went from thirty-seventh in the nation in voter turnout in 1996 to eleventh in 2012. Black turnout increased by 65 percent between 2000 and 2012, and it exceeded white turnout in 2008 and 2012. But after winning control of the governorship and the state legislature in 2012, the GOP passed a sweeping new voting law that eliminated same-day registration, shortened the early voting period, barred counties from extending voting in the event of long lines, and imposed one of the nation's strictest and most racially biased voter ID laws. According to one analysis, Republican legislators "gathered . . . data on the types of identification blacks had and didn't have, and then tailored the list of vote-worthy IDs to favor whites." When the law was eventually struck down in federal court, the court observed that it targeted African Americans "with almost surgical precision."

This was lawfare—legislation that was ostensibly aimed at combating fraud but in reality was designed to dampen turnout among lower-income, minority, and young voters. As the former Republican strategist Stuart Stevens recognizes, the Republicans "are not where the country is. And they know that, which is why they want to change the way people vote. It's just a variation of the poll tax and the literacy test." A former Republican legislative aide in Wisconsin observed in a 2015 GOP caucus meeting that Republican senators "were giddy about the ramifications" of a new voter ID law, with many of them highlighting the "prospects of suppressing minority and college voters." Of the eleven states with the highest African American turnout in 2008, seven adopted new voting restrictions after 2010, and of the twelve states with the highest Hispanic population growth between 2000 and 2010, nine passed restrictive voting laws during the same period.

Studies have found that to date, voter ID laws have had only a modest effect. But that doesn't make them any less harmful. When the welterweight boxing champion Antonio Margarito fought Shane Mosley with loaded gloves in 2009, he was suspended from

professional boxing for a year—even though he lost the fight. Antidemocratic behavior does not become acceptable when it's ineffective. Besides, marginal effects matter. The 2000 presidential
election was decided by 537 votes in the state of Florida. The 2020
election was decided by about 40,000 votes across three states.
Even modest changes in turnout can distort the results of close
elections.

Republican politicians might have feared losing elections in the
early twenty-first century, but many of the party's voters feared
losing something far bigger: their country—or more accurately,
their place in it. Throughout American history, white Protestants
had sat atop a seemingly unmovable racial hierarchy. From the
founding until the 1960s, positions of power and prestige were
occupied, almost without exception, by white Protestant men.
Even into the late 1980s, every single American president, vice
president, House Speaker, Senate majority leader, chief justice of
the Supreme Court, chairman of the Federal Reserve, and chairman of the Joint Chiefs of Staff was a white man. Every single U.S.
governor was white until 1989. Every Fortune 500 CEO was
white until 1987. Americans who did not identify as white during
this period held a lower status. This racial hierarchy guaranteed
white Americans a certain minimum standing in society—a "glass
floor below which the white citizen could see but never fall."
W.E.B. Du Bois called this the "psychological wage" of whiteness.
For nearly two hundred years, this racial hierarchy was taken for
granted.

This changed dramatically in the twenty-first century. Not

only was America no longer overwhelmingly white, but once-entrenched racial hierarchies were weakening. Challenges to white Americans' long-standing social dominance left many of them with feelings of alienation, displacement, and deprivation. A 2015 PRRI survey asked Americans whether they thought American culture and way of life had changed "mostly for the better" or "mostly for the worse" since the 1950s. Whereas a large majority of African Americans, Hispanic Americans, and religiously unaffiliated Americans said things had changed for the better since the 1950s, 57 percent of whites and 72 percent of white evangelical Christians said things had changed for the worse.

But the reaction went beyond nostalgia. The leveling of long-standing social hierarchies generated a sense of unfairness among many whites. When one grows up with a certain guaranteed standing in society, the loss of that special status can feel like an injustice. Indeed, many white Americans began to feel like victims. Surveys showed that whites' perception of "anti-white bias" rose steadily beginning in the 1960s; by the early twenty-first century, a majority of white Americans believed that discrimination against whites had become at least as big a problem as discrimination against Blacks.

These feelings were turbocharged by the Obama presidency. Although President Obama was a political moderate, research by the political scientist Michael Tesler shows that his election had a powerful radicalizing effect on Americans' political attitudes. Obama's presidency made the transition to multiracial democracy plain for all Americans to see. The mere presence of an African American family in the White House, displayed on television screens day after day, made the new demographic and political realities impossible to ignore. Many white Americans feared that the country they had grown up in was being taken away from them.

Much of the resistance to multiracial democracy took the form of white Christian nationalism, or what the sociologist Philip Gorski describes as the belief that "the United States was founded by (white) Christians, and that (white) Christians are in danger of becoming a persecuted (national) minority." "White Christians" were now less a religious group than an ethnic and political one. Although white evangelical Christians were most likely to hold these beliefs, a growing number of conservative white Catholics and secular white nationalists did too. So although it was white Protestants who used to sit atop America's social hierarchies and white evangelical Protestants who flocked to the GOP in the late twentieth century, the "white Christians" who came to dominate the Republican Party in the early twenty-first century were a religiously diverse group of Americans united by a desire to "mak[e] white Christianity culturally dominant again."

White Christian nationalism helped fuel the Tea Party movement, which emerged in February 2009—barely a month after Obama took office. Following nationwide protests on April 15, 2009, the Tea Party mushroomed into a mass movement with hundreds of local organizations, nearly half a million members, and some forty-five million supporters. The Tea Party was a classic reactionary movement, constituted disproportionately by older, white, and evangelical Christian Americans who were determined to "take their country back." Surveys showed Tea Party members to be overwhelmingly anti-immigrant, anti-Muslim, and resistant to ethnic and cultural diversity. According to the political scientists Christopher Parker and Matt Barreto, Tea Partiers perceived themselves to be "losing their country to groups they fail to recognize as 'real' Americans."

So while RNC leaders debated strategy in the wake of the 2012 defeat, many rank-and-file Republicans felt as if they were suffering a more existential loss. Popular right-wing media commentators encouraged this despair. On election night in 2012, the Fox News host Bill O'Reilly declared that "the white establishment is now the minority. . . . It's not traditional America anymore." The following day, Rush Limbaugh told his listeners, "I went to bed last night thinking we're outnumbered. . . . I went to bed . . . thinking we've lost the country."

Not only did the Republicans' white Christian base radicalize in the face of a perceived existential threat, but it effectively captured the party. How did that happen?

For most of the twentieth century, racial resentment wasn't a partisan matter. *Both* parties counted racial conservatives— defenders of traditional racial hierarchies—among their rank and file. Indeed, many conservative southern whites remained Democrats through the 1990s. But Republican politicians spent four decades recruiting southern, conservative, and evangelical whites into a single tent, establishing the GOP as the undisputed home for white Christians who feared cultural and demographic change. According to the political scientist Alan Abramowitz, the proportion of white Republicans who scored high on survey-based "racial resentment" scores increased from 44 percent in the 1980s to 64 percent during the Obama era.

The Republican Party was not, of course, a monolithic entity.

Not all Republican voters were racial conservatives. But by the Obama era, racially conservative whites had become a solid majority in the party.

This mattered a lot: the Republicans' radicalizing voters exerted influence through primaries, where extremist challengers—many of them backed by the Tea Party—either defeated mainstream Republicans or pulled them to the right. The process of radicalization was facilitated by the evisceration of the Republican Party leadership. The rise of well-funded outside groups (sponsored by the Koch brothers and other billionaires) and influential right-wing media such as Fox News left the party especially vulnerable to capture.

Confronted by an activist and primary voter base that one Republican pollster described as "angry about everything," GOP leaders struggled to steer away from white grievance politics. Republicans in Congress tried to rally the party behind immigration reform, the 2013 autopsy report's main policy recommendation. The soon-to-be House Speaker, Representative Paul Ryan, pleaded with right-wing media figures to accept a bill that offered undocumented immigrants a path to citizenship. In a telephone call with Rush Limbaugh, however, Ryan was rebuffed. Limbaugh "cut him off immediately," telling him, "Paul, I know where you're coming from. But at the end of the day my listeners don't want to hear it." Indeed, surveys showed that most Republicans opposed legislation that provided a path to citizenship. After Majority Leader Eric Cantor lost a primary to a Tea Party activist who campaigned against immigration, House Republicans gave up on immigration reform.

The 2016 presidential primaries offered another opportunity

for the Republicans to pursue a more inclusive path. The early front-runner, Jeb Bush (a fluent Spanish speaker who married a Mexican citizen), embraced the 2013 autopsy. One of his top aides, Sally Bradshaw, helped write the report. According to Bradshaw, the Bush campaign sought to "encourage the party to shift with the changing demographics." Bush told his aides, "I'm not a grievance candidate. I won't run a grievance campaign."

Donald Trump took a different approach. He went with the crowd, often playing to its worst impulses. Trump would test out ideas during campaign rallies. "The audience tells you where to go," he said. Trump quickly learned that the Tea Party's racially tinged mantra of "take our country back" was the key to winning over the racial conservatives who now dominated the Republican primary electorate. Whereas his Republican rivals were reluctant to use openly racist, nativistic, or demagogic appeals, Trump readily crossed those lines. His unique willingness to say and do things that other Republicans rejected as bigoted, racist, or cruel allowed him to dominate the market for white grievance votes. As the political scientist Ashley Jardina writes, Trump's campaign signaled to white voters that he intended to "maintain the racial hierarchy." Indeed, studies show that white Republicans who perceived their group's status to be threatened were most likely to support Trump in the primaries. As Ezra Klein aptly put it, "Trump didn't hijack the Republican Party. He understood it."

Trump's presidency accelerated the GOP's radicalization. His success showed that white identity politics was a winning formula within the party, which led many Republican politicians—new and old—to emulate his style and positions. At the same time, many Republicans who refused to jump on the Trump bandwagon either retired or were defeated in primaries. By 2020, no anti-Trump faction of any significance remained in the Republican Party, nearly extinguishing voices of conservative opposition to Trump's extremism.

The Trump presidency left the Republican Party deeply immersed in white resentment politics. A 2021 survey found that 84 percent of Trump voters said they "worry that discrimination against whites will increase significantly in the next few years." Many Trump supporters also embraced the "great replacement theory," which claimed that a cabal of elites was using immigration to replace America's "native" white population. Originally promoted by fringe white supremacists in Europe, the "great replacement theory" took root in the United States after 2016. During the 2017 Unite the Right white supremacist rally in Charlottesville, Virginia, marchers chanted, "You will not replace us!" and "Jews will not replace us!" The white supremacists who committed mass killings of Latinos in El Paso, Texas, in 2019 and African Americans in Buffalo, New York, in 2022 wrote manifestos embracing the "great replacement theory."

Right-wing media figures spurred them on. Laura Ingraham told her viewers, "Democrats . . . want to replace you, the American voters, with newly amnestied citizens and an ever increasing number of chain migrants." The most influential peddler of the "great replacement theory" was Tucker Carlson, the host of the most watched cable news program on American television. According to an investigation by *The New York Times,* on more than four hundred occasions between 2017 and 2021, Carlson or his invited guests claimed that elites were using immigration to force demographic change. Carlson told viewers that the Democrats were trying to

> change the racial mix of the country. That's the reason. To reduce the political power of people whose ancestors lived here and dramatically increase the proportion of Americans newly arrived from the Third World. . . . It's horrifying. . . . In political terms, this policy is called the "great replacement"—the replacement of legacy Americans with more obedient people from faraway countries.

By the end of Trump's presidency, then, fear and resentment pushed a strikingly large number of Republicans toward extremism. A 2021 survey sponsored by the American Enterprise Institute found that 56 percent of Republicans agreed with the statement that "the traditional American way of life is disappearing so fast that we may have to use force to save it." The stage was set for an assault on democracy itself.

Earlier we listed three basic principles that democratic parties must follow: they must always accept the results of fair elections, win or lose; they must unambiguously reject the use of violence to gain or hold on to power; and they must break ties to antidemocratic extremists. How has the Republican Party fared?

Let's begin with accepting election results. Few principles are more essential to democracy than admitting defeat. When parties lose elections, they must be able to recognize their opponent's victory, regroup, and work to rebuild their lost majorities. The Republican Party has lost this ability.

Donald Trump had a long history of refusing to accept defeat. During the 2016 presidential race, he repeatedly told supporters that the election was rigged against him, and he stated on several occasions—including the final presidential debate—that he might not accept the results if he lost. After losing the 2016 popular vote, Trump rejected the result, insisting, "I won the popular vote if you deduct the millions of people who voted illegally." He also claimed fraud after the Democrats won the 2018 midterm elections.

So it should have been no surprise that President Trump denied the results of the 2020 election. In his speech at the 2020 Republican National Convention, Trump declared, "The only way they can take this election away from us is if this is a rigged election." He repeated that claim throughout the fall campaign.

In November 2020, for the first time in American history, a sitting president refused to accept defeat. Late on election night, as the vote count began to favor Joe Biden, President Trump announced that the election was a "fraud on the American public. . . . We were getting ready to win this election. Frankly we did win this election. . . . This is a major fraud on our nation." Despite pleas from his advisers, Trump never publicly accepted the outcome of the election or conceded defeat. Instead, he waged a two-month campaign to overturn the election results, pressuring dozens of governors, state election officials, and state legislative leaders to tamper with or undo the results. He pressed Georgia's secretary of state, Brad Raffensperger, to commit old-school fraud, telling him, "I just want to find 11,780 votes"—one more than Biden's official lead in the state. And he even discussed the idea of deploying the National Guard to seize voting machines across the country, leading a terrified CIA director, Gina Haspel, to tell the chairman of the Joint Chiefs of Staff, General Mark Milley, "We are on the way to a right-wing coup." Finally, Trump's inner circle hatched a plan to block Biden's victory by disrupting the certification of the Electoral College vote. As part of this plan, allies in six states won by Biden prepared false certificates declaring Trump the winner. Trump then (unsuccessfully) lobbied Vice President Mike Pence, who presided over the joint session of Congress that counted the votes, to declare these states' elections "disputed" and refuse to count their electoral votes, leaving Trump a majority of the remaining votes.

But it wasn't just Trump who refused to accept defeat; it was the bulk of the Republican Party. For weeks after the election, most GOP politicians refused to publicly recognize Biden's victory. As of December 16, 2021, only twenty-five Republican members of Congress had done so. The Republican Accountability Project evaluated the public statements of all 261 Republican members of Congress, asking whether they expressed doubt about the legitimacy of the election. A striking 224 of 261 (or 86 percent) of them had. And on January 6, nearly two-thirds of House Republicans voted against certification of the results.

Many top Republican leaders assisted Trump's effort to overturn the election. South Carolina's senator Lindsey Graham called Georgia's secretary of state, Raffensperger, and asked whether he could disqualify all mail-in ballots in counties with high rates of signature mismatches—potentially turning the election in that state. Utah's senator Mike Lee texted the White House chief of staff, Mark Meadows, saying that "if a very small handful of states were to have their legislatures appoint alternative slates of [Electoral College] delegates, there could be a path" to overturning the election. He later told Meadows he was working "14 hours a day" to persuade state legislatures to send competing slates of electors to the Electoral College. Texas's senator Ted Cruz proposed the creation of an ad hoc "electoral commission" that would carry out an "emergency 10-day audit" of the election, creating an opportunity for swing-state legislatures to send competing slates of electors.

State-level Republicans aided these efforts. Seventeen Republican state attorneys general filed a lawsuit with the Supreme Court seeking to invalidate the results in Georgia, Pennsylvania, Michigan, and Wisconsin. In a study of Republican state legislators in the nine most closely fought states in the 2020 presidential race, *The New York Times* found that 44 percent of GOP legislators took steps to "discredit or overturn" the results of the election. In Arizona, Pennsylvania, and Wisconsin, an overwhelming majority did so.

From top to bottom, then, the bulk of the Republican Party refused to publicly accept the results of the 2020 election. "The Big Lie," as it was known, became an article of faith among Republican activists and a virtual litmus test for candidates in Republican primaries.

In addition to refusing to accept defeat, Republicans violated the second principle of democratic politics: the unambiguous rejection of violence. After 2016, but especially after 2020, a growing number of GOP politicians engaged in violent rhetoric and condoned violent behavior. A few Republican congresspeople, including Lauren Boebert, Matt Gaetz, Paul Gosar, and Marjorie Taylor Greene, maintained ties to paramilitary groups such as the

Proud Boys and the Oath Keepers and began to traffic in violent rhetoric, even alluding to the assassination of rivals in Congress.

In April 2020, armed protesters with ties to the state Republican Party blocked traffic and gathered around the statehouse in Lansing, Michigan, to protest Governor Gretchen Whitmer's COVID restrictions. President Trump applauded them, tweeting, "Liberate Michigan!" Two weeks later, they stormed the Michigan state capitol.

During the summer of 2020, several Republican congresspeople called for violence against Black Lives Matter protesters. Representative Matt Gaetz tweeted, "Now that we clearly see Antifa as terrorists, can we hunt them down like we do those in the Middle East?" Republican leaders embraced Kyle Rittenhouse, the seventeen-year-old who crossed state lines with a rifle and killed two protesters in Kenosha, Wisconsin. Trump received Rittenhouse at Mar-a-Lago, while Marjorie Taylor Greene sponsored a bill to award him a Congressional Gold Medal. The Republicans also championed Mark and Patricia McCloskey, a St. Louis couple who drew their guns on unarmed Black Lives Matter protesters, choosing the McCloskeys as featured speakers at the 2020 GOP convention.

The violent rhetoric mounted after the 2020 election. Election officials in Arizona, Georgia, Michigan, Pennsylvania, Wisconsin, and other swing states received death threats from Trump supporters in the aftermath of the election. A 2022 poll of election officials found that one in six had experienced threats on the job and that 30 percent knew someone who had left their post at least partly out of fear. In Wisconsin, some county GOP websites told Republicans to "prepare for war."

Finally, President Trump incited a violent insurrection seeking
to block the peaceful transfer of power. On the morning of January 6, he urged his supporters to march on the Capitol to stop the
certification of the Electoral College vote. When the attack began,
he refused to intervene and stop it. Instead, he *aided* the insurrection by refusing, for more than three hours, to approve requests to
send in the National Guard. At 6:00 P.M., as the Capitol was being
cleared, Trump told his followers to "remember this day forever."
Trump never denounced the assault on the Capitol. Instead, he
condoned it, telling a reporter, "Some people were saying it's
1776. If it's rigged, if it's being stolen, why not charge the Capitol?" Trump later described the insurrection as "the greatest movement in the history of our Country to Make America Great
Again."

Top Republican leaders forcefully denounced the attack on the
Capitol, but several GOP politicians responded more ambigu-
ously. Representative Andrew Clyde compared it to a "normal
tourist visit," while Senator Ron Johnson—uncannily echoing
French conservatives in the wake of the February 6, 1934, riots—
said he "never really felt threatened" by the insurrectionists because they were "people that love this country." Representative
Marjorie Taylor Greene later declared that the January 6 insurrection would have succeeded had she been in charge of it, adding
that under her leadership the insurrectionists "would have been
armed." When the House of Representatives created a committee
to investigate the attack on the Capitol, the RNC accused it of
persecuting "ordinary citizens engaged in legitimate political dis-
course."

The Republican flirtation with violence continued after January 6. During the 2022 primary season, *The New York Times* found more than a hundred Republican television ads in which candidates brandished or fired guns. We can think of no other major party in any contemporary Western democracy in which candidates so openly embraced violence.

Just as important as the open authoritarianism of leaders like Trump and Marjorie Taylor Greene, however, was the Republican Party's enabling of it. Authoritarian forces only succeed when they are tolerated and protected by mainstream politicians. When faced with antidemocratic behavior from their own partisan camp, loyal democrats publicly denounce such behavior, sever ties to individuals and groups responsible for such behavior, and, when necessary, join forces with partisan rivals to isolate antidemocratic extremists and hold them accountable. And crucially, they will do so even if it runs counter to their political interests. Breaking with antidemocratic extremists is the third principle of democratic behavior.

Liz Cheney behaved like a loyal democrat after the 2020 election. Although she was a hard-line conservative and bitter rival of the Democrats, Cheney not only recognized Biden's victory but denounced President Trump's effort to overturn the results, calling it a "crusade to undermine our democracy." Cheney broke with Trump after the January 6 insurrection, declaring, "The President of the United States summoned this mob, assembled the mob, and lit the flame of this attack." On January 13, 2021, she was one of ten Republican House members to vote to impeach Trump. Finally, Cheney worked with partisan rivals to hold Trump accountable. She joined seven Democrats on the U.S. House Select Committee to Investigate the January 6th Attack on the United States Capitol, serving as vice-chair.

Holding Trump accountable for January 6 was not in Cheney's short-term self-interest. After voting to impeach Trump, she received hundreds of death threats and was removed from the House Republican leadership, expelled from the Wyoming Republican Party, censured by the Republican National Committee, and defeated in a primary by a Trump-backed challenger. Loyalty to democracy derailed her political career.

Nine other GOP representatives voted to impeach Trump, and seven Republican senators voted to convict him. Their votes took political courage. Indeed, a majority of the seventeen Republicans who voted to impeach or convict Trump either retired or were defeated in primaries before the 2022 election.

Unfortunately, these seventeen loyal democrats were a small minority. Most Republican leaders acted as semi-loyal democrats. They professed to play by democratic rules but in reality enabled authoritarian behavior. The Senate majority leader, Mitch McConnell, and the House minority leader, Kevin McCarthy, followed the semi-loyalist's playbook to a T. They engaged in appeasement throughout Trump's presidency, acquiescing to Trump's antidemocratic behavior and protecting him from impeachment and removal. Both McConnell and McCarthy knew that Biden won the 2020 election and were troubled by Trump's refusal to accept defeat. Both men were appalled by the January 6 insurrection, blamed Trump for it, and privately told colleagues he should be removed. McConnell called the assault on the Capitol an act of "terrorism" carried out by people who had been "fed wild falsehoods by the most powerful man on earth." McCarthy held Trump responsible for the attack and told House colleagues that he should resign. Both McCarthy and McConnell considered the Twenty-fifth

Amendment as a possible means of removing Trump, and McConnell initially backed impeachment, declaring, "If this isn't impeachable, I don't know what is."

When it became clear that most Republican voters remained loyal to Trump, however, GOP leaders reverted to appeasement. McCarthy underwent a "head-snapping reversal," ceasing all criticism of Trump's antidemocratic behavior and soon visiting him at Mar-a-Lago. In the end, McCarthy was among the 197 House Republicans who voted against impeachment, and McConnell joined the 43 of 50 Senate Republicans who voted for acquittal. Led by McConnell, Republican senators blocked the creation of an independent commission to investigate the January 6 insurrection. This was textbook semi-loyalty.

But Republicans didn't just protect Trump. They continued to embrace him. Before departing the White House, Trump reportedly told the RNC chair, Ronna McDaniel, that he planned to leave the GOP and form his own party. A party that was committed to democracy would have parted ways with a leader who had just attempted a coup. But the RNC, desperate to keep Trump, threatened to stop paying his legal bills and withhold his campaign email list unless he stayed. And most leading Republicans, including McConnell and McCarthy, said they would support him if he were the party's future nominee.

Republican leaders perfectly exemplified what we earlier called the "banality of authoritarianism." McCarthy and McConnell did not actively seek to undermine democracy; they simply prioritized their career goals over its defense. Both leaders calculated that their political interests were better served by enabling Trump's authoritarianism than by opposing it. McConnell believed that an independent January 6 commission would undermine the Republicans' ability to win back a Senate majority in 2022. And McCarthy sought, above all, to be Speaker of the House. There were many Trump allies in the House Republican caucus. Had McCarthy backed impeachment or a January 6 commission, he might have lost their support, putting his future speakership in jeopardy. In an interview on the monument-filled National Mall, the journalist Jonathan Karl asked McCarthy why he didn't hold Trump accountable for January 6 out of principle. "Who knows," Karl said, "if you do the right thing, maybe there will be a statue of you out here someday." McCarthy laughed and replied, "Where's the statue for Jeff Flake?" referring to the former Arizona senator who confronted Trump and was forced into an early political retirement. McCarthy thus joined a long line of semi-loyal politicians—in interwar Europe, Cold War Latin America, and contemporary Hungary, Thailand, and Venezuela—who were willing to sacrifice democracy on the altar of political expediency.

Should we really expect politicians to step up and defend democracy? Another country, Argentina, shows how it can be done. In 1987, Argentina was a fragile democracy. The country had suffered *six* military coups between 1930 and 1976. Both major parties, the Peronists and the Radical Civic Union, had been semi-loyal in the past, supporting coups against their rivals—thereby condemning Argentina to half a century of instability and democratic failure. As we saw earlier, Argentina returned to democracy in 1983, following a brutal military dictatorship. The transition wasn't easy. The Peronists were out of power, and the new president, Raúl Alfonsín of the Radical Civic Union, confronted soaring inflation and widespread labor unrest. As a result, his public support collapsed. In April 1987, during Easter week, a group of military officers known as *Carapintadas* (or painted faces, for their camouflage face paint) rebelled, seizing Campo de Mayo, a major military base near Buenos Aires. Many of the *Carapintadas* had fought heroically in Argentina's losing war against Great Britain over the Falkland Islands. Their hostility toward Alfonsín was rooted in the president's embrace of human rights trials for military officers involved in brutal repression during the dictatorship.

For the opposition Peronists, the rebellion posed a dilemma. The *Carapintadas* shared Peronism's nationalist ideology, and several of them, including the coup leader, Aldo Rico, openly sympathized with Peronism. Some right-wing Peronists had ties to the *Carapintadas*. Although they did not support the uprising outright, they sympathized with the rebels, whom they viewed as "heroes from the Malvinas [Falklands], guys who were badly paid, victimized." But even Peronists who did not sympathize with the rebels looked at Alfonsín's plummeting popularity and were tempted to keep their distance from him. Eager to win back the presidency, they asked themselves, "Why should we help this guy?"

But the party's president, Antonio Cafiero, thought differently. Cafiero was a loyal democrat. He considered President Alfonsín an adversary, not an enemy. With the support of his allies in Peronism's ascendant Renewal faction, Cafiero decided to visit the presidential palace in a public demonstration of support for the government. The images of President Alfonsín and the leader of the opposition together on the balcony of the palace—viewed on live television by millions of Argentines—were powerful. Had Peronist leaders responded to the coup attempt with silence or ambiguity, or had they subtly justified or condoned it, the *Carapinta-*

das might have gained some traction. They might have been emboldened. Instead, they were left isolated and weakened. And Argentina never again succumbed to a coup.

Cafiero's act took courage. He aspired to the presidency, and he would face a competitive primary for his party's nomination. Indeed, his rival for the nomination, Carlos Menem, responded differently to the uprising. When a party official called him and urged him to join Cafiero at the presidential palace, Menem, who was about a four-hour drive away, demurred, saying he couldn't make it in time. Menem was in no hurry to appear in public with an unpopular president from the rival party. Although he didn't support the coup, he also "didn't want to complicate his presidential bid."

In raw political terms, Menem's instincts were sound. Amid a serious economic crisis, President Alfonsín's downward slide in the polls accelerated—to the point where anyone associated with him was tarnished politically. Sure enough, Cafiero's public endorsement of the president proved to be an "albatross." Menem, on the other hand, won the primary. As one journalist put it, Cafiero had "embraced a president who was failing," an audacious act that "didn't do him any political good." But as the Peronist leader José Luis Manzano observes, Cafiero "didn't want to be president at any cost." He and other Peronist leaders acted as loyal democrats, breaking with their party's semi-loyal past. And if Cafiero paid a political price for closing ranks behind an unpopular rival, Manzano reminds us, "what we got in return was priceless. We kept our democracy."

Is it fair, though, to characterize the entire Republican Party as antidemocratic? Certainly, many GOP politicians are loyal democrats. The Republican Accountability Project looked into this, giving a "democracy grade" to all Republican members of Congress in 2021, based on six criteria:

1. Did they sign on to the amicus brief that accompanied Texas's lawsuit to the Supreme Court seeking to nullify votes cast in Michigan, Wisconsin, Pennsylvania, and Georgia?
2. Did they object to the certification of Electoral College votes on January 6, 2021?
3. Did they make public statements casting doubt on the legitimacy of the 2020 election?
4. Did they seek to hold President Trump accountable for January 6 by voting to impeach or convict him?
5. Did they vote to create an independent commission to investigate the January 6 insurrection?
6. Did they vote to hold Steve Bannon in contempt of Congress for refusing to comply with a subpoena to testify before the House Select Committee to investigate the January 6 attack?

These six criteria are, in our view, a reasonably good measure of a Republican congressperson's commitment to democracy. The first three speak directly to the principle of accepting the results of elections, and the latter three speak to a willingness to condone extremist violence.

The scores are revealing. More than 60 percent (161 of 261) of Republican members of Congress adopted undemocratic positions on at least five of the six questions, earning a grade of F. Another fifty-four Republicans adopted antidemocratic positions on at least four of the questions. Only sixteen Republicans adopted consistently democratic positions and thus earned an A. By this measure, then, a large majority of Republicans in Congress adopted *consistently antidemocratic positions* after the 2020 election and January 6, and more than 80 percent of them adopted mostly antidemocratic positions. Only 6 percent of Republicans behaved in a consistently democratic manner, and most of them had retired or lost primaries by 2022.

Between November 2020 and January 2021, then, the Republican Party refused to accept electoral defeat, attempting to overturn the results of an election; it tolerated a violent insurrection—indeed party leaders encouraged it; and it didn't break with antidemocratic extremists. Not only did the party's leader, Donald Trump, remain in good standing in the party, but most Republican leaders said they would back him if he were the party's 2024 presidential candidate. In other words, the GOP *violated all three basic principles of democratic behavior.*

We might take comfort in the fact that the Trump-led Republican Party has never represented the majority of Americans. Trump never won the popular vote, and most Americans opposed him every day of his presidency. And when they got the chance, Americans punished Trumpism at the ballot box—in 2018, 2020, and 2022. After the 2020 elections, the Democrats controlled the presidency, the House, and the Senate. Democracy's self-correcting mechanisms seemed to work: Republican extremism appealed to only a minority of Americans, and in a democracy, of course, parties must build *majorities* to govern.

Or so one would think.

CHAPTER 5

FETTERED MAJORITIES

On July 17, 2020, the civil rights icon and Georgia congressman John Lewis died at the age of eighty. He was the first Black lawmaker to lie in state in the Capitol. As a young civil rights leader, Lewis had helped make the historic 1965 Voting Rights Act (VRA) a reality. On March 7, 1965, the twenty-five-year-old Lewis had led a peaceful march across the Edmund Pettus Bridge in Selma, Alabama. The marchers were brutally attacked by Alabama state troopers, who beat Lewis to the ground, cracking his skull. The horrifying violence of "Bloody Sunday," captured on television by ABC News, riveted the country and spurred Congress into action. Five months later, the Voting Rights Act was signed into law.

The VRA helped secure American democracy by authorizing the federal government to preemptively review—and block—discriminatory voting laws introduced in parts of the country that

had a history of severe racial discrimination in voting. The VRA
passed with strong bipartisan support. In 1982, the Senate renewed
it by a vote of 85–8. Even the former segregationist leader Strom
Thurmond voted for it. In 2006, the VRA was renewed for another twenty-five years by a 330–33 vote in the House and a 98–0
vote in the Senate. In a speech on the Senate floor, the Republican
majority leader, Mitch McConnell, described the VRA as a "landmark for all Americans, African-American and White."

In 2013, however, a conservative majority on the Supreme
Court overrode this bipartisan consensus—as well as polls showing
that most Americans believed the Voting Rights Act was still
necessary—and struck down a key provision of the legislation: the
coverage formula in Section 4. The court argued that the standard
used to assess which jurisdictions must submit changes to voting
procedures to the Federal Justice Department before going into
effect (a rule known as "preclearance") was unconstitutional. As
Chief Justice John Roberts wrote for the conservative majority in
Shelby County v. Holder, "A statute's 'current burdens' must be justified by 'current needs.'" He continued, "The coverage formula
met that test in 1965, but no longer does so." In Roberts's mind,
the VRA's preclearance requirements were no longer necessary.
Writing for the minority, Justice Ruth Bader Ginsburg warned
that "throwing out preclearance when it has worked and is con-
tinuing to work to stop discriminatory changes is like throwing
away your umbrella in a rainstorm because you are not getting
wet."

Ginsburg's analogy proved prescient. In the wake of the decision, states and counties previously subject to federal supervision
aggressively purged their voter rolls and closed hundreds of poll-

ing stations, particularly in Black neighborhoods. And in the eight years that followed the *Shelby* ruling, twenty-six states—including ten that had previously been subject to federal government preclearance—passed restrictive voting laws, many of which disproportionately affected nonwhite voters.

Calling the *Shelby County* ruling a "dagger in the heart of the Voting Rights Act," John Lewis implored Congress to pass legislation to reinstate the protections that the court had dismantled. Eventually, Democrats did just that. Representative Terri Sewell, whose Alabama district included Selma, sponsored the Voting Rights Advancement Act, which restored much of the original VRA. The bill passed the House in December 2019, with an ailing John Lewis sitting in the chair's seat to gavel the final vote. Before the vote, Representative Sewell honored Lewis's lifelong commitment to voting rights, declaring, "To say thank you . . . doesn't seem adequate." But then the bill's legislative progress came to a sudden halt. Republicans controlled the Senate, and the majority leader, McConnell, refused to hold a vote or even allow floor debate on the Voting Rights Advancement Act.

Seven months later, Lewis died. McConnell took to the Senate floor to praise Lewis as a "monumental figure" who made "huge personal sacrifices to help our nation move past the sin of racism." But the Senate still refused to take up the voting rights bill. At Lewis's memorial service, ex-President Barack Obama stood at Martin Luther King Jr.'s historic pulpit in Ebenezer Baptist Church in Atlanta and to a packed chamber of dignitaries eulogized Lewis, calling him a "founding father" of a "fuller, fairer, better America." He then declared, "You want to honor John? Let's honor him by revitalizing the law that he was willing to die for. And by the way, naming it the John Lewis Voting Rights Act, that is a fine tribute."

The stars seemed to align for such a tribute in 2021. The 2020 election gave Democrats control of the presidency, the House, and the Senate. A new voting rights bill, now named the John R. Lewis Voting Rights Advancement Act, passed the House in August 2021. Although the bill had majority support in the Senate (fifty Democrats and one Republican voted to advance it to the floor for debate), it was blocked in November 2021 by a filibuster—the U.S. Senate rule requiring a supermajority of sixty votes to end debate and proceed to a vote.

Two months later, the Democrats tried again, folding the John R. Lewis Voting Rights Advancement Act into the broader Freedom to Vote Act. The legislation standardized voting laws across the country, reversing many of the restrictive measures undertaken by states in 2021; it established same-day registration, expanded early voting, restored voting rights to convicted felons who had served their time, and limited partisan gerrymandering. A January 2022 survey found that 63 percent of Americans supported the bill. Another poll found that solid majorities were in favor of expanded access to early and mail-in voting, greater access to same-day registration, and limits on gerrymandering. Again, however, the Democratic majority could not secure the sixty votes needed to overcome a filibuster. When frustrated Democrats attempted to modify the filibuster rules to allow voting rights legislation to pass with a simple majority, two Democratic senators, Joe Manchin of West Virginia and Kyrsten Sinema of Arizona, balked.

Back in 1890, critical voting rights legislation designed to secure free and fair elections (the Lodge bill) passed the House and enjoyed majority support in the Senate before dying at the hands of a filibuster—removing one of the final obstacles to Jim Crow and single-party rule in the South. One hundred and thirty years later, the parallels were hard to ignore.

The dismantling of the Voting Rights Act makes plain a simple fact: many of America's venerated political institutions are not very democratic; indeed, they were not made for democracy. Five unelected Supreme Court justices dismantled an unmistakably democratizing law, the VRA, which had been passed and renewed on multiple occasions by bipartisan legislative majorities. In 2019, when efforts to restore the VRA were blocked by a Republican Senate majority, that majority represented seven million fewer voters than the Senate Democratic minority that backed it. In January 2022, when majorities in both houses of Congress—and more than 60 percent of Americans—backed voting rights legislation, it was blocked by a minority in the Senate. How did we get to a place where a partisan minority can wield such power?

Part of the answer is that democracy *needs* rules that limit the power of majorities. Modern democracy is not simply a system of majority rule; it combines majority rule *and* minority rights. Early defenders of limited government feared excessive concentrations of power—not only in the hands of kings, but also in the hands of popular majorities. And so the form of democracy that emerged in the West between the late eighteenth and the twentieth centuries, which today we call "liberal" democracy, is based on two pillars: collective self-rule (majority rule) and civil liberties (minority rights). Although liberal democracy cannot exist without free and fair elections, not everything can or should be up for grabs in elections. In the words of the former Supreme Court justice Robert H. Jackson, some domains of social and political life should be placed "beyond the reach of majorities." This is the role of what political scientists call "counter-majoritarian institutions."

Two domains in particular must be protected from majorities. The first is civil liberties. This includes the basic individual rights that are necessary for any democracy, such as freedom of speech, press, association, and assembly. But it also includes a range of other domains in which our individual life choices should be free from the interference of elected governments or legislative majorities. Elected governments, for example, should not have the power to determine whether or how we worship; they should not decide what books we may read, what movies we may watch, or what may be taught in universities; and they shouldn't decide the race or gender of the people we marry. Although the scope of rights to be protected will always be a matter of some dispute (and will likely change over time), there clearly exists a broad range of individual liberties that, in the words of Justice Jackson, "may not be submitted to vote; they depend on the outcome of no elections."

The U.S. Bill of Rights enshrines individual liberties, in effect roping them off from the whims of temporary majorities. But these rights remained ill-defined and unevenly protected for much of American history. This was made plain in one of the most famous cases to ever appear before the Supreme Court. In 1935, in the small, mostly Catholic town of Minersville, Pennsylvania, ten-year-old William Gobitis refused to salute the flag during the Pledge of Allegiance at the beginning of the school day. According to one account, "The teacher tried to force his arm up, but William held on to his pocket and successfully resisted." The next day, the boy's older sister did the same. It turned out that their parents were Jehovah's Witnesses who believed—and taught their children—that saluting the flag was a form of idolatry; not saluting the flag was thus a matter of religious conscience. As William's sister explained to her teacher, "Miss Shofstal, I can't salute the flag anymore. The Bible says at Exodus chapter 20, we can't have any other gods before Jehovah God." The children's actions prompted local outrage: their family's grocery store was boycotted and threatened with mob attack. The school district passed a local ordinance requiring the pledge, and the children were expelled from school.

The case eventually found its way to the Supreme Court, which ruled in 1940 in favor of Minersville, requiring the Pledge of Allegiance of everyone. In other words, the preferences of the town's majority were given precedence over individual freedom of conscience. The court's decision had terrible consequences: towns across America began to pass laws requiring flag saluting, which was accompanied by an outbreak of violence against Jehovah's Witnesses. In one incident, a mob of twenty-five hundred in Kennebunk, Maine, burned a Jehovah's Witnesses Kingdom Hall to the ground. Majorities can be abusive and dangerous.

In 1943, however, the Supreme Court reversed its stance on the Minersville case, helping to lay the basis for the protection of individual rights in the United States. As Justice Jackson explained in his influential majority opinion, elected "village tyrants" may assault individual rights in the name of majorities. So constitutional safeguards like the U.S. Bill of Rights and independent supreme courts with the power of judicial review can offer critical protection to individuals and minorities against majority abuse. Without strong mechanisms to secure individual rights of the sort sought by the Jehovah's Witnesses, or by Japanese Americans during World War II, or by African Americans and members of other religious, ethnic, political, or sexual minorities, democracy as we know it cannot exist.

Majorities must also be constrained in a second area: the rules of democracy itself. Elected governments must not be able to use their temporary majorities to entrench themselves in power by changing the rules of the game in ways that weaken their opponents or undermine fair competition. This is the specter of "majority tyranny": the possibility that a government will use its popular or parliamentary majority to vote the opposition—and democracy—out of existence. Consider Tanzania, a country that freed itself from European colonial rule in the early 1960s, ushering in a period of great hope and idealism. Tanzania's independence movement was led by Julius Nyerere and the Tanganyika African National Union (TANU) party. Like George Washington, Nyerere was revered as a national hero and enjoyed widespread support. In parliamentary elections held a year before independence in December 1961, TANU won seventy of seventy-one seats. In 1962, Nyerere won Tanzania's founding presidential election with 98 percent of the vote, compared with 1.9 percent for the runner-up, Zuberi Mtemvu. Nyerere and TANU thus had an unmistakable popular majority. They then used that majority to wipe out the opposition. Parliament first passed the 1962 Preventive Detention Act, which allowed the government to jail its opponents. It then rewrote the constitution to outlaw the opposition completely and establish single-party rule. Nyerere's party is still in power today.

The opposition's right to compete on a level playing field is another essential minority right. Democracies must create mechanisms that protect the democratic process from majorities that would subvert it. The process of constitutional amendment should therefore be difficult so that the rules of the game cannot simply be recast to the advantage of present-day incumbents. One way to do this is through rules that prevent simple majorities from amending the constitution. Most democracies require supermajorities (at least two-thirds of the legislature) to amend or rewrite the constitution. Other democracies intentionally inject a delay to this counter-majoritarianism, requiring the approval of two successive elected parliaments. Independent judiciaries with constitutional review power, meaning they have the authority to strike down unconstitutional laws, are another counter-majoritarian check on majority tyranny. Federalism and staggered elections (in which different offices are up for election in different years) also help check majorities, because they disperse power and reduce the likelihood that a single party will control all branches and levels of government.

The threat of majority tyranny remains ever present. In Hungary, we saw how the government of Viktor Orbán used its parliamentary majority to impose constitutional and electoral reforms that eviscerated judicial checks on Orbán's power and disadvantaged the opposition. And in 2023, the government of Prime Minister Benjamin Netanyahu in Israel attempted to push through reforms aimed at weakening the judiciary. One proposed law would enable a simple parliamentary majority to overturn Su-

preme Court rulings that struck down legislation, effectively
doing away with judicial review. For many observers, the measures were an assault on democracy. According to the former
prime minister Ehud Barak, they placed Israeli democracy in "imminent danger of collapse." In both Hungary and Israel, it was too
easy for simple majorities to change the rules of democracy. In
Hungary, only two-thirds of a single parliamentary chamber are
required to rewrite the constitution, and first-past-the-post electoral rules allowed Orbán's Fidesz party to capture two-thirds of
parliament despite winning just 53 percent of the vote. Israel has
no written constitution, so many democratic rules can be changed
by a simple parliamentary majority. That's too low a barrier.

Most democrats agree that individual liberties and the opposition's right to fair competition must be placed beyond the reach of
majorities. All democracies must therefore be tempered by a degree of counter-majoritarianism. But democracies must also empower majorities. Indeed, a political system that does *not* grant
majorities considerable say cannot be called a democracy. This is
the danger of counter-majoritarianism: rules designed to fetter
majorities may allow partisan minorities to *consistently thwart* and
even *rule over* majorities. As the eminent democratic theorist Robert Dahl warned, fear of "tyranny of the majority" may obscure an
equally dangerous phenomenon: tyranny of the minority. So just
as it is essential that some domains be placed beyond the reach of
majorities, so too is it essential that other domains remain *within the
reach of majorities*. Democracy is more than majority rule, but without majority rule there is no democracy.

Two domains must always remain within the reach of majorities: elections and legislative decision making. First, those with

more votes should prevail over those with fewer votes in deter-
mining who holds political office. There is no theory of liberal
democracy that justifies any other outcome. When candidates or
parties can win power against the wishes of the majority, democracy loses its meaning.

Second, those who win elections should govern. Legislative
majorities should be able to pass regular laws—provided, of course,
that such laws do not violate civil liberties or undermine the democratic process. From a democratic standpoint, supermajority rules
that allow a parliamentary minority to permanently block regular,
lawful legislation backed by the majority are difficult to defend.
Supermajority rules like the Senate filibuster are often cast either as
essential safeguards for minority rights or as mechanisms for compromise and consensus building. But such rules provide partisan
minorities with a powerful weapon: a veto. When such vetoes ex-
tend beyond the protection of civil liberties or the democratic process itself, they allow legislative minorities to impose their
preferences on the majority.

The political theorist Melissa Schwartzberg adds an important
observation: while supermajority rules may protect minority
rights in theory, in *practice* they often end up advancing the interests of other, more privileged minorities. In the United States,
counter-majoritarian institutions far more often protected southern slaveholders, large farming interests, and other wealthy elites
than they protected vulnerable minorities such as African Americans during Jim Crow or Japanese Americans in the 1940s.

Indeed, counter-majoritarian institutions that thwart electoral
and legislative majorities are often associated with authoritarianism,
not liberal democracy. For example, Thailand's military leaders

have long used counter-majoritarian institutions to win power without winning elections. After dismantling democracy in a 2014 coup, the Thai military, under the new ruler, General Prayuth Chan-ocha, sought to return to constitutional rule *without actually giving up power.* So the army established a bicameral parliamentary system with an elected 500-member House and a military-appointed 250-member Senate. The prime minister would be elected by a simple majority in a joint session of both houses. Because the military appointed all 250 senators, pro-military parties had to win only 126 of 500 House seats to ensure that General Prayuth would be elected prime minister. Even though the opposition party won the most seats in the House election in 2019, Prayuth was easily elected.

Similarly, when Chile democratized in 1989, it did so with a highly counter-majoritarian constitution imposed by the military dictator Augusto Pinochet. The 1980 constitution stipulated, for example, that nine of the Senate's forty-seven members would be appointed by the armed forces and other members of the outgoing dictatorship. When democratic elections were held in 1989, the opposition *Concertación* coalition won 55 percent of the vote and twenty-two of thirty-eight elected seats in the Senate. But thanks to the nine appointed senators, Pinochet's conservative allies gained a majority in the upper house, which stymied many of the new democratic government's reform efforts.

So not all counter-majoritarian institutions strengthen democracy. We must distinguish clearly between those that protect minorities, preserving democracy, and those that privilege minorities by granting them unfair advantage, thereby subverting democracy. In a professional soccer match, rules that ensure fair competition or protect players by banning dangerous and unfair play are essential. But rules that would allow one team to begin with a goal advantage, or which would award victory to a team that scored fewer goals, would be considered patently unfair.

Counter-majoritarianism also has a temporal dimension. Present-day majorities may be held in check by decisions made in the past—sometimes the distant past. This happens in two ways. First, since constitutions may endure for decades and even centuries, one generation inevitably ties the hands of majorities generations into the future. Legal theorists have called this the problem of the dead hand. The more difficult a constitution is to change, the firmer the grip of the dead hand.

Eighteenth-century radicals such as Jefferson and Thomas Paine were skeptical that a founding generation had the right to fetter future generations. Here, they echoed John Locke, who asked: Do parents ever have the right to shackle their children with future commitments? Jefferson engaged in a lively debate with James Madison over this question, asking his friend and ally "whether one generation of men has a right to bind another." His own answer was no. "The dead," he wrote to Madison, "should not govern the living." Jefferson even proposed an "expiration date" for constitutions, suggesting that they be rewritten every nineteen years—or once a generation. Though rejected by Madison, this Jeffersonian principle was incorporated into France's revolutionary constitution of 1793, which explicitly stated, "A people always have the right of revising, amending, and changing their Constitution. One generation cannot subject to its laws future generations." (The constitution was sidelined within months and replaced within two years.)

Madison and others recognized that there was value to entrenching constitutions. Indeed, the *whole point* of a democratic constitution is to establish a set of rights that are protected from the transient whims of present-day majorities. When it comes to the right to vote, freedom of expression, and other basic rights, we *should* be constrained by past generations. Madison also saw, with great prescience, that there are benefits to inheriting a stable, functioning constitution rather than having to rewrite the rules every twenty years. Bolivia and Ecuador have changed constitutions at a rate of about once a decade since independence in the 1820s. They have never sustained stable democracies, showing us the cost of not having a set of widely accepted rules that transcend politics. Nowhere has the Jeffersonian model given rise to a functional democracy.

And yet there is something to Jefferson's perspective. Constitutions are extraordinarily counter-majoritarian; they bind *generations* of majorities. The problem is that constitutional framers are fallible. Even the most brilliant among them cannot see far into the future. As the Federalist Noah Webster put it, it would be "consummate arrogance" to assume that America's founders had "all possible wisdom" to "foresee all possible circumstances" and "judge for future generations better than they can judge for themselves." The founders themselves recognized this. During the Philadelphia Convention, the Virginia delegate George Mason warned that the new constitution "will certainly be defective."

So constitutions should bind future generations—but not too tightly. If the barriers to change are too cumbersome, present-day majorities risk being trapped in an "iron cage" of rules that don't reflect society's needs and prevailing values. When this happens, *intergenerational counter-majoritarianism* becomes a serious problem.

The judicial branch is prone to another variant of this problem, especially when judges are appointed to powerful positions with no expiration date—no term limits or retirement age. Judicial review empowers judges—some appointed decades earlier—to strike down laws or policies of present-day majorities. It was this problem that provoked Franklin Roosevelt's 1937 "court packing" plan. Not only had Roosevelt just been overwhelmingly reelected with 61 percent of the popular vote, but he faced an unprecedented challenge in the Great Depression, which had prompted a reconsideration of the role of government in the economy. Roosevelt's New Deal program, which reflected this new thinking, was initially thwarted by a conservative Supreme Court majority composed of justices who were over seventy years old and had done their legal training in the nineteenth century. Again, judicial review can be legitimate and democracy enhancing. But when the justices doing the constitutional reviewing remain on the bench for decades, long after those who appointed them have left office, public policy may recede further and further beyond the reach of present-day majorities.

Democracies cannot survive without some essential countermajoritarian institutions. But they also cannot survive—at least as democracies—with excessively counter-majoritarian institutions. And this is where the United States finds itself today.

The U.S. constitutional system contains an unusually large number of counter-majoritarian institutions. These include the following:

- The Bill of Rights, which was added to the Constitution in 1791, just after the Constitutional Convention in Philadelphia.

- A Supreme Court with lifetime appointments for justices and power of judicial review, or the authority to strike down as unconstitutional laws passed by congressional majorities.
- Federalism, which devolves considerable lawmaking power to state and local governments, beyond the reach of national majorities.
- A bicameral Congress, which means that two legislative majorities are required to pass laws.
- A severely malapportioned Senate, in which all states are given the same representation, regardless of population.
- The filibuster, a supermajority rule in the Senate (not in the Constitution) that allows a partisan minority to permanently block legislation backed by the majority.
- The Electoral College, an indirect system of electing presidents that privileges smaller states and allows losers of the popular vote to win the presidency.
- Extreme supermajority rules for constitutional change: a two-thirds vote of each house of Congress, plus approval by three-quarters of U.S. states.

Of these, the Bill of Rights is the most unambiguously protective of democracy. Others are double-edged. An independent Supreme Court with judicial review power can be critical to protecting minority rights, but lifetime tenure allows unelected justices to thwart majorities for multiple generations. Extensive judicial review power, moreover, may be used to strike down majority-backed laws that do not threaten democracy or fundamental rights. Federalism is often viewed as a bulwark against dangerous national majorities, but for much of American history it has permitted state and local governments to egregiously violate civil and basic democratic rights. Supermajority rules for constitutional change are necessary to protect democracy, but the U.S. Constitution is extraordinarily difficult to reform, and comparative research suggests that the world's most democratic countries have fewer obstacles to reform.

Then there are the counter-majoritarian institutions that are clearly undemocratic, in that they empower partisan minorities at the expense of electoral and legislative majorities. One is the Electoral College, which allows a candidate with fewer votes to win the presidency. Another is the Senate, which dramatically over-represents citizens of less populated states (such as Wyoming and Vermont) at the expense of populous states (such as California and Texas) and allows partisan minorities to use the filibuster to permanently block legislation backed by large majorities.

America has always been excessively counter-majoritarian. Indeed, this feature was baked into the Constitution. Why?

One reason is historical timing. America has the world's oldest written constitution. It is an eighteenth-century document, a product of a pre-democratic era. Modern democracy, with equal rights and full suffrage, did not exist anywhere in the world at the time of the founding. The founders' ideas regarding popular sovereignty were quite radical. The constitutional order they created—a republic, rather than a monarchy, with no property requirements for officeholders, competitive elections for the presidency and the House, and, within a few decades, broad suffrage for white men—was more democratic than anything existing in Europe at the time. Still, the founders did not aspire to build what we would today call a democracy. Many of them openly rejected democracy. The Massachusetts delegate Elbridge Gerry, for example, called it "the worst . . . of all political evils." Neither the right to vote nor civil liberties, two essential elements of modern democracy, were included in the original Constitution. And guided by an outsized fear of popular majorities, the founders were quick to embrace institutions that checked or constrained them.

But the problem is not just *when* the Constitution was written; it's also *how* it was written. Many Americans revere the Constitution as a virtually unassailable document. They view counter-majoritarian institutions like the Senate and the Electoral College as part of a carefully calibrated system of checks and balances designed by extraordinarily prescient leaders. This is a myth. The framers were a talented group of men who forged the world's most enduring constitution. But our counter-majoritarian institutions were *not* part of a well-thought-out master plan. Indeed, two of America's most prominent framers, Hamilton and Madison, *opposed* many of them.

The founders might have been inspired by classical Greek and Roman writers, but most of them were experienced and pragmatic politicians who sought, above all, to forge a lasting union of thirteen independent states. The stakes were high. America's first constitution, the 1781 Articles of Confederation, had proven unworkable, and delegates to the 1787 Constitutional Convention feared the country stood at the brink of civil war. If the convention failed and the union broke apart, America risked a descent into instability and violence. Not only would the country's emerging economy be threatened, but crucially, the states would be vulnerable to British, French, and Spanish geopolitical ambition and military intervention. Under intense pressure to reach an agreement, the convention's fifty-five delegates did what leaders navigating transitions usually do: they improvised and compromised.

Founders of a new constitutional order often face an immense challenge: they must secure cooperation of diverse groups, some of which are powerful enough to "kick over the board"—and abruptly end the game—if their demands are not met. When small but influential groups can credibly threaten to derail a difficult transition, founding leaders often conclude that they have no choice but to grant them outsized privileges. During Poland's 1989 transition from communism, the anticommunist opposition agreed to a· pact guaranteeing the outgoing Communist Party 65 percent of the seats in the first elected parliament. The Chilean dictator Augusto Pinochet only agreed to leave power after being assured that he would remain in charge of the military, that the armed forces would retain considerable power, that human rights trials would be off the agenda, and that nine of the country's forty-seven senators would be appointed by the outgoing authoritarian government. In South Africa, the ruling National Party agreed to the dismantling of apartheid once they had secured a range of protections for the white minority, including cabinet representation and a vice presidency in the first elected government. In these cases, counter-majoritarianism is a product not of high-minded efforts to balance majority rule and minority rights but rather of a series of particular concessions aimed at placating a powerful minority that threatens to sabotage the transition.

The U.S. founding was similarly fraught. Two explosive issues seemed poised to wreck the framers' plans to forge a constitutional consensus as they gathered in Philadelphia in the summer of 1787: the role of smaller states in the union and the institution of slavery.

Representatives of small states like Delaware worried that their interests would be swamped by larger states like Virginia and Pennsylvania. The states had existed as semi-independent entities since the Revolutionary War; they had developed strong, almost nation-like, identities and interests, which they jealously guarded. Thus, many of their representatives demanded that states be given equal representation in the new political system. In other words, statehood, not population, would be the principal basis for representation.

The demands of the five southern slave states centered on protecting slavery as an institution. This was a nonnegotiable issue for the South. Southern delegates resisted the creation of any mechanism in the new Constitution that would potentially endanger it. But southern slaveholders were a minority, both in the convention and in America. Overall, the population of the eight northern states roughly matched that of the five southern states. However, since 40 percent of the southern population were enslaved people who had no voting rights and because southern states had more restrictive voting laws, the North had a much larger voting population and would likely prevail in any national election. So representatives of the southern slave states insisted on counter-majoritarian protections, "as close to ironclad as possible," to ensure slavery's survival under the new republic.

Madison saw how a schism over slavery might shatter the embryonic union. Seven weeks into the convention, he observed that the greatest fault line running through it was not between big and small states but between northern and southern states. Representatives of the southern slave states regarded the protection of slavery as a matter of existential importance. Their principal demand was, in the words of the historian Sean Wilentz, to "keep slavery completely outside the national government's reach," or, at the very least, to "make it impossible for the government to enact anything concerning slavery without the slaveholding states' consent." If this demand were not met, they threatened to abandon the convention. Although many northern delegates were personally opposed to slavery, and although a majority of delegates, led by Madison, insisted on not explicitly recognizing slavery as a form of property in the Constitution, few (if any) of them were committed to an antislavery constitution.

To reach an agreement, the representatives of small states and southern slave states would have to be mollified. So they were granted various concessions. The new Constitution not only permitted slavery: it safeguarded the institution, and, as Wilentz put it, "strengthened the slaveholders' hand in national politics." Protections included a twenty-year congressional ban on the abolition of the slave trade, a clause mandating the return of fugitive slaves, and another that empowered the federal government to put down domestic rebellions (implicitly including slave revolts). The biggest victory for the southern states, however, was the notorious "three-fifths clause," which allowed them to count enslaved people as part of each state's population (five slaves counted as three free persons) for the purposes of legislative apportionment, even though slaves had no rights. This expanded the slave states' representation in the House, which also increased their influence in the Electoral College. In this way, the southern slaveholding minority achieved its demand for what the South Carolina delegate Charles Pinckney called "something like an equality." For example, in 1790, Massachusetts's voting population was greater than Virginia's, but since

Virginia had 300,000 slaves, it was given five more representatives to Congress than Massachusetts; likewise, New Hampshire and South Carolina had an equal number of free citizens, but since South Carolina had 100,000 slaves, it received two more House seats than New Hampshire. Overall, the three-fifths clause increased the South's representation in the House of Representatives by 25 percent. This gave the southern states control of nearly half of the House, which was enough to "thwart any national lawmaking regarding slavery that lacked their approval."

The issue of slavery—and *protecting* slavery—thus powerfully shaped the drafting of America's Constitution. The word "slavery" didn't appear in the final document, but its institutional legacies were far-reaching. Never has a silence echoed so loudly.

Although the three-fifths clause became moot after the Civil War, other counter-majoritarian compromises endured. Chief among these was the structure of the U.S. Senate. Small-state delegates insisted that all states be given equal representation in the political system—a highly anti-majority arrangement that would give Delaware, with its fifty-nine thousand residents, the same political representation as Massachusetts, Virginia, and Pennsylvania, each of which had between five and seven times as many residents. Many of the founders, including Hamilton and Madison, strongly opposed the idea of equal representation of states. As Hamilton argued at the convention, people, not territories, deserved representation in Congress:

As states are a collection of individual men[,] which ought we to respect most, the rights of the people composing them, or the artificial beings resulting from the composition? Nothing could be more preposterous or absurd than to sacrifice the former to the latter.

Hamilton, criticizing the Articles of Confederation, argued that the equal representation of states "contradicts that fundamental maxim of republican government, which requires that the sense of the majority should prevail." "It may happen," he wrote in Federalist No. 22, that a "majority of states is a small minority of the people of America." Likewise, Madison described equal representation in the Senate as "evidently unjust" and warned that it would allow small states to "extort measures [from the House] repugnant to the wishes and interests of the majority." James Wilson of Pennsylvania also rejected equal state representation, asking, like Hamilton, "Can we forget for whom we are forming a government? Is it for *men,* or for the imaginary beings called states?" Wilson backed Madison's so-called Virginia Plan, presented on the first day of deliberations. Under this proposal, representation in both the House and the Senate would be proportional to the population of each state. But the smaller states, particularly Connecticut, Delaware, and New Jersey, adamantly refused to accept a constitution that did not grant them equal representation in at least one congressional chamber.

The convention nearly collapsed when the Delaware delegate Gunning Bedford threatened that his state would exit the union if states were not given equal representation, ominously warning that "the small [states] will find some foreign ally of more honor and good faith, who will take them by the hand and do them justice."

Benjamin Franklin, the conciliatory elder statesman who had

remained mostly silent during the acrimonious debate, intervened at this moment of impasse, calling for a group prayer. A group of delegates eventually concluded that if they wanted to preserve the union, they had to make this concession to the small states. A deal was struck. Under the so-called Connecticut Compromise, the House of Representatives would be elected via a majoritarian principle, with representation proportionate to the population of the state (based, of course, on the new three-fifths clause), but the Senate would be composed of two senators per state, no matter the size. This arrangement was not part of a well-thought-out plan. It was a "second best" solution to an intractable standoff that threatened to derail the convention and perhaps destroy the young nation. (Madison himself opposed the Connecticut Compromise and voted against it.)

Likewise, the Electoral College was not a product of constitutional theory or farsighted design. Rather, it was adopted by default, after all other alternatives had been rejected.

The question of how to select the new republic's president was the "most difficult" the framers confronted during the convention, according to the Pennsylvania delegate James Wilson. At the time, most independent nations were monarchies; the framers had few good models for the new republic, and most of them were ancient. They had to design a non-monarchical executive "from scratch."

How to choose their chief magistrate? The initial draft proposal, backed by Madison and embedded in the Virginia Plan, called for Congress to choose the president—a system not unlike the parliamentary model of democracy that would later emerge in Europe during the nineteenth century. Parliamentarism eventually became a common type of democracy, but at the time many delegates feared the president would be overly beholden to Congress, so the system was rejected. James Wilson argued for popular election of the president. This is how all other presidential and semi-presidential democracies—from Argentina to France to South Korea—elect their executives today. But at the time, there were no presidential democracies, and in Philadelphia in 1787 most delegates were still too distrustful of the "people" to accept direct elections, and the proposal was twice voted down by the convention. Southern delegates were particularly opposed to direct presidential elections. As Madison recognized, the South's heavy suffrage restrictions, including the disenfranchisement of the enslaved population, left it with many fewer eligible voters than the North. Because the slaveholding South seemed certain to lose any national popular vote, the constitutional scholar Akhil Reed Amar writes, direct elections were a "dealbreaker" for them.

Once again, the convention was deadlocked, unable to agree on a method of selecting the president. The delegates debated the issue for twenty-one days and held thirty separate votes—more than for any other issue. Every proposed alternative was voted down. Finally, as the convention was drawing to a close in late August, the matter was handed off to its Committee on Unfinished Parts. They proposed a model that had been used to "elect" monarchs and emperors under the Holy Roman Empire, a confederation of more than a thousand semi-sovereign territories and lordships in central Europe. When the emperor died, local princes and archbishops gathered in a Council of Electors (*Kurfürstenrat*), usually in Frankfurt, Germany, to vote on a new emperor. This is similar to how popes have been chosen since the Middle Ages. Even today, with the passing of a pope, the Sacred College of Car-

dinals convenes in Rome to "elect a successor." America's constitutional framers deployed a variant of this "medieval relic" in a
non-monarchical setting, which came to be known as the Electoral
College.

The historian Alexander Keyssar calls the Electoral College a
"consensus second choice," adopted by a convention that could
not agree on an alternative. Madison personally viewed direct elections as the "fittest" method to choose a president, but he ultimately recognized that the Electoral College generated the "fewest
objections," largely because it provided additional advantages to
both the southern slave states and the small states. The number of
electoral votes assigned to each state would be equal to that state's
House delegation plus its two senators. This arrangement satisfied
the southern states because House representatives would be elected
under the three-fifths clause, and it satisfied the small states because
the Senate was based on equal state representation. In this way,
both sets of states had a greater say in the selection of the president
than they would have had in a system of direct popular election.

The Electoral College never did what it was designed to do.
Hamilton expected it to be composed of highly qualified notables,
or prominent elites, chosen by state legislatures, who would act
independently. This proved illusory. The Electoral College immediately became an arena of party competition. As early as 1796,
electors acted as strictly partisan representatives.

Two other important counter-majoritarian institutions—
judicial review and the Senate filibuster—are not mentioned in the
Constitution. They emerged in the early years of the republic. The
Constitution (Article III) required that Congress create a Supreme

Court, which it did in the First Congress in 1789. The Constitution also explicitly stated that federal judges could enjoy lifetime tenure (conditional on "good behavior")—an idea that had emerged in England in response to judges' excessive dependence on the Crown. The framers' decision not to impose term limits or a mandatory retirement age should not be surprising. They were not concerned about long tenures on the court. Life expectancy was shorter at the time of the founding, and importantly, the position of Supreme Court justice lacked the status and appeal that it has today. The court didn't even have its own building, and in the republic's early years justices spent most of their time in inns and on the road as they traveled "the circuit." As a result, there was little expectation that justices would stay in their positions. The first chief justice, John Jay, left his position after 5.5 years to serve as governor of New York. Indeed, the six justices of the first Supreme Court appointed by President George Washington served an average of only 8.3 years, compared with an average of 25.3 years for justices who have left the bench since 1970.

The powers of the Supreme Court were left rather vague. The framers clearly aimed to establish the supremacy of federal law over state law (something that was lacking in the ill-fated Articles of Confederation), but the idea of judicial review of federal legislation was never resolved in the convention or explicitly incorporated into the Constitution. There were no existing models of judicial review to borrow from; judges lacked such authority in England. Madison's proposal for a "council of revision," composed of federal judges and the president, that would review congressional legislation was rejected, because delegates worried about judges intervening in the lawmaking process. Ultimately, it appears, the framers never reached a consensus on the issue of a judicial veto of federal legislation, so it was never spelled out in the Constitution.

Judicial review emerged gradually, not by design but in judicial practice during the 1790s and early years of the nineteenth century. On the eve of Thomas Jefferson's inauguration in March 1801, the outgoing president, John Adams, a rival Federalist, worked until 9:00 P.M. finalizing the appointment of new judges to fill vacancies created by the Judiciary Act of 1801, a law passed by the lame-duck Congress that increased the number of federal judges. It was a classic case of what we now call court packing. When the new Jefferson administration refused to process the appointment of an incoming Federalist justice of the peace appointed by Adams, Chief Justice John Marshall, a Federalist, resolved the dispute. In *Marbury v. Madison,* he accommodated the new administration's wish not to grant William Marbury his commission while simultaneously (and deftly) asserting the court's authority to decide when a law departed the bounds of the Constitution. Judicial review then took hold gradually over the course of the nineteenth century.

Like judicial review, the Senate filibuster is not enshrined in the Constitution, even though many Americans associate it with our constitutional system of checks and balances. The filibuster is a classic counter-majoritarian institution. It allows a minority of senators (since 1975, forty of one hundred) to prevent legislation from coming to a vote, which means that in practice a supermajority of sixty votes is needed to pass most laws. The filibuster is often viewed as an essential—even constitutional—minority right. Lyndon Johnson once called it "the fountainhead of all our freedoms."

The Texas senator Phil Gramm described it as "part of the fabric of American democracy." They were both wrong.

Many of the framers of the Constitution, including Hamilton and Madison, strongly opposed supermajority rules in Congress. America's first Congress, under the Articles of Confederation, had operated under such rules and proved utterly dysfunctional. In the wake of its failure, both Hamilton and Madison embraced the principle of majority rule, which Madison later called "the vital principle of republican government." In *The Federalist Papers,* Madison explicitly rejected the use of supermajority rules in Congress on the grounds that "the fundamental principle of free government would be reversed. It would no longer be the majority that would rule; the power would be transferred to the minority." And Hamilton argued (in Federalist No. 22) that a supermajority rule would "subject the sense of the greater number to that of the lesser number." Under such rules, he observed,

> we are apt to rest satisfied that all is safe, because nothing improper will likely to be done; but we forget how much good may be prevented, and how much ill may be produced, by the power of hindering that which is necessary from being done, and of keeping affairs in the same unfavorable posture in which they may happen to stand at particular periods.

With the exception of treaty ratification and the removal of impeached officials, the Philadelphia Convention rejected all proposals for supermajority rules in regular congressional legislation.

The original U.S. Senate had no filibuster. Rather, it adopted the so-called previous question motion, which allowed a simple majority of senators to vote to end debate. The rule was little used, however, and in 1806, following recommendations by the former vice president Aaron Burr, the Senate eliminated it. Although the historical record is thin, Burr's rationale seems to have been that the rule was rarely employed (John Quincy Adams noted in his memoirs that it had been used once in the previous four years), and that when it was, it was largely with the purpose of *avoiding* debate on a particular issue. There is no evidence that Burr or anyone else intended for the rule change to protect partisan minorities or ensure any sort of "right" to unlimited debate. As the congressional scholar Sarah Binder put it, Senate majorities lost the means to end debate—and thus force a vote—"by mistake."

For a few decades, it didn't matter. There were no organized filibusters until the 1830s (or by some accounts, 1841), and the practice was so rare that it didn't even have a name until the 1850s. In the 1840s and 1850s, however, southern senators led by John C. Calhoun began to frame unlimited debate—a de facto minority veto—as a constitutional minority right. Still, senators largely refrained from using it. There were only twenty successful filibusters between 1806 and 1917—fewer than two a decade.

Filibuster use picked up in the late nineteenth century: in the run-up to World War I, a filibuster of a bill to arm U.S. merchant ships in the face of German U-boat attacks convinced President Wilson and Senate leaders of the need to create some mechanism to close debate. So in 1917, the Senate passed Rule 22, under which a vote of two-thirds of senators could end debate (a practice known as cloture) and force a vote on legislation. Although many senators supported a simple majority cloture rule (which would have restored the system of the original Senate), the two-thirds rule carried the day.

The Senate now had what was effectively a supermajority rule, in which a one-third minority could prevent legislation from coming to a vote (in 1975, this threshold was raised to two-fifths). This minority veto power was used to block antilynching legislation in 1922, 1937, and 1940 (despite more than 70 percent public support), as well as bills to abolish the poll tax in 1942, 1944, and 1946 (despite more than 60 percent public support). Still, filibusters remained relatively rare for much of the twentieth century—in part because they were hard work. Senators had to physically hold the floor—by speaking continuously—to sustain a filibuster. After reforms in the 1970s, however, senators only needed to signal their intent to filibuster to party leaders—via a phone call or, today, an email—to put the supermajority rule in effect. As filibustering became costless, what had once been rare became a routine practice. Filibuster use skyrocketed in the late twentieth and early twenty-first centuries, to the point where today it is "widely accepted that legislation of any importance requires at least sixty votes to pass." In other words, the filibuster evolved into what was effectively a supermajority rule for all Senate legislation.

This is a dramatic change. Prior to the late twentieth century, a de facto minority veto existed but was rarely used. Now it is almost always used. Gregory Koger calls it a "quiet revolution." There was no collective decision to adopt a regular supermajority rule in the Senate. "It just happened, and it happened so quietly we barely noticed."

Although the filibuster's defenders drape it in America's founding traditions, in reality, it emerged by accident and was little used for most of our history. The ironclad minority veto we know today is a recent invention.

We have been taught since grade school that our Constitution is a hallowed document, to be viewed under glass. We imagine that our founding institutions were part of a grand design—a carefully crafted blueprint for a well-functioning republic. Such a story obscures the history of compromise, concessions, and second-best solutions that produced them. It also conflates essential democracy-enhancing institutions with unnecessary and even undemocratic ones. When we treat our founding institutions as a coherent and fixed set of checks and balances, we lump together rules that protect civil liberties and ensure a level playing field with ones that give privileged and partisan minorities a leg up in winning elections and legislative battles. The former are necessary for democracy; the latter are antithetical to it.

Opinion surveys make clear that a majority of Americans hold broadly inclusive values and embrace the principles of liberal and multiracial democracy. But our institutions are frustrating that majority. As one important political observer noted almost three-quarters of a century ago, "The American majority [is] an amiable shepherd dog kept forever on a lion's leash." It's not unfettered majorities that threaten us today. It's *fettered majorities* that are the problem.

CHAPTER 6

MINORITY RULE

In February 1909, rural landowners from across Germany descended on the capital city of Berlin for Agrarian Week, the annual gathering of the country's largest agricultural association. Meeting in an impressive four-thousand-seat circus hall, Germany's agricultural titans (sometimes called Bread Lords) debated their political future. As the convention discussed the perils of free trade and socialism, one aristocrat, Baron Franz von Boldenschwingh, proclaimed to the cheering audience,

> Gentlemen, I know that in some places people are shy to criticize Judaism or to name oneself as an opponent of Judaism. It is a weakness of our times to not want to call things by their proper name.

Like many of Germany's big landowners, Baron von Bodel-
schwingh feared the decline of "Christian" culture in the countryside and the rise of "Jewish newspapers" in the rapidly growing
cities. But he then turned to the issue that was the focus of his
speech: the redrawing of district boundaries for Germany's parliamentary elections:

> With all emphasis, I would like to speak out against a
> changing of the electoral constituency boundaries which
> will reduce the influence of the countryside. And I would
> like to add: from my view, any of the MPs from one of the
> parties that is close to us that have come out uncondition-
> ally for the redrawing of electoral districts, should find no
> support and no contact from us.

The German aristocrat's keen interest in the arcane topic of
electoral boundaries was motivated by alarm: he was aware that
predominantly rural-based conservative forces were swimming
against the tides of history. As Germany industrialized during the
late nineteenth century, its cities had expanded at breakneck speed.
Jobs were increasingly found in urban centers, and real estate de-
velopers gobbled up farmland on the outskirts of the cities, building block after block of new tenement and middle-class housing.
The great plains and farmland, especially in the east, were empty-
ing. In the booming cities, a more liberal, cosmopolitan culture
was on the rise. And with the number of workers living in the
cities multiplying, so, too, was support for the political left. The
working-class Social Democratic Party exploded onto the scene,

garnering more votes than any other party in the 1893 parliamentary elections—and in every election through World War I.

But the Social Democrats' ability to win and exercise national
power was limited by the country's political institutions. The imperial constitution, designed in 1871, equipped conservatives with
procedural weapons that effectively thwarted popular rule. The
conservative king had the power to appoint cabinets irrespective
of how citizens voted. An indirectly elected second chamber
(Bundesrat) was dominated by elites. And most power in Germany's federal system lay with the states, which remained highly undemocratic.

That left the national parliament (Reichstag) as the country's
most democratic institution. In 1871, before Germany's urban
boom, parliamentary districts had been drawn up in a surprisingly
fair way: they were equal in size (one MP per 100,000 residents);
moreover, all men had the right to vote. But as Baron von Bodel-
schwingh recognized in 1909, the recent mass exodus of voters
from the countryside to the city benefited his conservative allies
enormously. If conservatives maintained the electoral boundaries
created back in 1871, they would be increasingly overrepresented.
As more and more working-class voters moved into the same small
set of crowded urban districts, each with only one member of parliament, the Social Democrats would run up larger and larger vote
margins to win those few seats, wasting vast numbers of votes. In
other words, fixed election districts amid large-scale urbanization
skewed politics increasingly against the cities. Rural districts contained shrinking numbers of voters but maintained the same
representation in parliament, giving rural-based conservatives

outsized political weight. It was a form of what the political scientists Jacob Hacker and Paul Pierson call "creeping counter-majoritarianism."

By 1912, in the typically rural conservative district of Heiligenbeil-Preussische Eylau, a mere eight thousand voters earned a parliamentary seat; in the typical industrial and mining district of Bochum-Gelsenkirchen-Hattingen, by contrast, a full sixty thousand voters were needed to win a parliamentary seat. The consequences were devastating for the political left: in 1907, Social Democrats won the most votes, with 29 percent of the national vote, but they ended up with only forty-three seats, placing them in a distant fourth place. At the same time, the Conservative Party won only 9 percent of the national vote but ended up with sixty seats. The electoral system was tilted in favor of conservatives, effectively locking in minority rule until the imperial political system collapsed after World War I.

When partisan minorities capture counter-majoritarian institutions, it can enable those on the losing side of history to cling to power. For years, Germany's conservatives maintained their political dominance despite losing elections. They adopted policies opposed by majorities and vetoed policies backed by majorities.

It's one thing for minorities to occasionally frustrate or temporarily defeat majorities in one-off political fights. That can happen in the normal give-and-take of democratic politics. But it is another thing for a partisan minority to *consistently* defeat or impose policies on larger majorities and, worse still, use the system to entrench its advantages. When this happens, you have minority rule, not democracy.

. . .

Something similar is happening in America today. Like nineteenth-century European conservatives, America's conservative party is now consistently given a leg up by political institutions that remain frozen in place despite sweeping societal change. Democracy is supposed to be a game of numbers: the party with the most votes wins. But in America today, parties that win electoral majorities often don't have the chance to govern and sometimes don't even win.

The U.S. system has always contained institutions that empower minorities at the expense of majorities. But only in the twenty-first century has counter-majoritarianism taken on a *partisan* cast—that is, regularly benefiting one party over another in national politics.

The framers didn't intend to create a system of partisan minority rule; they didn't even anticipate the rise of political parties. They imagined a world where local elites without party affiliation would serve as responsible statesmen in pursuit of the public good. As we have seen, the original beneficiaries of counter-majoritarianism in the U.S. Constitution were small or low-population states, which negotiated a set of built-in advantages at the Philadelphia Convention.

But two things changed over time. First, as the country expanded and America's population grew, the asymmetry between low- and high-population states increased dramatically. In 1790, a voter in Delaware (the least populous state) had about thirteen times more influence in the U.S. Senate than a voter in the most populous state, Virginia. In 2000, by contrast, a voter in Wyoming has nearly seventy times more influence in the U.S. Senate than a voter in California.

But there was another change: America urbanized. At the time of the founding, the United States was overwhelmingly a country of small towns and vast expanses of sparsely populated farmlands and forests. All states—large and small—were rural. As America industrialized during the nineteenth century, however, people flocked to urban areas in search of work. In 1920, the U.S. Census Bureau announced, to great public fanfare, that for the first time in U.S. history more Americans lived in cities than in the countryside.

The rise of cities fundamentally altered politics. By 1920, the most populous states were now also among the most urban (for example, New York, Illinois, Pennsylvania), while the least populous were more rural (Wyoming, Nevada, Vermont). What began as a strictly small-state bias had become a *rural*-state bias. This meant that rural jurisdictions were now overrepresented in three of America's most important national political institutions: the U.S. Senate, the Electoral College, and—because presidents nominate Supreme Court justices and the Senate confirms them—the Supreme Court.

Even though America's constitutional system favored rural interests for much of the twentieth century, however, it had no clear-cut partisan bias. This is because for most of the twentieth century both parties had urban *and* rural bases. Rural voters in the Northeast and the Midwest were solidly Republican, but (white) southern rural voters were overwhelmingly Democratic. Democrats were stronger in most northeastern cities, but many western cities were Republican strongholds. Since both parties had urban and rural wings, rural overrepresentation did not consistently favor either side.

This has changed in the twenty-first century. With the rise of the postindustrial knowledge economy, urban centers have become engines of economic dynamism and good jobs, while rural areas and older manufacturing centers have stagnated. At the same time, immigration has increased the ethnic and cultural diversity of many of these dynamic urban centers. As the political scientist Jonathan Rodden has shown, these changes in economic and political geography have had important consequences across Western democracies. Left-of-center parties—the Labour Party in Great Britain, the Social Democrats and Greens in Germany, the Democrats in the United States—have increasingly become the home of urban voters, who tend to be more secular, cosmopolitan, and tolerant of ethnic diversity, whereas right-leaning—and often far-right-wing—parties increasingly represent small-town and rural voters, who tend to be more socially conservative and less supportive of immigration and ethnic diversity.

In the United States, this shift was exacerbated by the race-driven transformation of the party system. Before the civil rights movement rural voters in the South were overwhelmingly Democratic. Elsewhere, they leaned Republican. After the civil rights revolution, the (white) rural South gradually moved into the Republican camp.

Today, then, Republicans are predominantly the party of sparsely populated regions, while Democrats are the party of the cities. As a result, the Constitution's small-state bias, which became a *rural* bias in the twentieth century, has become a *partisan bias* in the twenty-first century. We are experiencing our own form of "creeping counter-majoritarianism."

·   ·   ·

America risks descending into minority rule—an unusual and un-democratic situation in which a party that wins fewer votes than its rivals nevertheless maintains control over key levers of political power.

To understand how this works, imagine a basketball game. In U.S. professional basketball, teams score one point for a free throw, two points for a regular shot, and three points for a shot from be-yond the three-point line. But imagine a game in which those rules apply only to one team (call it Team Normal), and the other team (Team Extra) is given *four* points for each shot it makes beyond the three-point line. Games would still sometimes be competitive, with uncertain results. If Team Extra won by, say, thirty points, without even attempting any four-point shots, it would win fair and square. In other instances, Team Normal might dominate, winning the game by, say, twenty points *despite* the four-point rule. But in close games, things get complicated. Think about a game in which each team makes the same number of free throws and regular shots but Team Normal makes ten shots beyond the three-point line while Team Extra makes eight shots beyond the three-point line. Under standard rules, Team Normal would win the game by six points. But under the new rules, Team Extra would win by two points. The loser becomes the winner. Again, these rules won't always determine the outcomes: Team Extra may perform so well that it doesn't need its built-in advantage to win; or Team Normal may perform well enough to win despite Team Extra's built-in advantage. But in close games, Team Extra will win more often than it ordinarily would.

The U.S. political system increasingly functions this way. The mapping of the partisan divide onto the urban-rural divide risks converting some of our most important institutions into pillars of minority rule.

One pillar is the Electoral College, which distorts the popular vote in two ways. First, nearly all states (with the exception of Maine and Nebraska) allocate Electoral College votes in a winner-take-all manner. This means that if a candidate wins a state by a narrow margin of 50.1 percent to 49.9 percent, the candidate will receive 100 percent of the state's electoral votes. This disproportionality creates problems when states' electoral votes are aggregated in the Electoral College, because it allows the loser of the national popular vote to win.

Consider how the 2016 election played out in the states of Wisconsin (10 electoral votes), Michigan (16 electoral votes), Pennsylvania (20 electoral votes), and New York (29 electoral votes). Donald Trump won Wisconsin, Michigan, and Pennsylvania by narrow margins (23,000 votes, 11,000 votes, and 54,000 votes, respectively), which allowed him to capture all 46 of those states' electoral votes. Hillary Clinton won New York by 1.7 million votes, carrying its 29 electoral votes. Summing up the votes in those four states, Clinton won the popular vote by 1.6 million votes, but Trump won the Electoral College vote among those states by 46 to 29. The loser won.

The Electoral College's winner-take-all system may benefit losing candidates of either party. Indeed, in the 1960s, it was conservative Republicans who thought it was unfair. The Republican senator Karl Mundt of South Dakota proposed a constitutional amendment to reform the Electoral College, which he said gave "dictatorial power" to "a few huge American cities and a handful of big so-called 'pivotal' states."

However, a second distortion in the Electoral College, the small-state bias, clearly favors the Republicans. Remember that the number of presidential electors allotted to each state is equal to the size of its congressional delegation: the number of representatives in the House plus the number of senators. Because the U.S. Senate heavily overrepresents sparsely populated states, the Electoral College has a modest rural bias of about twenty votes in the 538-seat college, which gives the Republicans a small but potentially decisive advantage. In 2000, for example, the small-state bias added an estimated eighteen votes to George W. Bush's overall electoral vote. Since Bush defeated Al Gore by only five electoral votes, those eighteen votes were pivotal, turning the popular-vote loser into the president-elect.

One way in which analysts measure the Republican Party's current advantage in the Electoral College is by identifying the state that serves as the tipping point in a national election—in other words, the state that delivers the decisive 270th electoral vote to the winning candidate. If we rank states from the largest pro-Democratic margin (Vermont) to the largest pro-Republican margin (Wyoming) in the 2020 presidential election, Wisconsin was the tipping point state. As such, we'd expect it to track the national popular vote, which Biden won by 4.4 percentage points. But he won Wisconsin by only 0.6 points, a nearly 4-point gap. This is the Electoral College bias: Biden needed to win the popular vote by around 4 points to be elected president. Like in the basketball game described above, a 3-point Biden advantage would have led to a Trump victory.

The net result of this is that U.S. presidential elections have not been very democratic in the twenty-first century. Between 1992 and 2020, the Republican Party has lost the popular vote in every presidential election except 2004. In other words, the GOP won the most votes *only once* during a span of nearly three decades. And yet Republican Party candidates have won the presidency *three* times during that period, allowing the party to occupy the presidency for twelve of those twenty-eight years.

A second pillar of minority rule—one with an even more marked partisan bias—is the U.S. Senate. Sparsely populated states representing less than 20 percent of the U.S. population can produce a Senate majority. And states representing 11 percent of the population can produce enough votes to block legislation via a filibuster.

The problem is now compounded by partisan bias. The GOP's dominance in low-population states allows it to control the U.S. Senate without winning national popular majorities. Senators are elected to staggered six-year terms, with a third of the chamber up for election every two years. That means it takes three elections over a six-year cycle to fully renovate the Senate. Although the Republicans have won the national popular vote for the Senate in a few individual elections (for example, in 2002, 2010, and 2014), the Democrats have won an overall popular majority for the Senate in *every six-year cycle since 1996–2002.* And yet the Republicans controlled the Senate for most of this period. So more often than not, the party with fewer votes controlled the Senate.

How big is the Senate's pro-Republican bias? Consider the 2020 election. Drawing on the tipping state logic above, there is a five-point gap between the 2020 presidential election results in the median state—the one that yields a Senate majority—and the 2020 national presidential vote. This means that the Senate's parti-

san bias was such that Democrats had to win the nationwide popular vote for Senate by about *five points* to gain control of the Senate.
Over the past few decades, the size of the pro-Republican bias has
varied from election to election, ranging from a low of two points
to a high of nearly six points. But one thing has been constant: the
GOP has enjoyed an advantage in the Senate for decades.

Or look at it another way: At no time during the twenty-first
century have Senate Republicans represented a majority of the
U.S. population. Based on states' populations, Senate Democrats
have continuously represented more Americans since 1999. In the
2016 election, for example, the Republicans won a fifty-two-seat
Senate majority. But their senators represented only 45 percent of
Americans. In 2018, the GOP won a fifty-three-seat majority, but
again, its senators represented only a minority (48 percent) of
Americans. After the 2020 election, which left the Senate evenly
split, the fifty Democratic senators represented 55 percent of
Americans—41.5 million more people than the fifty Republican
senators. The pattern continued in 2022: the GOP continued to
hold more Senate seats (forty-nine) than its vote share (42 percent).
So getting to fifty senators requires considerably fewer votes for
the Republicans than for the Democrats. As one commentator
puts it, "The makeup of the Republican coalition these days is so
ideally suited to winning elections in sparsely populated states that
it takes political malpractice and misfortune on an almost comical
scale for the conservative party not to win control."

The Supreme Court constitutes a third pillar of minority rule.
The court's partisan bias is indirect but nevertheless is consequential. Given the nature of the Electoral College and the Senate, Supreme Court justices may be nominated by presidents who lost the

popular vote and confirmed by Senate majorities that represent only a minority of Americans. And given the Republican advantage in the Electoral College and the Senate, such justices are more likely to be Republican appointees.

This has certainly been the case in the twenty-first century. Four of nine current Supreme Court justices—Clarence Thomas, Neil Gorsuch, Brett Kavanaugh, and Amy Coney Barrett—were confirmed by a Senate majority that collectively won a minority of the popular vote in Senate elections and represented less than half of the American population. And three of them—Gorsuch, Kavanaugh, and Coney Barrett—were also nominated by a president who lost the popular vote. Had majorities prevailed in presidential and Senate elections, then, three—and possibly four—of the Supreme Court's most conservative justices would not be on the court. In all likelihood, three of these seats would have been filled by Democratic appointees.

Thanks to the growing divergence between electoral majorities and the composition of the Supreme Court, Americans have a court that is increasingly—and often glaringly—at odds with public opinion. Historically, scholars of the Supreme Court argue, justices have tempered their decisions to avoid straying too far from the people's will. That appears to no longer be the case. Recent research has found a growing gap between Supreme Court rulings and majority public opinion in the United States. This trend is no accident: the court's conservative majority was imposed by a partisan minority.

A fourth pillar of minority rule, which is not anchored in the Constitution, is an electoral system that *manufactures* artificial majorities and sometimes allows parties that win fewer votes to

control legislatures. Nearly all U.S. congressional and state legislative elections employ a first-past-the-post (or winner-take-
all) system. States are carved up into districts with one legislator
elected per district. The first-place candidate in each election wins
the seat, and all rival candidates lose. The outcome is the same
whether the election is a 50.1 percent to 49.9 percent nail-biter or
an 80 percent to 20 percent landslide. Recall that in the twenty-
first century, the Democratic Party's voters are concentrated in
metropolitan centers, whereas Republican voters, based in small
towns and suburbs, tend to be more evenly distributed. As a result, Democrats are more likely to "waste" votes by racking up
large majorities in urban districts while losing in most non-urban
ones. This "inefficient" distribution of voters, combined with
single-member districts, can allow the party with fewer votes to
win legislative majorities.

The problem is most visible in state legislatures. Often viewed
as the heart of our democracy, state legislatures are sometimes described as the bodies that are "closest to the people" and thus most
representative of the popular will. The Supreme Court chief justice Earl Warren called them "the fountainhead of representative
government," while Justice Neil Gorsuch has touted them as the
true "people's representatives." But in reality, America's state legislatures are prone to minority rule.

To see how this works, we can look at Pennsylvania, a major
battleground state where Democrats have routinely won statewide
popular majorities in the twenty-first century but Republicans
have typically dominated the legislature. Since 2000, the Democrats have won five of Pennsylvania's six gubernatorial elections
and four of five presidential races. They have often won a majority

of the vote for the state legislature, too, but this hasn't always translated into a majority of the state legislative seats. In 2018, for example, the Democrats won 55 percent of the vote in the state's legislative elections, but the Republicans retained a 110–93 seat majority in the state house.

If we compare three typical state legislative districts in the 2018 election, we can see how this unfolds. First, consider Pennsylvania's 70th Legislative District, a densely populated, 45 percent nonwhite district just outside Philadelphia, where the Democratic legislator Matt Bradford, an attorney who once worked for the United Steelworkers, overwhelmingly won his 2018 race with 16,055 votes, compared with his Republican challenger's 7,112 votes. Contrast this with the nearby District 71, a more sparsely populated, 84 percent white district, where the Republican candidate Jim Rigby, a former Ferndale Borough police chief, eked out a closely fought race, defeating his Democratic rival 11,615 to 10,661. Then look at District 144 in southeastern Pennsylvania, a mostly rural district where the Republican Todd Polinchock, a retired navy pilot, narrowly beat his Democratic rival 15,457 to 14,867. If we add up the total votes across the three districts, the Democrats won more votes by a margin of 41,583 to 34,184. But the Republicans captured two of the three seats. This pattern occurred across Pennsylvania in 2018, and it regularly occurs across many U.S. states today. Democrats often win a majority of the statewide vote, but since their voters are packed into overwhelmingly Democratic districts while Republicans win more closely fought races, Republicans can win legislative majorities even while winning fewer votes.

Although geographic sorting clearly plays a role here, many

state legislatures also intentionally sort voters by drawing the lines in ways that favor the party in power. After each decennial U.S. census, states are required to redraw election boundaries to keep institutions up-to-date with population changes. Since the Supreme Court decisions in *Baker v. Carr* (1962) and *Reynolds v. Sims* (1964), legislative districts must also be equally sized in terms of population. But they don't have to be similarly shaped. State legislatures may carve up districts in highly irregular ways, redrawing district lines to place rival party voters into a small number of districts and spreading out the remainder across other districts, thereby diluting the rival party's vote. Rival parties will thus win a few districts with big majorities but lose many more districts as a result.

This is gerrymandering, and it's as old as the republic itself. Both major parties have long engaged in it. But two things changed in the early twenty-first century. First, the growing concentration of Democratic voters in the cities made Republican gerrymandering easier. That is, geographic sorting had already done much of the work for them, effectively giving them a "head start." And second, polarization and Republican radicalization, particularly after Barack Obama's election in 2008, raised the stakes of redistricting, transforming what had once been a low-drama, bureaucratic exercise into a well-funded, nationally coordinated, high-tech, and no-holds-barred enterprise.

Indeed, in 2010, the Republican Party launched a national gerrymandering strategy called the Redistricting Majority Project, or REDMAP. Financed by wealthy Republican donors, REDMAP was a nationally coordinated plan to win control of state legislatures and redraw district lines in the Republicans' favor. In a strategy not unlike that of Viktor Orbán after his party's massive parliamentary victory in Hungary in 2010, Republicans used their landslide victory in the 2010 midterms to gain control of the redistricting process in numerous battleground states, ranging from Wisconsin and Michigan to Virginia and North Carolina. As in Hungary, the strategy paid off. In Wisconsin, after Republicans aggressively gerrymandered the state's election boundaries in 2011, Democrats won the popular vote for the state assembly in 2012 (50 to 49 percent), but Republicans remained safely in control of the state house, capturing sixty of ninety-nine seats. The former assembly member Andy Jorgensen described the gerrymandered election as "a corrupt way of taking power you didn't win. This is an episode of *The Sopranos*." Minority rule continued in the Wisconsin legislature for the rest of the decade. In 2018, the Democrats won 53 percent of the state assembly vote, compared with 45 percent for the Republicans, and yet the GOP secured a 63–36 advantage in the state house. Republicans also won control of state legislatures despite losing the popular vote in Michigan, North Carolina, Pennsylvania, and Virginia.

Geographic sorting and gerrymandering have produced what one analyst has called "manufactured majorities." Between 1968 and 2016, there were 121 instances in state legislatures in which the party that received fewer votes statewide nevertheless won a majority of seats in the state house, and there were 146 instances in which the losing party won control of state senates. Whereas in the past both parties occasionally benefited from manufactured majorities, today, thanks to the urban-rural divide, the Republicans are almost always the beneficiary.

. . .

Commentators today frequently describe our national political system as stalemated between two evenly matched parties. Scholars and pundits alike tell us that a major source of America's democratic ills—for example, polarization and gridlock—is an unusual degree of partisan "parity." Presidential elections are determined by razor-thin margins; the U.S. Senate is evenly split. But such claims obscure the fact that parity is *manufactured* by our institutions. Electoral College outcomes are indeed decided by the narrowest of margins, and the two parties' seat shares in the Senate are closely matched. But when we look at American voters, we find less parity: the Democratic Party has, as we have noted, won the popular vote in all but one presidential election since the 1980s and every six-year cycle in the Senate since the 1990s. That's anything but parity. Parity in Washington emerges only after our votes pass through the distortionary channels of our institutions.

America has not yet fully succumbed to minority rule. Electoral majorities still generally prevail in many arenas, including the House of Representatives and gubernatorial and other statewide elections. In other arenas, including the presidency, minority rule remains episodic rather than entrenched. But instances of minority rule are growing more frequent.

This has real consequences. Imagine an American born in 1980 who first voted in 1998 or 2000. The Democrats would have won the popular vote in every six-year cycle in the U.S. Senate and all but one presidential election during her adult lifetime. And yet she would have lived most of her adult life under Republican presidents, a Republican-controlled Senate, and a Supreme Court dominated by Republican appointees. How much faith should she have in our democracy?

. . .

The emergence of minority rule matters not only because it allows losers to win. It also has insidious effects on public policies that affect people's lives. Public opinion never translates perfectly into policy. Citizens tend to be inconsistent and shifting in their policy views, and those views don't always shape their voting choices. In addition, organized (and often well-financed) interest groups exert considerable influence over policy and legislation, frequently in ways that diverge from majority public opinion. But institutions also matter, and the more that political institutions overrepresent partisan minorities, the more likely it is that majority opinion will be thwarted or ignored. If decisions on contentious issues are made by senators or justices who are "beyond the reach of majorities," then we shouldn't be surprised when policies are out of sync with majority views.

A clear example of this is the politics of abortion. The Supreme Court's 2022 decision in *Dobbs v. Jackson* eliminated the constitutionally protected right to an abortion, throwing the issue to Congress and state legislatures. In his majority opinion, Justice Samuel Alito wrote that it was time to "heed the Constitution and return the issue of abortion to the people's elected representatives." In his concurring opinion, Justice Brett Kavanaugh argued that the ruling restored "the people's authority to address the issue of abortion through the processes of democratic self-government."

But our counter-majoritarian institutions have untethered the views of "the people's elected representatives" from the views of the people themselves. A June 2022 Monmouth University poll showed that only 37 percent of Americans approved of the decision to overturn *Roe v. Wade*.

Similarly, a May 2022 Gallup poll found that 55 percent of Americans identified as "pro-choice" while only 39 percent identified as "pro-life." According to the Pew Research Center, 61 percent of U.S. adults say abortion should be legal in all or most cases, while only 37 percent believe abortion should be illegal in all or most cases. Despite broad majority support for abortion rights, however, counter-majoritarian institutions have thwarted the attempts of Democrats in Congress to codify *Roe*. The Women's Health Protection Act, which would have prevented states from restricting abortion rights, passed the House but was dead on arrival in the Senate, falling well short of the sixty-vote threshold needed to break the filibuster.

Abortion laws have thus come down to the states. Thirteen U.S. states had so-called trigger laws, designed to automatically reinstate partial or total abortion bans upon the overturn of *Roe*. According to the Guttmacher Institute, another thirteen states were likely to enact abortion bans in the aftermath of the *Dobbs* ruling. Several of these bans emerged out of heavily gerrymandered legislatures and flew in the face of state-level public opinion. The political scientists Jacob Grumbach and Christopher Warshaw analyzed polling data to determine support for abortion rights in the states. They found that majorities of the public support legal abortion rights in about forty states, while only about ten states have clear antiabortion majorities. This means that as many as sixteen states could pass restrictive abortion laws that are opposed by a majority of the state's population. According to Grumbach and Warshaw, "This imbalance only runs one direction: There are no states where the citizenry supports an abortion ban but the state government does not."

Take Ohio, for example. Grumbach and Warshaw found that only about 44 percent of Ohioans support making abortion illegal. But when *Roe v. Wade* was overturned, Ohio became home to one of the most restrictive abortion laws in the nation. The state's so-called heartbeat bill (which took effect after the *Dobbs* decision but was later suspended due to legal appeals) bans abortions when a fetal heartbeat can be detected—usually around six weeks into pregnancy. The law makes no exceptions for rape or incest. According to a 2019 poll, only 14 percent of Ohioans supported an abortion ban even in cases of rape and incest. There are, of course, some states (such as West Virginia and Arkansas) where majorities do in fact oppose legal abortion. Restrictive laws in these states will thus bring abortion policy into closer alignment with majority opinion. But overall, Grumbach finds that "after [*Dobbs*], and after the laws it triggers, 14 million fewer Americans will live under their preferred abortion policy."

There is an even larger gap between public opinion and policy on the issue of gun control. A series of mass school shootings in recent decades—including those in Columbine (1999), Sandy Hook (2012), Parkland (2018), and Uvalde (2022)—generated broad public support for stricter gun laws. According to polling conducted by Morning Consult/Politico in the wake of the mass shooting in Uvalde, Texas, 65 percent of Americans support stricter gun control laws, while only 29 percent oppose them. Broad public support also emerged for specific gun safety policies. Surveys by Gallup and Pew have consistently found more than 60 percent support for a law banning the manufacture, sale, or possession of semiautomatic or "assault" weapons and more than 80 percent support for laws requiring universal background checks for gun purchases. But such legislation has consistently failed in the U.S. Senate. This is, in part, because the Senate vastly overrepresents gun owners: the twenty states with the highest rates of gun ownership contain barely a third as many people as the twenty states with the lowest rates of gun ownership. But these states are all equally represented in the Senate. Together with the filibuster, this overrepresentation has made the Senate the graveyard of gun control legislation.

In the aftermath of the Sandy Hook massacre, parents of the victims lobbied for legislation to establish universal background checks for gun purchases. They were successful in the House, which passed a universal background check bill in 2013. The bill gained the support of fifty-five senators. But that, of course, wasn't enough, and it died at the hands of a filibuster. The forty-five senators who opposed the bill represented 38 percent of Americans. The House passed similar universal background check legislation in 2015, 2019, and 2021, but all three bills were killed in the Senate. And in July 2022, the House passed a bill banning certain semiautomatic weapons. A Fox News poll in June had found 63 percent nationwide public support for the ban. But because the bill's supporters again could not muster the sixty votes needed to overcome a filibuster, it was never taken up by the Senate.

Gun policy also flies in the face of public opinion at the state level. In Ohio, 2018 polling found large majorities in favor of gun control. More than 60 percent of Ohioans supported bans on semi-automatic weapons and high-capacity magazines, and more than 70 percent supported a mandatory waiting period for gun purchases. More than 75 percent did not support arming teachers. But the Republican-dominated state legislature took a different route.

Instead of passing gun control legislation, it passed a bill allowing for the concealed carry of handguns without a permit, alongside Texas, Tennessee, and Montana. This, even though only 20 percent of Americans support such legislation. And in the wake of the 2022 Uvalde shooting, Ohio fast-tracked a bill designed to arm teachers.

In the words of the *New York Times* columnist Jamelle Bouie: "Few Americans want the most permissive gun laws on offer. But those who do have captured the Republican Party and used its institutional advantages to both stop gun control and elevate an expansive and idiosyncratic view of gun rights to the level of constitutional law."

America's counter-majoritarian institutions also consistently hamper efforts to reduce poverty and inequality, even though solid majorities support these efforts. Consider the problem of America's stagnating wages. A federally mandated minimum wage was first established in the United States during the New Deal (at twenty-five cents per hour). It increased steadily for three decades, peaking in value after the 1966 amendments to the Fair Labor Standards Act (a cornerstone of President Lyndon Johnson's War on Poverty), which established a $1.60 minimum wage (about twelve 2020 dollars) beginning in 1968. The effect on working people's income was dramatic. During the 1960s and 1970s, an individual working full time at the minimum wage could earn enough to keep a family of three above the national poverty line.

Since 1968, however, the federal government has failed to regularly adjust the minimum wage to keep up with inflation, and real wages earned by those at the bottom end of the income distribution have eroded steadily. Between 1968 and 2006, the value of the minimum wage declined by 45 percent. In 2020, workers earning the federal minimum wage had about a third less money to spend each month on food and rent than they had fifty years earlier. Today, a three-person household living off a federal minimum wage falls substantially below the poverty line.

For decades, Americans have overwhelmingly supported raising the minimum wage. And yet it has hardly budged. Since the last increase, in July 2009 (to $7.25 an hour), efforts to raise it have consistently been blocked in Congress. In 2014, a bill to increase the minimum wage to $10.10—a measure that, according to polls, was backed by two-thirds of Americans—obtained only fifty-four of the sixty votes needed to advance in the Senate. The Raise the Wage Act, which would have increased the federal minimum wage to $15 an hour, passed the House of Representatives in 2019. The Congressional Budget Office estimated that the bill would boost the pay of 27 million American workers and lift 1.3 million households out of poverty. In a Hill-HarrisX poll of registered voters, 81 percent expressed support for a minimum-wage increase in general and 55 percent supported a $15/hour minimum wage. But the Senate refused to take up the legislation.

The most recent effort to raise the national minimum wage came in 2021. The 2021 American Rescue Plan (the COVID stimulus bill) initially included a national $15/hour minimum-wage provision. According to a Pew survey, 62 percent of Americans supported the initiative. A CBS News poll at the time found 71 percent support for a higher minimum wage. But neither popular support nor a Democratic Party majority in the Senate was enough to guarantee passage. Once the Senate parliamentarian ruled that a minimum-wage increase was not a budgetary provision that could be passed through reconciliation (the special Senate procedure that overrides the filibuster on certain spending bills), it was clear that the $15/hour minimum wage would die in the Senate.

The failure to deal with stagnating wages over the past fifty years has made America an outlier in terms of both poverty and inequality. The political scientists Lane Kenworthy and Jonas Pontusson examined ten rich democracies, including the United States, that experienced rising household income inequality as they entered the twenty-first century. In nine of those ten countries, governments responded with more aggressive policies of redistribution. Only the United States did not.

Scholars have linked the rise of radical right-wing populism in the United States to the persistent failure to address problems of stagnating incomes and rising inequality. Counter-majoritarian institutions are not the only reason that American democracy has failed to respond to the needs of working- and middle-class voters—weakened labor unions and the outsized influence of big money weigh heavily as well. But rules enabling legislative minorities to routinely ignore the will of the majority are a powerful contributing factor.

The threat to democracy goes beyond the thwarting of public opinion. There is a risk today that America's counter-majoritarian institutions will reinforce and even entrench minority rule.

We often think of America's democratic system as self-correcting. The competitive pressure of elections and checks and balances created by the Constitution are supposed to limit and eventually reverse authoritarian movements.

But this is not always the case. In the hands of an antidemocratic party, institutions that are designed to protect minorities may reinforce and even *strengthen* authoritarianism.

For one, counter-majoritarian institutions may reinforce authoritarian extremism by shielding minority parties from competitive pressures. Minority parties may use counter-majoritarian advantages to seemingly defy the laws of political gravity and hold on to power while appealing to only a narrow extremist base. When that happens, the self-correcting nature of the electoral marketplace disappears.

A day after the January 6, 2021, attack on the Capitol, the Republican National Committee held its traditional four-day winter meeting in a chandelier-adorned ballroom at the ocean-side Ritz-Carlton resort on Amelia Island, Florida. If there was ever a moment for self-reflection on the GOP's future, this was it. America had just experienced an unprecedented assault on its democracy, and President Trump had played a major role in it. Not only that, but the Trump-led Republicans had failed electorally. Trump was only the third president in the last eighty-eight years to fail to win reelection. Moreover, the party had lost control of the House *and* the Senate. It was a clean sweep. Indeed, Trump was the first president since Herbert Hoover to lose the House, the Senate, and the presidency all in his first term in office.

In the world of electoral politics, defeat is normally costly. It brings internal recrimination, tarnishes reputations, weakens leaders, and sometimes derails careers. But none of that was evident on

Amelia Island in January 2021. As *The New York Times* observed, Republican leaders seemed to be "operating in a parallel universe." As Trump headed for a second impeachment and a possible criminal investigation, the gathering of GOP state chairs and committee members bathed him in adoration. They did not rethink their strategy or alter their platform. The RNC chair, Ronna McDaniel, Trump's preferred candidate, was unanimously reelected. In her speech, McDaniel never even mentioned Trump's defeat. In other words, the Republicans reacted to a devastating electoral setback by doubling down on Trumpism. As David Bossie, a Maryland committeeman, put it, "You don't have to throw out everybody when there's nothing fundamentally wrong." "This room, they're in denial," observed the New Jersey committeeman Bill Palatucci, one of the few attendees who worried publicly about the damage Trump had done to the GOP's "brand." His was a lonely voice on Amelia Island. His fellow Republicans were nearly unanimous in endorsing the defeated president, insisting, as the Alabama committeeman Paul Reynolds did, that Trump and his followers "make us a better party."

The Trump-dominated Republican Party ran election-denying candidates in congressional races across the country in the 2022 midterm elections, and again it underperformed. After three consecutive disappointing elections in 2018, 2020, and 2022, some Republican leaders began to recognize that Trumpist extremism was costing the party votes. Still, however, the party did not change course. Ronna McDaniel, the Trump ally, was reelected again in January 2023; her only challengers were pro-Trump election deniers. House Republicans also failed to break with Trump. After Kevin McCarthy was elected House Speaker in January

2023, he declared that he wanted to "especially thank President Trump. . . . I don't think anybody should doubt his influence. He was with me from the beginning." GOP congressional leaders made no effort to isolate or remove extremists. Representatives Marjorie Taylor Greene and Paul Gosar, who had been stripped of past committee memberships due to violent rhetoric, were given new committee assignments. So even if some Republican politicians began, hesitatingly, to contemplate a future without Trump in 2023, they showed little interest in rethinking the party's program or breaking with Trumpism's extremist base.

It is hard to imagine such behavior in a country without excessively counter-majoritarian institutions. The GOP's reluctance to moderate, even in the wake of successive electoral disappointments, can only be understood in light of the fact that manufactured majorities in the Senate and the Electoral College remained tantalizingly within reach.

Normally, political parties change course when they lose elections. In this way, they resemble firms in a marketplace. If a company suffers repeated quarterly losses, it engages in self-reflection, develops a new strategy, and maybe even fires the CEO.

Likewise, after the Democratic Party lost three consecutive presidential elections in 1980, 1984, and 1988, a new generation of Democratic politicians, including Arkansas's governor, Bill Clinton, launched a process of political soul-searching. They founded new think tanks (like the Democratic Leadership Council) and challenged party leaders to rethink key elements of the party's platform and strategy. The Democrats changed course and moved to the political center and won the next two presidential elections. The British Labour Party underwent a similar transformation after spending the 1980s and much of the 1990s in the political wilderness.

For more than two centuries, competition has been regarded as a kind of magical elixir. Theorists and practitioners often cite the philosopher John Stuart Mill's formula for defeating antidemocratic ideologies. In Mill's famous phrase, it is the "collision of adverse opinions" that allows the truth to triumph over untruth. Similarly, James Madison argued in Federalist No. 10 that "if a faction consists of less than a majority, relief is supplied by the republican principle, which enables the majority to defeat its sinister views by regular vote." Democracy, then, should be self-correcting: Competitive elections create a feedback mechanism that rewards parties that are responsive to voters and punishes those who are not. Losing parties are thus compelled to moderate and broaden their appeal to win again in the future.

But there is a hitch: electoral arrangements that overrepresent certain territories or groups, allowing parties to win elections *without capturing the most votes,* weaken the incentive to adapt. Without competitive pressure to broaden their appeal, parties may turn inward and radicalize.

This is what has happened to the Republican Party in the early twenty-first century. The rural bias of American institutions enabled the GOP to win the presidency and control the Senate (and eventually the Supreme Court) even as it lost the national popular vote time and time again. The Republicans became the beneficiaries of a kind of "constitutional protectionism"—institutions that dull the incentive to compete. Republicans enjoyed an automatic head start in national elections, which partially shielded them from competitive pressure.

The electoral crutch afforded by our institutions threatens American democracy by reinforcing Republican extremism. Since Republicans can win and exercise power *without building national electoral majorities,* they lack the normal incentives to adapt to the fundamental changes taking place in American society. If you can regularly win the most important offices in the land without broadening your appeal, then why do it? Republican politicians have thus fallen into a self-reinforcing spiral: their conservative base is pushing them into extremism, and the electoral protection offered by counter-majoritarian institutions has weakened their incentive to resist that push.

American democracy can only survive with a Republican Party that is capable of winning national majorities—one that can compete for votes in the cities and among younger and nonwhite citizens. Only when the Republicans can legitimately win national elections again will their leaders' fears of multiracial democracy subside. Only then can we expect the party to abandon violent extremism and play by democratic rules, win or lose. For these things to happen, the Republicans must become a truly multiethnic party. Our institutions have weakened the GOP's incentive to change course in this way. And that's a serious problem. As long as the Republican Party can hold on to power without broadening beyond its radicalized core white Christian base, it will remain prone to the kind of extremism that imperils our democracy today.

Not only do counter-majoritarian institutions reinforce authoritarian extremism, but they may also help to entrench it—by empowering a partisan minority, which then uses that power to solidify control over other institutions. In politics, power begets power. Between 2016 and 2020, a president who lost the popular vote used his party's manufactured Senate majority to shift the Supreme Court substantially to the right. With the court on board, minority rule can be even further entrenched.

This has in fact begun to happen: the Supreme Court has acted to reinforce minority rule in highly gerrymandered state legislatures. Wisconsin's egregiously drawn election maps, which have been shown to be among the most extreme in American history, were struck down by a federal court in 2016. But in 2018, the Supreme Court—now with Neil Gorsuch aboard—reversed the decision and allowed the gerrymandered districts to stand (effectively ducking a decision on procedural grounds). A year later, with Anthony Kennedy now retired and replaced by Brett Kavanaugh, a 5–4 court majority ruled (in *Rucho v. Common Cause*) that federal courts lack the authority to decide cases of partisan gerrymandering in the states. As Chief Justice John Roberts's majority opinion put it, "Partisan gerrymandering claims present political questions beyond the reach of federal courts." A counter-majoritarian Supreme Court, packed by a counter-majoritarian Senate, helped to shore up minority rule in the states.

It could get worse. Increasingly unable to win the popular vote for president, some Republicans have come up with radical new schemes to subvert the electoral process. One of these involves a heretofore fringe legal theory called the "independent state legislature doctrine." Articles I and II of the Constitution grant state legislatures the authority to set the manner for choosing presidential electors. Article II states, "Each State shall appoint, in such Manner as the Legislature therefore may direct, a Number of Electors." Traditionally, this clause has been interpreted as referring to each state's general lawmaking process, which includes things like state constitutions, state supreme courts, governors' vetoes, and citizen referenda. Using an unorthodox reading of the letter of the law, however, some conservatives have argued that Article II gives state legislatures the exclusive power to set the rules for elections. Thus, according to the independent state legislature doctrine, Richard Hasen writes, state legislatures possess "virtually unlimited powers over the rules for running presidential and congressional elections—even if their use means violating the state's own constitution and ignoring its interpretation by the state supreme court."

As we have seen, Republicans controlled several key state legislatures—including in Michigan, North Carolina, Pennsylvania, and Wisconsin—in the 2010s despite losing the statewide popular vote. Under the constitutional reinterpretation proposed by the doctrine, these state legislatures could potentially engage in bold power plays, including awarding themselves the right to unilaterally determine election winners or appoint the state's electors.

The notion that state legislatures, rather than voters, should choose the president of the United States may seem ludicrous, and it is obviously undemocratic. Indeed, the doctrine has long been dismissed as far outside the mainstream. But variants of it have been endorsed in writing by the Supreme Court justices Alito, Gorsuch, Thomas, and Kavanaugh. Justice Coney Barrett could join them.

If the presidency were to be determined by state legislatures that are themselves governed by partisan minorities, America will have fully descended into minority rule.

Although such a scenario remains unlikely, it is clear that America's excessively counter-majoritarian institutions have left us vulnerable to undemocratic situations in which electoral minorities prevail over majorities. As we saw in 2016, America's countermajoritarian institutions can manufacture authoritarian minorities into governing majorities. In other words, far from checking authoritarian power, our institutions have begun to augment it.

The past decade has taught us a sobering lesson: the United States is especially prone to democratic crisis and even backsliding. Many Western societies, from the U.K. and France to Germany, the Netherlands, and all of Scandinavia, have experienced a backlash against growing diversity in the twenty-first century. Yet their democracies remain relatively healthy. How have they done it?

CHAPTER 7

AMERICA THE OUTLIER

In the spring of 1814, twenty-five years after the ratification of America's Constitution, a group of 112 Norwegian men—civil servants, lawyers, military officials, business leaders, theologians, and even a sailor—gathered in Eidsvoll, a rural village forty miles north of Oslo. For five weeks, while meeting at the manor home of the businessman Carsten Anker, the men debated and drafted what is today the world's *second* oldest written constitution.

Like America's founders, Norway's independence leaders were in a highly precarious situation. Norway had been part of Denmark for more than four hundred years, but after Denmark's defeat in the Napoleonic Wars, the victorious powers, led by Great Britain, decided to transfer the territory to Sweden. This triggered a wave of nationalism in Norway. Unwilling to be traded away "like a herd of cattle," as one observer at the time put it, Norwegians asserted their independence. So they elected the 112-man constitutional assembly that gathered at Eidsvoll.

Inspired by the ideals of the Enlightenment and the promise of self-government, Norway's founders viewed the American experience as a model. After all, the Americans had just done what the Norwegians now aspired to do: declare independence from a foreign power. The Norwegian press had spread news of the American experiment across the country, casting George Washington and Benjamin Franklin as heroes. Although the press didn't always get the story right (it described the American president as a "monarch," reported that Washington had been "appointed dictator of the United States for four years," and referred to the vice president as a "viceroy"), many of the men gathered at Eidsvoll were quite familiar with the workings of the American system. Christian Magnus Falsen, a prominent independence advocate who took a leading role in the constitution-writing process, even christened his son "George Benjamin" after Washington and Franklin. Falsen was deeply influenced by Madison and Jefferson, too, later declaring that parts of the Norwegian constitution were based "nearly exclusively" on the American model.

After the constitution was approved in May 1814, Norway declared independence. It didn't last. The Swedish army invaded in July, forcing Norway into a "union" with Sweden. However, Norway was allowed to retain its new constitution and political system. The 1814 constitution governed Norway during the subsequent semi-independent period and after full independence in 1905. It remains in place today.

Although Norway's constitutional framers were inspired by America's founding experience, their initial creation was hardly revolutionary. Norway remained a hereditary monarchy, and kings retained the right to appoint cabinets and veto legislation (although their vetoes could now be overridden by parliament). Members of parliament (Storting) were indirectly elected by regional electoral colleges, and voting was limited to men who met certain property requirements. Urban elites also gained a powerful built-in advantage in the Storting. Norway was overwhelmingly rural in 1814: about 90 percent of the electorate lived in the countryside. Because many peasants owned land and could therefore vote, wealthy urban elites feared being overwhelmed by the peasant majority. As one Norwegian political scientist puts it, the elite viewed peasants as a "potential time bomb." So the constitution established a fixed two-to-one ratio of rural to urban seats in parliament—a ratio that dramatically overrepresented cities, since rural residents actually outnumbered urban residents by ten to one. This was the so-called Peasant Clause. Majority rule was further diluted by bicameralism, because the lower house of parliament elected an upper chamber called the Lagting. And finally, Article 2 of the 1814 constitution established the "Evangelical-Lutheran religion" as the "official religion of the state" and required that at least half of government ministers be members of the church.

So Norway's 1814 constitution, like America's in 1789, included a range of undemocratic features. In fact, early nineteenth-century Norway was considerably less democratic than the United States.

Over the next two centuries, however, Norway underwent a series of far-reaching democratic reforms—all under its original constitution. Parliamentary sovereignty was established in the late nineteenth century, and Norway became a genuine constitutional monarchy. A 1905 constitutional reform eliminated regional electoral colleges and established direct elections for parliament. Property restrictions on voting were eliminated in 1898, and universal (male and female) suffrage was established in 1913.

After 1913, Norway was a democracy. However, one major counter-majoritarian institution remained: the Peasant Clause. By the mid-twentieth century, urbanization had reversed the nature of the malapportionment due to the Peasant Clause. With half the population now living in cities, a fixed two-to-one rural-to-urban seat ratio now increasingly overrepresented *rural* voters. Like the U.S. Senate, then, the Peasant Clause threatened majority rule by inflating the political power of sparsely populated areas—to the benefit of conservative parties. Unlike in the United States, however, the major political parties negotiated a constitutional reform that eliminated the Peasant Clause in 1952. Norway took additional steps toward majority rule when it reduced the voting age to eighteen in 1978 and eliminated its upper chamber of parliament in 2009.

But Norway didn't stop democratizing. As Norwegian society and global norms changed in the late twentieth and early twenty-first centuries, constitutional and democratic rights were expanded in new ways. Indigenous minorities, for example, gained new protections. In the late 1970s, the government was preparing to construct a massive hydroelectric plant on a river that would have submerged a Sami village and its reindeer grazing lands. This triggered a massive protest campaign—including demonstrations and hunger strikes—by Sami activists, who were supported by environmentalists and local fishermen. In 1981, fourteen Sami women occupied the Norwegian prime minister's office, shaking up Norway's politics and placing Sami rights firmly on the political agenda. A 1988 constitutional amendment guaranteed the protection of Sami language and culture.

Rights continued to expand over the next quarter century. A 1992 constitutional amendment guaranteed Norwegians the right to a healthy environment. In 2012, the constitution was amended once again, this time to abolish Norway's official religion and guarantee equal rights to "all religious and philosophical communities." And in 2014, Norway adopted a set of sweeping constitutional human and social rights protections, including for children to be granted "respect for their human dignity," the right to education, and the right to subsistence (through work or, for those who could not support themselves, government assistance). In total, Norway's constitution was amended 316 times between 1814 and 2014.

Two centuries of reform have transformed Norway into one of the most democratic countries on earth. On Freedom House's Global Freedom Index (which ranges from 0 to 100), most established democracies received a score above 90 in 2022. A handful of countries including Canada, Denmark, New Zealand, and Uruguay received a score above 95. Only three countries received a perfect score of 100: Finland, Sweden, and Norway. Freedom House scores countries on twenty-five separate dimensions of democracy. Norway receives a perfect score on all of them.

Norway's story of transformation is impressive, but it is not unusual. Other European political systems started in an equally undemocratic place, with a variety of institutions that kept popular majorities in check. Most of them, like Norway, were ruled by monarchies. With few exceptions, only men with property could vote. Voting was usually indirect: citizens voted not for candidates but for local "notables"—civil servants, priests, pastors, landowners, or factory owners—who in turn selected members of parliament. And in Latin America, where founding leaders took the U.S. Constitution as a model after gaining independence in the early nineteenth century, all presidents were indirectly elected, via electoral colleges or legislatures, prior to 1840.

In addition, early electoral systems were skewed to favor wealthy landowners. Cities—home to Europe's growing working classes— were often massively underrepresented in parliament, compared with rural districts. In Britain's notorious "rotten boroughs," a few dozen voters sometimes had their very own representative.

In most countries, there were also extensive *legislative* checks on popular majorities, including undemocratic bodies with the power to veto legislation. In Britain, the House of Lords, an unelected body composed of hereditary peers and appointees, had the authority to block all legislation that did not involve taxes. Canada also created an appointed Senate after it gained independence in 1867. Most nineteenth-century European political systems possessed similar upper chambers, composed of hereditary members and appointees from the Crown and the church.

Parliaments everywhere thus offered excessive protection to minority interests. An extreme example was Poland's eighteenth-century parliament (Sejm), in which each deputy in the two-hundred-member body possessed *individual veto over any bill*. The

French political philosopher Jean-Jacques Rousseau regarded Poland's *liberum veto* (Latin for "I freely object") as, in the words of
one legal analyst, a "tyranny of the minority of one." The system's
defenders characterized it as a "privilege of our liberty." But it
brought political life to a grinding halt. Between 1720 and 1764,
more than half of Poland's parliamentary sessions were shut down
by individual vetoes or filibusters before any decisions were made.
Unable to conduct government business or raise public funds for
defense, Poland fell prey to military interventions by neighboring
Russia, Prussia, and Austria, whose armies dismembered its territory, literally erasing Poland from the map for more than a century. (The dysfunctionality of the *liberum veto* was not lost on
America's founders, including Alexander Hamilton, who cited
Poland as an example of the "poison" of "giv[ing] a minority a
negative upon the majority.")

Although other countries steered clear of the *liberum veto,* states
across Europe lacked rules to halt parliamentary debate, allowing
small legislative factions to routinely scuttle legislative majorities.
This filibuster-like behavior grew so widespread in Europe that the
German legal theorist George Jellinek warned in 1904 that "parliamentary obstruction is no longer a mere *intermezzo* in the history
of this or that parliament. It has become an international phenomenon which, in threatening manner, calls in question the whole
future of parliamentary government."

Across the West, then, early political systems placed elections
and parliaments beyond the reach of popular majorities, ensuring
not just minority rights but outright minority rule. In that world
of monarchies and aristocracies, America's founding Constitution,

even with its counter-majoritarian features, stood out as comparatively democratic.

Over the course of the twentieth century, however, most of the countries that are now considered established democracies dismantled their most egregiously counter-majoritarian institutions and took steps to empower majorities. First, they did away with suffrage restrictions. Universal male suffrage first came to France's Third Republic in the 1870s. New Zealand, Australia, and Finland were pioneers of female enfranchisement in the late nineteenth and early twentieth centuries. By 1920, virtually all adult men and women could vote in most of western Europe, Australia, and New Zealand (Belgium, France, and Switzerland were slower to grant women's suffrage).

Indirect elections also disappeared. By the late nineteenth century, France and the Netherlands had eliminated the powerful local councils that had previously selected members of parliament; Norway, Prussia, and Sweden did the same in the early twentieth century. France experimented with an electoral college for a single presidential election in the late 1950s but then dropped it. Electoral colleges gradually disappeared across Latin America. Colombia eliminated its electoral college in 1910; Chile did so in 1925; Paraguay in 1943. Brazil adopted an electoral college in 1964 under military rule but replaced it with direct presidential elections in 1988. Argentina, the last country in Latin America with indirect presidential elections, dropped its electoral college in 1994.

Most European democracies also reformed their electoral systems—the rules that govern how votes are translated into representation. Countries across continental Europe and Scandinavia abandoned first-past-the-post election systems when they democratized at the turn of the twentieth century. Beginning in Belgium in 1899, Finland in 1906, and Sweden in 1907 and then diffusing across Europe, coalitions of parties from across the spectrum pushed successfully for proportional representation with multi-member districts (meaning multiple members of parliament are elected from a single district) to bring parties' share of the seats in parliament more closely in line with their share of the popular vote. Under these new rules, parties that won, say, 40 percent of the vote could expect to win about 40 percent of the seats, which, as the political scientist Arend Lijphart has shown, helps to ensure that electoral majorities translate into governing majorities. By World War II, nearly all continental European democracies used some variant of proportional representation, and today 80 percent of democracies with populations above one million do so.

Undemocratic upper chambers were tamed or eliminated beginning, in the first decades of the twentieth century, with Britain's House of Lords. Britain suffered a political earthquake in 1906 when the Liberal Party won a landslide election, displacing the Conservatives (or Tories), who had governed for more than a decade. The new Liberal-led government launched ambitious new social policies, which were to be paid for with progressive taxes on inherited and landed wealth. Outnumbered by more than two to one in Parliament, the Conservatives panicked. The House of Lords, which was dominated by conservative-leaning hereditary peers, came to the Tories' rescue. Inserting itself directly into politics, the unelected upper chamber vetoed the Liberal government's all-important tax bill of 1909.

By convention, the House of Lords could veto some legislation, but not tax bills (fights over taxation had sparked the English Civil War in the 1640s). The House of Lords nonetheless voted down the ambitious budget bill, breaking all precedent.

The Lords justified this unusual move by claiming their chamber was a "watchdog of the constitution." The Liberal Chancellor of the Exchequer, David Lloyd George, the main author of the budget bill, dismissed this, calling the House of Lords a plutocratic body—"not a watchdog," but rather the "poodle" of the Conservative Party leader. In a speech to a roaring crowd in London's East End, the sharp-tongued Lloyd George ridiculed the aristocrats who inherited their seats in the House of Lords as "five hundred ordinary men, accidently chosen from among the ranks of the unemployed," and asked why they should be able to "override the deliberate judgement of millions."

Facing a constitutional crisis, the Liberals drew up the Parliament Act, which would strip the House of Lords of its ability to permanently veto *any legislation* at all. The battle lines were drawn. If the House of Lords lost its veto, its conservative members warned, political apocalypse would follow. It wasn't just taxes they feared. They worried about other items on the Liberal-led majority's agenda, including plans to grant Catholic Ireland greater autonomy, which Conservatives viewed as a fundamental affront to the traditional (Protestant) vision of British national identity. Lord Lansdowne, a conservative member of the Lords, predicted that the passage of the Parliament Act would lead to

measures inflicting irreparable injury upon our most cherished institutions. The Crown is not safe, the Constitution is not safe, the Union is not safe, the Church is not safe, our political liberties are not safe—literally no institution, however much revered and respected in this country, [will be] beyond the reach of [this] majority.

Ultimately, the bill passed not only the House of Commons but also the House of Lords. It took some hardball. The Lords were persuaded only after the Liberal government, with the king's support, threatened to swamp the House of Lords by appointing hundreds of new Liberal peers to the body if they did not relent. With the bill's passage, the House of Lords lost the ability to block laws passed by the elected House of Commons (although it could delay them). One of Britain's most powerful counter-majoritarian institutions had been substantially weakened. And rather than trigger a political apocalypse, the reform paved the way for the construction of a fuller, more inclusive democracy over the course of the twentieth century.

Several other emerging democracies abolished their aristocratic upper chambers outright after World War II. New Zealand eliminated its House of Lords–like Legislative Council in 1950. Denmark abolished its nineteenth-century upper chamber (Landsting) in 1953 via referendum. Sweden followed suit in 1970. By the early twenty-first century, two-thirds of the world's parliaments were unicameral. The result was not—as defenders of upper chambers frequently warned—political chaos and dysfunction. New Zealand, Denmark, and Sweden went on to become three of the most stable and democratic countries in the world.

Another way to democratize historically undemocratic upper chambers is to make them more representative. This was the path

taken by Germany and Austria. In Germany, in the wake of World
War II, this development was particularly striking because West
Germans wrote a new constitution and rebuilt their democracy
under the watchful eye of American occupying forces. In August
1948, German constitutional experts gathered at the site of a medieval Augustinian monastery (Herrenchiemsee) in southeastern
Bavaria to begin to draft a democratic constitution. One of the
constitutional designers' main tasks was to revamp the country's
nineteenth-century second chamber (Bundesrat), which had historically been composed mostly of appointed civil servants.

The intense two-week convention that followed produced a
constitution that was nearly complete, except for this second
chamber. The designers had not yet agreed on a structure. When
party leaders gathered the following month in Bonn's Parliamentary Council under the chairmanship of the future chancellor
Konrad Adenauer, they considered several options. Despite the
outsized role played by American occupying forces, the designers
of Germany's constitution rejected the U.S. Senate model of equal
representation for Germany's federal states. Instead, representation
in the Bundesrat would be based roughly on states' populations. So
Germany's second federal chamber remained in place but was made
more representative. Today, the smallest German states each send
three representatives to the Bundesrat, medium-sized states send
four representatives, and the largest states send six representatives.
With this structure, Germany's postwar framers combined principles of federalism and democracy.

Most twentieth-century democracies also took steps to limit
minority obstruction *within* legislatures, establishing a procedure—
known as cloture—to allow simple majorities to end parliamen-

tary debate. The term "cloture" originated during the early days
of the French Third Republic. In the 1870s, the provisional government of Adolphe Thiers faced daunting challenges. France had
just lost a war to Prussia, and the new Republican government had
to contend with the revolutionary Paris Commune on the left and
forces seeking to restore the monarchy on the right. The new government needed to show it could legislate effectively. However,
the National Assembly was renowned for its marathon debates and
inaction on pressing issues. Pushed by Thiers, the Assembly created a cloture motion through which a parliamentary majority
could vote to rein in an otherwise endless debate.

Britain carried out similar reforms. In 1881, the Liberal prime
minister, William Gladstone, pushed through a "cloture rule" that
allowed a majority of MPs to end debate so that Parliament could
move to a vote. The Australian Parliament adopted a similar cloture rule in 1905. In Canada, opposition minorities in Parliament
had filibustered several important bills, including one introduced
by the Conservative prime minister, Robert Borden, in 1912. The
Naval Aid Bill, which aimed to respond to the rise of German sea
power by bolstering Canada's navy, was filibustered by the opposition Liberals for five months. The debate, which at times stretched
past midnight, took a physical toll on the prime minister, who developed such severe boils that he was forced to take the floor with
his "neck swathed in bandages." The ordeal, which Prime Minister
Borden described as "the most strenuous and remarkable that had
ever occurred in Canadian Parliamentary history," led the government to push through a cloture rule—allowing a simple majority
to end debate—in April 1913.

The trend of eliminating filibusters and other supermajority rules has continued in recent years. For much of the twentieth century, Finland's parliament had a delaying rule under which a one-third minority could vote to defer legislation until after the next election. The rule was abolished in 1992. Denmark still has a rule in which a one-third parliamentary minority may call a public referendum on nonfinancial legislation, and if 30 percent of the adult population votes against (a high bar given voter turnout), it is blocked. However, this rule has not been used since 1963.

Iceland's parliament (Althingi) has long had an old-fashioned talking filibuster. The secretary-general of the Althingi, Helgi Bernódusson, described it as "deeply rooted in the Icelandic political culture." Each year, the media designated the title of Speech King of the Althingi to the member of parliament who delivered the longest speeches. Earning the title was "regarded as an honor." Efforts to curb the filibuster in the early twenty-first century met with considerable resistance, because it was viewed as threatening members of parliament's "freedom of speech." In 2016, Bernódusson declared, "There are no indications at present that it will be possible to curb filibustering in the Althingi. The Speaker's hands are tied by the rules and the Members of Parliament have their way. The Althingi is stuck in the filibuster rut." Three years later, however, after a record-breaking 150-hour filibuster on a European Union energy law, the parliament curbed the filibuster through new limits on speeches and rebuttals.

Amid this broad pattern of reform, there is one area in which many democracies moved in a more counter-majoritarian direction in the twentieth century: judicial review. Prior to World War II, judicial review existed in only a few countries outside the

United States. But since 1945, most democracies have adopted some form of it. In some countries, including Austria, Germany, Italy, Portugal, and Spain, new constitutional courts were created as "guardians" of the constitution. In other countries, including Brazil, Denmark, India, Israel, and Japan, existing supreme courts were given this guardian role. One recent study of thirty-one established democracies found that twenty-six of them now possess some type of judicial review.

Recall that judicial review can be a source of intergenerational counter-majoritarianism. Democracies outside the United States have attenuated this problem by replacing life tenure with either term limits or a mandatory retirement age for high court justices. For example, Canada adopted a mandatory retirement age of seventy-five for its Supreme Court justices in 1927. This was done in response to two aging justices who refused to retire, including one who did so in a dispute over the size of his pension and who became inactive in court deliberations, and another whom Prime Minister Mackenzie King described in his diary as "senile."

Similarly, Australia established a retirement age of seventy for High Court justices in 1977, after the forty-six-year tenure of Justice Edward McTiernan came to an inglorious end. McTiernan had been appointed to the court in 1930, and by the 1970s the octogenarian's voice was often "difficult for counsel to understand." In 1976, McTiernan broke his hip swatting a cricket with a rolled-up newspaper at the Windsor Hotel in Melbourne. In an apparent effort to nudge him into retirement, the chief justice refused to build a wheelchair ramp in the High Court building, citing costs. McTiernan retired, and when Parliament took up the issue of establishing a retirement age, opposition was "virtually nonexistent." Members of Parliament argued that a retirement age would help "contemporize the courts" by bringing in judges who were "closer to the people" and held "current day sets of values."

Every democracy that has introduced judicial review since 1945 has also introduced either a retirement age or term limits for high court judges, thereby limiting the problem of long-tenured judges binding future generations.

In sum, the twentieth century ushered in the modern democratic era—an age in which many of the institutional fetters on popular majorities that were designed by pre-democratic monarchies and aristocracies were dismantled. Democracies all over the world abolished or weakened their most egregiously counter-majoritarian institutions. Conservative defenders of these institutions anxiously warned of impending instability, chaos, or tyranny. But that has rarely ensued since World War II. Indeed, countries like Canada, Denmark, Finland, France, Germany, New Zealand, Norway, Sweden, and the U.K. were both more stable and more democratic at the close of the twentieth century than they were at the beginning. Eliminating counter-majoritarianism helped give rise to modern democracy.

America was not immune to these trends. It, too, took important steps toward majority rule in the twentieth century. The Nineteenth Amendment (ratified in 1920) extended voting rights to women, and the 1924 Snyder Act extended citizenship and voting rights to Native Americans. But it was not until the 1965 Voting Rights Act that the United States met minimal standards for universal suffrage.

America also (partially) democratized its upper chamber. The U.S. Senate, which has been provocatively described as "an American House of Lords," was indirectly elected prior to 1913. The Constitution endowed state legislatures, not voters, with the authority to select their states' U.S. senators. Thus, the 1913 ratification of the Seventeenth Amendment, which mandated the direct popular election of senators, was also an important democratizing step.

Legislative elections became much fairer in the 1960s as America's own "rotten boroughs" were eliminated. Prior to this, rural election districts across America contained far fewer people than urban and suburban ones. For example, Alabama's Lowndes County, with just over 15,000 people, had the same number of state senators as Jefferson County, which had more than 600,000 residents. This pattern repeated across America. The result was massive rural overrepresentation in legislatures. In 1960, rural counties contained 23 percent of the U.S. population but elected 52 percent of the seats in state legislatures. By contrast, urban and suburban counties contained two-thirds of the U.S. population but elected only one-third of the seats in state legislatures. In state legislative and national congressional elections, rural minorities had long governed urban majorities. In 1956, when the Virginia state legislature voted to close public schools rather than integrate them in the wake of the 1954 *Brown v. Board of Education* ruling, the twenty-one state senators who voted for closure represented fewer people than the seventeen senators who voted for integration. This rural bias tipped the partisan balance in many states, allowing parties representing electoral minorities to dominate state legislatures.

Between 1962 and 1964, a series of Supreme Court rulings ensured that electoral majorities were represented in Congress and state legislatures. Establishing the principle of "one person, one vote," the court rulings required all U.S. legislative districts to be roughly equal in population. In the words of the political scientists Stephen Ansolabehere and James Snyder, the consequences of the rulings were "immediate, complete, and stunning." Almost overnight, artificial rural majorities were wiped out in seventeen states. The equalization of voting power was a major step toward ensuring a semblance of majority rule in the House of Representatives and state legislatures.

A final spurt of constitutional reforms came in the 1960s and early 1970s. The Twenty-third Amendment (ratified in 1961) gave Washington, D.C., residents the right to vote in presidential elections; the Twenty-fourth Amendment (1964) finally prohibited poll taxes; and the Twenty-sixth Amendment (1971) lowered the age to vote from twenty-one to eighteen.

Although these twentieth-century reforms made America far more democratic than it had previously been, they did not go as far as in other democracies. Take the Electoral College. Whereas every other presidential democracy in the world did away with indirect elections during the twentieth century, in America the Electoral College remained intact. There were hundreds of attempts to reform or abolish it, but they all failed.

America also retained its first-past-the-post electoral system, even though it created situations of minority rule, especially in state legislatures. The United States thus joined Canada and the U.K. as the only rich Western democracies to not adopt more proportional election rules in the twentieth century.

America's heavily malapportioned Senate also remained intact. The 1962–64 Supreme Court rulings establishing the principle of "one person, one vote" in the House of Representatives did not apply to the U.S. Senate. As a result, America's state-level "rotten boroughs" persist.

America also maintained a minority veto *within* the Senate. Much like legislatures in France, Britain, and Canada, the absence of any cloture rule led to a marked increase in obstructionist tactics beginning in the late nineteenth century. And as in Canada, the filibuster problem took on added urgency in the face of German naval threats in the run-up to World War I. But Canada, like France and Britain, put in place a majoritarian 50 percent cloture rule, while the U.S. Senate adopted a nearly insurmountable super-majoritarian sixty-seven-vote cloture rule. The rule was modified from two-thirds to three-fifths in 1975, but it remained counter-majoritarian. America thus entered the twenty-first century with a "sixty-vote Senate."

Finally, unlike every other established democracy, America did not introduce term limits or mandatory retirement ages for Supreme Court justices. Today, in the Supreme Court, judges effectively serve for life. It's an entirely different story at the state level. Of the fifty U.S. states, forty-six imposed term limits on state supreme court justices during the nineteenth or twentieth century. Three others adopted mandatory retirement ages. Only Rhode Island maintains lifetime tenure for its supreme court justices. But among national democracies, America, like Rhode Island, stands alone.

The United States, once a democratic pioneer and model for other nations, has now become a democratic laggard. The endurance of our pre-democratic institutions as other democracies have dismantled theirs makes us a uniquely counter-majoritarian democracy at the dawn of the twenty-first century. Consider the following:

- America is the only presidential democracy in the world in which the president is elected via an Electoral College, rather than directly by voters. Only in America can a president be "elected against the majority expressed at the polls."

- America is one of the few remaining democracies that retains a bicameral legislature with a powerful upper chamber, and it is one of an even smaller number of democracies in which a powerful upper chamber is severely malapportioned due to the "equal representation of unequal states" (only Argentina and Brazil are worse). Most important, it is the world's only democracy with both a strong, malapportioned Senate *and* a legislative minority veto (the filibuster). In no other democracy do legislative minorities routinely and permanently thwart legislative majorities.

- America is one of the few established democracies (along with Canada, India, Jamaica, and the U.K.) with first-past-the-post electoral rules that permit electoral pluralities to be manufactured into legislative majorities and, in some cases, allow parties that win fewer votes to win legislative majorities.

- America is the only democracy in the world with lifetime tenure for Supreme Court justices. All other established democracies have either term limits, a mandatory retirement age, or both.

- Among democracies, the U.S. Constitution is the hardest in the world to change, for it requires supermajorities in two legislative chambers plus the approval of three-quarters of the states.

America is an outlier. And we are now more vulnerable to minority rule than any other established democracy. How did other
democracies outpace us? How did a country like Norway trans-
form itself from an early nineteenth-century monarchy into a system that, by any measure, is now *more* democratic than the United
States?

The simple answer is that Norway's constitution is easier to
change. In Norway, a constitutional amendment requires a supermajority of two-thirds support in two successive elected parliaments, but there is no equivalent to America's extraordinarily
difficult state-level ratification process. According to Tom Ginsburg and James Melton, the relative flexibility of the constitution
has allowed Norwegians to "update the formal text in ways that
keep it modern."

Americans are not so fortunate. As noted earlier, our Constitution is the hardest to amend in the democratic world. Among the
thirty-one democracies examined by Donald Lutz in his comparative study of constitutional amendment processes, the United
States stands at the top of the Index of Difficulty, exceeding the
next-highest-scoring countries (Australia and Switzerland) by a
wide margin. Not only do constitutional amendments require the
approval of two-thirds majorities in both the House and the Senate, but they must be ratified by three-quarters of the states. For
this reason, the United States has one of the lowest rates of constitutional change in the world. According to the U.S. Senate, there
have been 11,848 attempts to amend the U.S. Constitution. But
only twenty-seven of them have been successful. America's Constitution has been amended only twelve times since Reconstruction, most recently in 1992—more than three decades ago.

This has had important consequences. Consider the fate of the Electoral College. Again, the United States is the only democracy with this institution. No other provision of the U.S. Constitution has been the target of so many reform initiatives. By one count, there have been more than seven hundred attempts to abolish or reform the Electoral College over the last 225 years. The most serious push during the twentieth century came in the 1960s and 1970s. This was a period that saw three "close call" presidential elections (1960, 1968, and 1976), in which the winner of the popular vote very nearly lost the Electoral College. Following the 1960 election, the Tennessee senator Estes Kefauver, the chair of the Senate Judiciary Committee's Subcommittee on Constitutional Amendments, called for an end to the Electoral College, comparing its persistence to a "game of Russian roulette." When Kefauver died in 1963, he was succeeded as chair of the Subcommittee on Constitutional Amendments by the Indiana senator Birch Bayh. The Senate Judiciary chair James Eastland had been planning to disband the little-used subcommittee, but Bayh persuaded him to maintain it by offering to fund it with his own office's budget. But even Bayh recognized that his committee was "a graveyard. How often do you amend the Constitution, for heaven's sakes?"

After President Kennedy's assassination, however, Bayh took the lead in passing the Twenty-fifth Amendment, which clarified protocol in the case that the president dies or is incapacitated while in office. Bayh was initially skeptical about Electoral College reform, but as democratic changes swept the country in the mid-1960s, he reconsidered, and in 1966 he proposed a constitutional amendment to replace the Electoral College with direct presidential elections.

Americans were on board. A 1966 Gallup poll found 63 percent support for abolishing the Electoral College. That year, the U.S. Chamber of Commerce polled its members and found them nine to one in favor of the reform. In 1967, the prestigious American Bar Association added its endorsement, calling the Electoral College "archaic, undemocratic, complex, ambiguous, indirect, and dangerous."

Bayh's reform proposal was given a boost by the 1968 election, in which George Wallace's strong third-party performance nearly threw the race into the House of Representatives. A shift of just seventy-eight thousand votes in Illinois and Missouri would have cost Nixon his Electoral College majority and left the outcome to the House, where Democrats held a majority. The result frightened leaders of both parties, who began to rally behind Bayh's proposal.

By 1969, the movement to abolish the Electoral College "seemed unstoppable." The newly elected president, Richard Nixon, backed the initiative. So did the Democratic Senate majority leader, Mike Mansfield; the Republican minority leader, Everett Dirksen; the House minority leader, Gerald Ford; and key legislators like Walter Mondale, Howard Baker, and George H. W. Bush. Constitutional reform was backed by business (the Chamber of Commerce) *and* labor (AFL-CIO), by the American Bar Association, and by the League of Women Voters. As the Republican representative William McCulloch observed,

It has become a condition of American life that a citizen would always look forward to death, taxes, and electoral college reform. But today, across this land, there breathes a

new hope. Perhaps, at long last, electoral college reform is
an idea whose time has come.

In September 1969, the House of Representatives passed the
proposal to abolish the Electoral College 338–70—far more than
the two-thirds necessary to amend the Constitution. As the proposal moved to the Senate, a Gallup poll showed that 81 percent of
Americans supported the reform. A *New York Times* survey of state
legislators found that thirty state legislatures were ready to pass the
amendment, six others were undecided, and six were slightly opposed (thirty-eight states would be needed for ratification). Abolition seemed well within reach.

But like so many times in the past, the Senate killed the reform.
And like so many past reform efforts, opposition came from the
South. Alabama's senator James Allen declared, "The Electoral
College is one of the South's few remaining political safeguards.
Let's keep it." The longtime segregationist senator Strom Thurmond promised to filibuster the bill, and the Senate Judiciary
Committee chair, James Eastland, another segregationist, "slow-
walked it through the Judiciary Committee," delaying it by nearly
a year. When a cloture vote was finally held on September 17,
1970, fifty-four senators voted to end debate—a majority, but
well short of the two-thirds needed to end the filibuster. When a
second cloture vote was held twelve days later, fifty-three senators
voted for it. The bill died before it ever came up for a vote.

Bayh didn't give up. He reintroduced his Electoral College reform bill in 1971, 1973, 1975, and 1977. In 1977, following yet
another "close call" election, the proposal got some traction. President Jimmy Carter backed the initiative, and a Gallup poll found

that 75 percent of Americans supported it. But the bill was delayed and then, once again, filibustered in the Senate. When a cloture vote was finally held in 1979, it garnered only fifty-one votes. Afterward, *The New York Times* reported that supporters of Electoral College reform "conceded privately that they stood little chance of reviving the issue unless a president was elected with a minority of the popular vote or the nation came disturbingly close to such a result." As it turned out, they were wildly overoptimistic. Two presidents have been elected with a minority of the popular vote during the early twenty-first century, and yet the Electoral College still stands.

Another serious but ultimately unsuccessful effort to reform the Constitution came in the 1970s, with the Equal Rights Amendment (ERA), which, like recent reforms in Norway, would have enshrined equal rights for women. The ERA was first developed and introduced into Congress by the National Woman's Party in 1923. It was introduced into Congress every year after that, but for decades it was buried in the House Judiciary Committee. The ERA gained momentum during the 1960s, and in 1970, Representative Martha Griffiths succeeded in prying the legislation out of the Judiciary Committee and forcing a vote. In October 1971, the House approved the ERA 354–23. It went to the Senate, where in March 1972 it was approved 84–8. Hawaii ratified the ERA on the same day it passed the Senate, and Delaware, Nebraska, New Hampshire, Idaho, and Iowa ratified it over the next two days. By early 1973, thirty of the required thirty-eight states had ratified the ERA.

Conditions seemed favorable for ratification. Presidents Nixon, Ford, and Carter all backed the ERA, and both the Democratic and the Republican party platforms supported it in 1972 and 1976. Public opinion strongly favored ratification. A 1974 Gallup poll found 74 percent support for the ERA, and surveys generally ran two-to-one in favor of ratification throughout the 1970s.

And yet the process stalled. Five more states approved the ERA after 1973, bringing the total to thirty-five—just three states shy of ratification—in 1977. But even though Congress extended the deadline for ratification to 1982, no additional states signed on. Ten of the fifteen states that failed to ratify were in the South. Four decades later, polls show that nearly three in four Americans support the ERA. Yet the prospects for ratification remain slim.

Our excessively counter-majoritarian Constitution is not just a historical curiosity. It endangers our democracy by protecting and empowering an authoritarian partisan minority. But that Constitution is nearly impossible to reform. We are trapped, it seems, by our institutions. Is there no exit?

CHAPTER 8

DEMOCRATIZING
OUR DEMOCRACY

James Bryce, the British observer of American political life who traveled the country in the late nineteenth century conducting research for his influential two-volume book, *The American Commonwealth,* observed that wherever he went in the United States, Americans asked him, with no small degree of pride, "What do you think of our institutions?" Bryce, an Oxford historian who would go on to serve as British ambassador to the United States, noted,

> The institutions of the United States are deemed by inhabitants and admitted by strangers to be a matter of more general interest than those of the not less famous nations of the Old World. They are . . . institutions of a new type. . . .

They represent an experiment in the rule of the multitude, tried on a scale unprecedently vast, and the results of which everyone is concerned to watch.

Today, America is engaged in another—equally ambitious—experiment: the construction of a vast multiracial democracy. Again, the world is watching.

Previous efforts to build a multiracial democracy in America have failed. Unlike earlier periods, however, today's experiment has the support of most Americans. It is only in the twenty-first century that a solid majority has embraced the principles of diversity and racial equality.

But this majority alone isn't enough to save our democracy, because in America majorities do not really rule. Not only have steps toward a more inclusive politics triggered a fierce backlash among an authoritarian minority, but our institutions have amplified the power of that minority. The acute constitutional crisis triggered by the Trump presidency might have passed, but rather than regarding those four years as an exception, we should regard them as a warning. The conditions that gave rise to the Trump presidency—a radicalized party empowered by a pre-democratic constitution—remain in place.

We stand at a crossroads: either America will be a multiracial democracy or it will not be a democracy at all.

There are paths forward. Other countries' experiences, as well as our own history, offer some guidance. We aren't the first generation to face the rise of political movements that assault democracy from within. In the past, democracies have confronted such threats in several specific ways.

One strategy, born in the darkest days of 1930s Europe, is to corral all democratic-minded forces into a broad coalition to isolate and defeat antidemocratic extremists. Facing the specter of a global wave of fascism, many of Europe's new democracies came to the brink of collapse between the two world wars. In some countries, mainstream politicians responded by setting aside their intense ideological differences and forging broad left-right coalitions to defend democracy. Acute crises call for extraordinary cooperation; leaders of rival parties realized they needed to temporarily set aside their policy goals and forge a common pro-democratic front, both at election time and while governing. In Finland in the early 1930s, the leftist Social Democrats joined center and center-right parties in a broad-based Legality Front to face down the fascist Lapua Movement. In Belgium, the center-left Labor Party joined forces with the conservative Catholic Party and the centrist Liberals in a right-leaning unity government to defeat the fascist Rexist Party. In both cases, coalitions of pro-democratic parties succeeded in keeping extremist forces out of power (until the Nazis invaded Belgium in 1940).

Some American politicians used this containment strategy during the Trump presidency. The lifelong conservatives who founded "Never Trump" organizations like Republicans for the Rule of Law, Republican Voters Against Trump, and the Lincoln Project cooperated with the Democrats—a party they had spent their careers opposing—to defeat the Trump-led GOP in elections. Likewise, Representatives Liz Cheney and Adam Kinzinger, two conservative Republicans, risked their political careers by working closely with Democrats on the House Select Committee to Investigate the January 6th Attack on the United States Capitol. This is how containment should work.

Containment strategies were also employed in America's state legislatures. In Ohio and Pennsylvania after the 2022 midterm elections, Democrats aligned with more moderate Republicans to defeat extremist Republicans for the statehouse speakership. In Pennsylvania, an alliance of Democrats and Republicans elected a moderate Democrat; in Ohio, they elected a mainstream Republican, keeping election-deniers out of power.

These kinds of cross-party alliances—and perhaps even bipartisan tickets—may be critical in 2024 if the Republican Party continues on its extremist path.

Containment is only a short-term strategy, however. Democracy at its heart is about competition, so short-circuiting it for too long can be self-defeating. Progressive and conservative forces may need to close ranks temporarily to defend democracy, but ultimately voters should be able to choose between them. Indeed, evidence from Europe suggests that when "grand coalitions" remain in place for long periods of time, voters come to regard them as collusive, exclusionary, and illegitimate. Excessive mainstream party cooperation may lend plausibility to populist claims that the "establishment" is conspiring against them. So although containment can help keep antidemocratic forces out of power, it doesn't necessarily weaken them. And it might even strengthen them.

A second strategy for confronting authoritarians—known as militant or defensive democracy—also emerged out of the trauma of 1930s Europe. The idea is that government authority and the law can be used to *exclude* and *aggressively prosecute* antidemocratic forces. The strategy was first implemented in post–World War II West Germany. Haunted by the experience of Hitler's rise to power, the country's postwar constitutional designers didn't want their democratic government to stand by helplessly in the face of authoritarian threats from within. So they wrote a constitution that allowed for the *banning and restricting* of insurrectionist or "anti-constitutional" speech, groups, and parties. Used on rare occasions to investigate extremist left- and right-wing parties (most recently in 2021), the mere existence of this authority to investigate groups that assault the "democratic order" arguably has a deterrent effect on extremist forces. The model has spread across much of Europe.

Militant democracy may at first glance seem at odds with America's libertarian tradition, but the U.S. Constitution also possesses tools for combating antidemocratic extremism. As constitutional scholars remind us, Section 3 of the Fourteenth Amendment was adopted to explicitly prohibit "insurrectionists" from holding public office in the aftermath of the Civil War. Although it has rarely been used for this purpose, the Fourteenth Amendment offers a powerful tool to defend democracy from domestic enemies. America had never prosecuted a former president before 2023, but numerous other established democracies—from Japan and South Korea to France, Israel, and Italy—have done so, and their political systems were no worse off for it. Indeed, where presidents or prime ministers have committed serious crimes, it is essential for democracy to demonstrate that no one is above the law. Americans strongly agree that the full force of the law should be applied against those who violently assault our democracy. A 2021 Pew

survey found that 87 percent of Americans believed it was important to prosecute the January 6, 2021, Capitol rioters, and 69 percent believed it was "very important to do so."

Like containment, however, the exclusion strategy has pitfalls.
Most important, it is a tool that is easily abused. American history
is replete with instances of such abuse: the 1798 Alien and Sedition
Acts; the imprisonment of the socialist leader Eugene Debs; the
1919–20 Palmer Raids; the notorious House Un-American Ac-
tivities Committee and Senator Joseph McCarthy's political witch
hunts; and the surveillance, prosecution, and even killing of African American leaders and activists. Ideas of militant democracy
were also used to justify undemocratic bans on left-wing parties in
much of Latin America during the Cold War. So although using
the full force of the law against violent antidemocratic extremists
can be critical to defending democracy, the ever-present risk of
politicization and overreach requires that militant democracy be
used with extraordinary caution and restraint.

Forging broad coalitions to defend democracy and rigorously
enforcing the law against antidemocratic extremists can be indispensable strategies in the face of imminent authoritarian threats.
But they are short-term strategies—imperfect tools to fight dangerous fires. They are not long-term solutions. So we must also
consider more fundamental steps to shore up American democracy.

Here we return to a basic principle inspired by James Madison and
others: Extremist minorities are best overcome through electoral
competition. Madison believed that the need to win popular ma-

jorities would likely tame the most "sinister" political tendencies. But his formula requires that popular majorities *actually prevail* in elections. For that to happen, America must reform its institutions. The early twentieth century American reformer Jane Addams once wrote, "The cure for the ills of Democracy is more Democracy."

We agree. America's excessively counter-majoritarian institutions reinforce extremism, empower authoritarian minorities, and threaten minority rule. To overcome these problems, we must double down on democracy. This means dismantling spheres of undue minority protection and empowering majorities at all levels of government; it means ending constitutional protectionism and unleashing real political competition; it means bringing the balance of political power more closely in line with the balance of voter preferences; and it means forcing our politicians to be more responsive and accountable to majorities of Americans. In short, we must democratize our democracy, undertaking long overdue constitutional and electoral reforms that would, at minimum, bring America in line with other established democracies.

Americans are often skeptical of sweeping reform proposals—and for good reason. Reform is hard, especially in a political system with numerous institutional veto points and highly polarized parties. But reform never happens when it is never considered, so we ask readers to momentarily set aside concerns about *how* to bring about change—we'll get to that—and consider three broad areas of reform.

UPHOLD THE RIGHT TO VOTE. The right to vote is a core element of any modern definition of democracy. In representative democracies, citizens elect their leaders. Leaders can only be elected democratically if all citizens are able to vote. So if voting is costly or difficult for some citizens—if they have to stand in line for hours or travel long distances to vote—elections cannot be fully democratic.

In most democracies, this is not an issue. In a democracy, *people are supposed to vote*. So most democratic societies grant citizens a constitutional (or at least statutory) right to vote, and government authorities make it as easy as possible for people to vote. In some countries (Australia, Belgium, Brazil, Costa Rica, Uruguay), voting is obligatory; it is considered a civic duty, like paying taxes. In nearly all democracies, voter registration is automatic. Once citizens turn eighteen, their names are added to the rolls. And voting is made simple. Nearly all democracies in Europe and Latin America hold elections on the weekend, usually on a Sunday, so that work does not discourage or prevent people from voting. In most established democracies, voter turnout can reach as high as 80 percent. It's not rocket science: if governments make it simple for citizens to register and vote, most of them will vote.

In the United States, to the surprise of many, there is no constitutional or even statutory "right to vote." The Second Amendment affirmed Americans' right to bear arms, but nowhere does the Constitution recognize their right to suffrage. Later amendments specified that suffrage may not be denied on the basis of race (Fifteenth Amendment) or sex (Nineteenth Amendment), but never has the Constitution positively affirmed Americans' right to vote. Likewise, although there are many federal laws protecting voting, no single federal statute grants all adult citizens the right to cast a ballot. Unlike most established democracies, the United States has a long history of governments discouraging and even suppressing the vote. Even today, America is also one of the few countries on earth (Belize and Burundi are two others) in which responsibility for voter registration lies entirely with individual citizens.

Voting in America should be as straightforward as it is in democracies in Europe and elsewhere. This means we should do the following:

1. Pass a constitutional amendment establishing a right to vote for all citizens, which would provide a solid basis to litigate voting restrictions.

2. Establish automatic registration in which all citizens are registered to vote when they turn eighteen. This could be accompanied by the automatic distribution of national voting ID cards to all citizens. The burdens of the registration process should not deter anyone from voting.

3. Expand early voting and easy mail-in voting options for citizens of all states. It should be easy for all Americans to cast ballots.

4. Make Election Day a Sunday or a national holiday, so that work responsibilities do not discourage Americans from voting.

5. Restore voting rights (without additional fines or fees) to all ex-felons who have served their time.

6. Restore national-level voting rights protections. In the spirit of the 1965 Voting Rights Act, parts of which the Supreme Court struck down in 2013, we should reinstate federal oversight of election rules and administration. This could apply only in states and localities with a history of voting rights violations,

following the VRA model, or to all jurisdictions equally, following the model of the 1890 Lodge bill.

7. Replace the current system of partisan electoral administration with one in which state and local electoral administration is in the hands of professional, nonpartisan officials. This will help ensure fairness in the updating of voter rolls, access to polling places, and the voting and vote-counting processes. Nearly every other established democracy, from France and Germany to Brazil, Costa Rica, Japan, and South Africa, has nonpartisan referees to oversee elections.

ENSURE THAT ELECTION OUTCOMES REFLECT MAJORITY PREFERENCES.
Those who win the most votes should win elections. Nothing in democratic theory justifies allowing losers to win elections. The political philosopher John Stuart Mill wrote that democracy should "giv[e] the powers of government in all cases to the numerical majority." Unfortunately in U.S. presidential, Senate, and some state legislative elections, this frequently does not occur. Several steps can be taken to ensure that those who win electoral majorities actually govern:

8. Abolish the Electoral College and replace it with a national popular vote. No other presidential democracy permits the loser of the popular vote to win the presidency. Such a constitutional amendment very nearly passed as recently as 1970.

9. Reform the Senate so that the number of senators elected per state is more proportional to the population of each state (as in Germany). California and Texas should elect more senators than Vermont and Wyoming. Because Article V of the U.S.

Constitution stipulates that "no state, without its Consent, may be deprived of its equal suffrage in the Senate" (a form of *liberum veto*), we understand the barriers to such a reform are enormous. But because the structure of the Senate so subverts basic democratic principles, and with such great consequence, any list of important democratizing reforms must include it.

10. Replace "first-past-the-post" electoral rules and single-member districts for the House of Representatives and state legislatures with a form of proportional representation in which voters elect multiple representatives from larger electoral districts and parties win seats in proportion to the share of the vote they win. This would require repeal of the 1967 Uniform Congressional District Act, which mandates single-member districts for House elections. By ensuring that the distribution of seats in Congress more accurately reflects the way Americans vote, a proportional representation system would prevent the problem of "manufactured majorities," in which parties that win fewer votes in an election capture a majority of seats in the legislature. As the political scientist Lee Drutman writes, a proportional representation system "treats all voters equally, regardless of where they live. And it treats all parties the same, regardless of where their voters live."

11. Eliminate partisan gerrymandering via the creation of independent redistricting commissions such as those used in California, Colorado, and Michigan.

12. Update the Apportionment Act of 1929, which fixed the House of Representatives at 435, and return to the original design of a House that expands in line with population growth. At present, the ratio of voters to representatives in the House is

nearly *five* times higher than that of any European democracy. Expanding the size of Congress would bring representatives closer to the people, and, if the Electoral College and the current Senate structure remain in place, mitigate the small-state bias of the Electoral College.

EMPOWER GOVERNING MAJORITIES. Finally, Americans must take steps to empower legislative majorities by weakening counter-majoritarian legislative and judicial institutions:

13. Abolish the Senate filibuster (a reform that requires neither statutory nor constitutional change), thereby eliminating the ability of partisan minorities to repeatedly and permanently thwart legislative majorities. In no other established democracy is such a minority veto routinely employed.

14. Establish term limits (perhaps twelve or eighteen years) for Supreme Court justices to regularize the Supreme Court appointment process so that every president has the same number of appointments per term. Such a reform would place the United States in the mainstream of all other major democracies in the world. This would also limit the court's intergenerational counter-majoritarianism.

15. Make it easier to amend the Constitution by eliminating the requirement that three-quarters of state legislatures ratify any proposed amendment. Requiring two-thirds supermajorities in both the House of Representatives and the Senate for a constitutional amendment would bring America in line with most other established democracies, including federal democracies like Germany and India, as well as many U.S. states.

These reforms would have a simple yet powerful effect: they would allow majorities to win power and govern. Not only would our proposed reforms help stave off minority rule, but they would also eliminate constitutional protectionism, unleashing the competitive dynamics of democracy. Importantly, the reforms would compel the Republicans to build broader coalitions in order to win. In America today, these coalitions would necessarily be more diverse, which would dilute the influence of the most extremist elements in the Republican Party. A more diverse Republican Party capable of winning national majorities fair and square might be bad news in electoral terms for the Democratic Party, but it would be very good news for American democracy.

The reforms we propose might appear radical, but they are already in place in the vast majority of established democracies, including highly successful ones like Denmark, Germany, Finland, New Zealand, Norway, and Sweden. Making it simpler to vote, ending gerrymandering, replacing the Electoral College with a direct popular vote, eliminating the Senate filibuster, making Senate representation more proportional, ending lifetime tenure on the Supreme Court, and making it a little easier to reform the Constitution—all of these changes would simply catch us up to the rest of the world.

Still, even if these proposals make sense in *theory*, aren't they utterly unrealistic in practice? Given the nature of the American political system and the state of our politics today, one could argue the quixotic pursuit of hard-to-achieve reforms is a counterproductive distraction from the day-to-day incremental work of "real" politics. In 1911, Joe Hill, the Swedish-born American labor activist and songwriter, warned workers to beware of the idealistic promises of do-gooders when facing concrete problems. The song begins,

> *Long-haired preachers come out every night,*
> *Try to tell you what's wrong and what's right;*
> *But when asked how 'bout something to eat*
> *They will answer with voices so sweet:*

> *You will eat, by and by,*
> *In that glorious land above the sky;*
> *Work and pray, live on hay,*
> *You'll get pie in the sky when you die.*

Are democratic reforms "pie in the sky"? The barriers to change today are indeed high—from seemingly unmovable Republican opposition to the unparalleled difficulty of amending the U.S. Constitution. They may appear so insurmountable that it is tempting to set aside a list like ours in pursuit of more immediate goals, like winning the next election or crafting achievable legislation. As political realists, we sympathize with this perspective. Election victories and incremental policy improvements are critical, both to bettering people's lives and to protecting democracy.

But they are not enough. Even if many of our proposals are unlikely to be adopted in the near term, it is essential that ideas for constitutional reform become part of a larger national political debate. The most powerful weapon against change is silence. When an idea is viewed in mainstream circles as impossible, when politicians never mention it, when newspaper editors ignore it, when teachers don't bring it up in class, when scholars stop talking about it for fear of being seen as naive or out of touch—in short, when an ambitious idea is "unthinkable"—the battle is lost. Non-reform becomes a self-fulfilling prophecy.

Just because an idea is not taken seriously today doesn't mean it shouldn't be taken seriously—or that it won't be taken seriously in the future. During the early nineteenth century, the idea of ending slavery was considered unthinkable in mainstream America, and abolitionists were dismissed as dreamers. When the women's suffrage movement was born in the 1840s, no country in the world granted women the right to vote. Well into the twentieth century, mainstream America considered the idea of women's suffrage absurd. And for decades after the Civil War, the pursuit of racial equality and civil rights was seen as impracticable, if not impossible. In each case, the mainstream view changed radically. But for that to happen, someone had to start a public conversation.

The conversation about democratic reform is beginning. In 2020, the prestigious American Academy of Arts and Sciences issued a report, titled *Our Common Purpose,* which laid out a multifaceted reform agenda for American democracy. Organizations such as the Brennan Center for Justice, New America, and Protect Democracy have presented a range of innovative proposals to create a more proportional electoral system, end gerrymandering, expand voting rights, and improve the quality of elections. And in 2021, the White House formed a presidential commission on the reform of the U.S. Supreme Court, drawing on the expertise of retired judges, law professors, and other experts to explore avenues for institutional change. These are important steps. Change cannot be achieved if it is not even considered.

Talk and ideas aren't empty; they lay the groundwork for reform. When Sir Ralf Dahrendorf, the eminent German-born liberal member of the British House of Lords, was asked what explained the "great leap" in the creation of international institutions after World War II, he answered,

> If you go back and look at the origins of the postwar order . . . starting with the United Nations . . . the International Monetary Fund and the World Bank . . . and a whole lot of subsidiary institutions—if you look at the origins of that, you will find that most of the ideas were actually thought out during the war. . . . It is extremely important that when the moment comes in which it is possible to take a new leap forward in . . . institution building, the ideas are [already] there.

When institutional change happens, participants often quote the French poet Victor Hugo's line "Nothing is more powerful than an idea whose time has come." But an idea's time can only come if someone has proposed it.

Democratic reform will remain impossible, however, unless we rethink our attitude toward constitutional change. Unlike citizens of other established democracies, Americans tend to resist the notion that our Constitution has flaws or deficiencies that should be corrected, or that parts of it may be out of date. As Aziz Rana observes, many Americans embrace the Constitution with an "almost religious devotion." We treat the framers as if they were endowed with almost divine or supernatural powers, and we treat the Con-

stitution as if it were a sacred document—one that is "basically perfect." In other words, our society operates under the assumption
that our founding institutions are, in effect, best practice—across
history and in all contexts. The idea that the U.S. Constitution
cannot be improved upon is not based on empirical evidence or
serious debate. Rather, it is an article of faith.

That isn't how institutions work. Constitutions are never perfect at their inception. They are, after all, human creations. Recall
that the Electoral College was an improvised, second-best solution
that never functioned as its designers imagined; or that Madison
(like Hamilton) opposed equal state representation in the Senate
but was outvoted in the Philadelphia Convention. There is nothing sacred about these institutions. And even the best-designed
constitutions require occasional revision because the world in
which they operate changes—often dramatically. No set of rules is
ever "best practice" for all time and under all circumstances. National borders shift and populations expand. New technologies
allow people to do things that were unimaginable for earlier generations. Fundamental principles like equality and liberty may endure, but societal norms evolve in ways that compel us to change
how we define those principles.

John Roberts, later chief justice of the Supreme Court, recognized this when he championed judicial term limits in 1983, when
he was working in the Office of White House Counsel under President Ronald Reagan:

> The framers adopted life tenure at a time when people sim-
> ply did not live as long as they do now. A judge insulated
> from the normal currents of life for twenty-five or thirty

years was a rarity then, but it is becoming commonplace today. Setting a term of, say, fifteen years would ensure that federal judges would not lose all touch with reality through decades of ivory tower existence.

We also know more today about how institutions work. At America's founding, the very notion of representative democracy had not yet been invented. There were no elected presidents or parliamentary democracies. Monarchy was still ubiquitous. But in the 236 years since the U.S. Constitution was written, dozens of other democracies have emerged. Many of them have produced institutional innovations that have proven successful, from directly elected presidents to electoral systems based on proportional representation to independent national election authorities. These innovations have spread widely over the last century because leaders of new democracies consider them improvements.

Changes in the world around us do not always require constitutional change, but sometimes they do. The idea that certain institutions, set in stone, are always "best practice" flies in the face of years of social science research showing that institutions that function well in one context can become ineffective and even dangerously dysfunctional in another.

The founders actually knew this. *They* were not wedded to the original version of the Constitution. They recognized the limitations of their creation and believed that later generations would—and should—modify them. In 1787, just after the Philadelphia Convention, George Washington wrote, "The warmest friends and best supporters the Constitution has, do not contend that it is free from imperfections; but found them unavoidable." If problems arose from these imperfections, Washington wrote, "the remedy must come hereafter." He went on to write that the American people

> can, as they will have the advantage of experience on their Side, decide with as much propriety on the alterations and amendments which are necessary as ourselves. I do not think we are more inspired, have more wisdom, or possess more virtue, than those who will come after us.

Thomas Jefferson was especially critical of those who "look at constitutions with sanctimonious reverence, and deem them like the ark of the covenant, too sacred to be touched." In his view,

> laws and institutions must go hand in hand with the progress of the human mind. . . . We might as well require a man to wear still the coat which fitted him when a boy as civilized society to remain under the regimen of their barbarous ancestors.

Institutions that do not adapt may limp along for years and even decades. But they can grow sclerotic and eventually undermine the legitimacy of the political system. This is happening in twenty-first-century America. In 1995, less than 25 percent of Americans expressed dissatisfaction with their democracy. That figure has increased dramatically in recent years, reaching 55 percent in 2020. Although public dissatisfaction with democracy has grown all over the world, it has risen more sharply in the United States than in other Western democracies. According to the Pew

Research Center, only 41 percent of Americans said they were sat-isfied with democracy in 2021, compared with more than 60 per-cent in Australia, Canada, Germany, and the Netherlands and more than 70 percent in New Zealand and Sweden. Although we may wish to believe that our Constitution is "basically perfect," rigidly unchanging institutions are, in fact, prone to rot. And eventually, they fail.

American history has been punctuated by rare but meaningful moments of democratic progress. During Reconstruction, three major constitutional amendments (the Thirteenth, Fourteenth, and Fifteenth) and a series of far-reaching new laws opened up the political system (albeit only temporarily) to African Americans. Likewise, between 1913 and 1920, America witnessed the passage of three democratizing constitutional amendments: the Sixteenth, authorizing a direct income tax; the Seventeenth, establishing di-rect elections to the U.S. Senate; and the Nineteenth, constitu-tionalizing women's suffrage. Finally, a third period of sweeping democratic and constitutional reform began with the series of Su-preme Court decisions (1962–64) ending malapportionment in the U.S. House of Representatives, followed by the Civil Rights Act (1964) and the Voting Rights Act (1965). Indeed, much of what we value about contemporary American democracy was achieved via this series of constitutional and legislative changes—many of which were once considered impossible to achieve.

What can we learn from these reform episodes? For one, change doesn't depend on the arrival of a single transformative leader. Many of America's most important advances toward political and economic inclusion were made during the presidencies of individuals who, at the time, were seen as unlikely reformers: Woodrow Wilson, Franklin Delano Roosevelt, and Lyndon Johnson. None were radicals in their own right. Indeed, they were all products of the old regime that they would eventually help overturn. Wilson, for example, was a conservative southern Democrat—very distant from the northern middle-class Progressive movement that, with his support, gave rise to the Sixteenth, Seventeenth, and Nineteenth Amendments (in fact, Wilson opposed women's suffrage early in his presidency). Likewise, Franklin Roosevelt was an American aristocrat who nevertheless played a leading role in establishing basic union and worker rights during the 1930s. Finally, Lyndon Johnson made his career as a southern Democrat, ascending to power in the U.S. Senate with the support of influential segregationist figures such as Richard Russell. But by the 1960s, Johnson was spearheading the passage of the Civil Rights and Voting Rights Acts.

These leaders' transformations did not occur accidentally or overnight. They required robust political movements. A first step in this direction was getting reform on the public agenda. Indeed, critical to the success of any reform movement is the ability of advocates, organizers, public thinkers, and opinion makers to reshape the terms of political debate and gradually alter what others viewed as desirable or possible. The most significant instances of democratic reform in American history, from Reconstruction to women's suffrage to civil rights, were preceded by years of relentless legal, political, and public advocacy work.

For example, the Democratic Party's transformation from a defender of Jim Crow into an advocate of civil rights did not occur naturally, easily, or quickly. In the 1930s, long before racial equality was viewed as a national issue, activists in the NAACP and the Congress of Industrial Organizations (CIO) began to organize around civil rights inside the Democratic Party. Guided by labor leaders like Sidney Hillman and John L. Lewis, the CIO began to push Democrats to support not only progressive labor legislation but also civil rights bills such as antilynching laws and the abolition of poll taxes. CIO leaders also worked to shape the values of their rank-and-file members. *The CIO News,* which was distributed nationwide on a weekly basis to the homes of all CIO members, Black and white, featured long articles on civil rights issues (with titles like "CIO Attacks Filibuster on Lynching Bill"), including the reproduction of CIO leaders' speeches to African American groups. As one historian puts it, "Never before had the proponents of the black struggle reached so broad an audience."

But setting the agenda is only the beginning. Democratic reform also requires continuous political pressure. Meaningful change is usually driven by sustained social movements—broad coalitions of citizens whose activism shifts the debate and, eventually, the balance of political power on an issue. Campaigns by social movements—using a diversity of means, including petitions, door-to-door campaigns, rallies, marches, strikes, pickets, sit-ins, and boycotts—can reshape public opinion and alter media narratives.

Ultimately, social movements can change politicians' electoral calculations by creating new constituencies for reform and discrediting the defenders of the status quo. In the case of the civil rights movement, the legal struggle was spearheaded by the NAACP, but the grassroots campaign was carried out by organizations like the

Southern Christian Leadership Conference, which was based on a vast network of churches, and the Student Nonviolent Coordinating Committee.

Politicians like Wilson, Roosevelt, and Johnson did not become reform advocates on their own. Rather, they embraced inclusionary reforms only when large-scale social movements altered their political calculus. President Wilson faced pressure from northern middle-class progressives, many of whom had backed his rival, Theodore Roosevelt. Wilson "converted" to the cause of women's suffrage while president only after facing pressure from female activists in his home state of New Jersey, when the state held a referendum on the issue in 1915. President Franklin Roosevelt championed workers' rights during the Depression and amid waves of labor unrest, including the sit-down strike that brought Flint, Michigan's GM plants to a standstill in 1936–37. And President Johnson fully embraced civil rights amid intense mobilization from the civil rights movement, including high-profile events such as the 1963 March on Washington and the 1965 Bloody Sunday march in Selma.

Each of the above reform periods was the product of a long, grinding struggle. Every major reform movement took decades, and they all encountered roadblocks along the way. Successful movements must learn to cope with setbacks, including electoral defeats, internal divisions, unexpected leadership changes, and divisive foreign wars.

Consider the movement for (white) women's suffrage, which culminated in the Nineteenth Amendment in 1920. This was no short-term project. As Carrie Chapman Catt, president of the National American Woman Suffrage Association, founder of the

League of Women Voters, and chief architect of the Nineteenth Amendment, put it, "To the unimaginative man on the street," the Nineteenth Amendment looked "to come out of nowhere." Of course it didn't. It reflected the work of more than two generations of women activists. As Catt observed,

> To get the word male in effect out of the constitution cost the women of the country fifty-two years of pauseless campaign. . . . During that time they were forced to conduct fifty-six campaigns of referenda to male voters; 480 campaigns to urge Legislatures to submit suffrage amendments to voters; 47 campaigns to induce State constitutional conventions to write woman suffrage into State constitutions; 277 campaigns to persuade State party conventions to include woman suffrage planks; 30 campaigns to urge presidential party conventions to adopt woman suffrage planks in party platforms; and 19 campaigns with 19 successive Congresses. . . . Hundreds of women gave the accumulated possibilities of an entire lifetime, thousands gave years of their lives, hundreds of thousands gave constant interest and such aid as they could. It was a continuous, seemingly endless, chain of activity. Young suffragists who helped forge the last links of that chain were not born when it began. Old suffragists who forged the first links were dead when it ended.

The women's suffrage movement was scarred by defeat, infighting, and even a deep sense of betrayal, especially after female enfranchisement was pushed to the margins with the passage of the

Fifteenth Amendment in 1870. To survive, the movement had to adjust its strategy. Leaders like Elizabeth Cady Stanton and Susan B. Anthony worked to develop an "origin story" for the movement, elevating the importance of the movement's original 1848 Seneca Falls Convention. Their influential multivolume *History of Woman Suffrage,* published beginning in the 1880s, was written with the goal of giving the national movement coherence in the face of growing fragmentation and disarray.

Another challenge facing the women's suffrage movement was its deep roots in upper-class white nativism. But beginning around 1900, leaders like Catt made another shift, turning what had been a mostly elite upper-class movement into one that made inroads with trade unionists, recent immigrants, female socialists, the settlement movement, and Black women's clubs by arguing that the franchise would help cure a range of social ills, from illiteracy and poor sanitation to child labor. Catt showed an astute "willingness to tailor the suffrage message to regional and group differences."

Mobilization was also critical. Following the merger of the American Woman Suffrage Association and the National Woman Suffrage Association in 1890, the movement strengthened considerably. Membership in the new National American Woman Suffrage Association soared, increasing fivefold—from sixteen thousand to eighty-five thousand—between 1910 and 1920. Borrowing strategies used by suffrage movements in Great Britain and other countries, the movement adopted a more grassroots approach, going "precinct by precinct" to win the 1917 state referendum on women's suffrage in New York. Similar campaigns had achieved suffrage in other states, including California in 1911.

There may be a lesson here: suffrage reform was initially achieved, in many cases, at the state level, which helped build momentum for federal constitutional change.

Other major constitutional reforms also took time and relentless effort. The Seventeenth Amendment, which established the direct election of U.S. senators, was preceded by decades of failed initiatives. There were nearly a dozen congressional proposals for an amendment before 1872. The campaign for direct elections gained momentum in the late nineteenth century; twenty-five separate proposals were introduced to Congress between 1891 and 1893 alone. William Jennings Bryan and the Populist Party called for direct Senate elections in their 1892 platform, giving the issue new momentum. The House of Representatives approved the amendment five times between 1892 and 1902, but each time the Senate refused to even hold a vote. In 1906, William Randolph Hearst galvanized national attention further when he hired the popular novelist David Graham Phillips to write a sensationalist series of articles titled "The Treason of the Senate," a nine-installment series in *Cosmopolitan* magazine that depicted the selection of senators in state legislatures as a corrupt process dominated by wealthy special interests. In 1907, Oregon began holding an "advisory" popular vote to guide the legislature's selection of senators. By 1912, more than half of U.S. states had adopted this work-around. Finally, in 1913, after a full twenty-nine states had adopted the so-called Oregon System, the Seventeenth Amendment was ratified. Again, reforms began at the state level, ultimately making a federal constitutional amendment unescapable.

What is needed today, then, is not only a democratic reform

agenda but a democratic reform *movement* capable of mobilizing diverse citizens in a sustained nationwide campaign to ignite imaginations and change the terms of public debate.

That may seem like a tall order, but the stirrings of such a movement are already afoot. The Black Lives Matter campaign, born after the 2013 acquittal of the killer of the unarmed Black teenager Trayvon Martin, mobilized millions of Americans behind a core principle of democracy: equal treatment before the law. The May 2020 police killing of George Floyd triggered the largest protest movement in U.S. history. Between fifteen million and twenty-six million Americans—one in ten adult Americans—took to the streets. There were at least 5,000 protests—an average of about 140 per day—in the early summer of 2020. The protests reached every U.S. state and more than 40 percent of American counties, extending even into small towns. They were led overwhelmingly by young people, and they were strikingly multiracial: about half the protesters (54 percent) identified as white. And unlike the 1960s, when surveys consistently found that majorities of Americans opposed civil rights demonstrations, the Black Lives Matter protests were embraced by most Americans. Nearly three-quarters of Americans sympathized with the demonstrations during the summer of 2020. Although this support subsequently waned, 55 percent of Americans continued to support Black Lives Matter in 2021.

And it wasn't just Black Lives Matter. The Trump presidency spawned a massive civic movement in defense of democracy. New organizations—many of them bipartisan—emerged to defend civil and voting rights, safeguard elections, and uphold the rule of law, joining established organizations such as the ACLU, the

League of Women Voters, and the NAACP. Many news outlets established a "democracy beat" for their domestic politics coverage for the first time. Dozens of new national organizations to safeguard democracy emerged after the 2016 election. One prominent organization, Protect Democracy, was created in 2016 to "prevent our democracy from declining into a more authoritarian form of government." Protect Democracy filed lawsuits and Freedom of Information requests, helped craft legislation, and even developed new software, VoteShield, to help prevent undue purges of the voter rolls.

Another pro-democracy group, Black Voters Matter, was launched by LaTosha Brown. Brown was born in Selma, Alabama, a few years after Bloody Sunday and the passage of the Voting Rights Act. As a child, she watched her grandmother put on her best clothes and pull out her good pocketbook to go to the polling station. Brown would accompany her grandmother, feeling as if she were doing her part. "I didn't know what voting was," Brown says. "But I knew it was pretty special." So when lawmakers across the country began to purge voter rolls, close polling stations, and pass legislation making it harder for minority and lower-income citizens to vote, Brown felt compelled to respond.

In 2016, Brown and Cliff Albright created the Black Voters Matter Fund, which supported community-based efforts—mainly in the South—to fight the closure of polling stations, educate citizens about new registration and voting requirements, and mobilize voters. By 2020, the Black Voters Matter Fund was supporting more than six hundred groups in twelve states. The group organized bus caravans that toured the South, focusing especially on rural communities, where voter suppression laws tend to have the greatest effect. The 2020 "We Got Power" tour visited fifteen states and contacted more than ten million voters.

Young voters also joined the struggle for multiracial democracy during the Trump years. Gen Z is the most diverse generation in American history. It is also the most troubled by the state of contemporary American politics and, far and away, the most committed to the principles of multiracial democracy. According to a 2022 survey by the Harvard Institute of Politics, two-thirds of likely voters between the ages of eighteen and twenty-nine believe American democracy is "in trouble" or "failed." Similarly, Pew surveys found that two-thirds of Americans between the ages of eighteen and twenty-nine supported the Black Lives Matter movement in 2021. Younger Americans are more likely than older generations to support immigration and prefer diverse neighborhoods. This is the generation that will secure multiracial democracy in America.

Historically, young people have not voted. Only 39 percent of voters aged eighteen to twenty-nine voted in the 2016 election, compared with more than 70 percent of those over sixty. Because older voters were both more racially conservative and more pro-Trump than younger voters, and by a large margin, this turnout differential had far-reaching consequences for American democracy. But something changed during Trump's presidency. Young people—especially Gen Z—began to mobilize. In the wake of the February 2018 mass killing at a high school in Parkland, Florida, surviving high school students organized the 2018 March for Our Lives. More than two million people joined marches in 387 of the country's 435 congressional districts.

Although the March for Our Lives focused on combating gun

violence, its organizers launched a broader movement to register and mobilize new voters and helped spur a generation of pro-democracy activists. Santiago Mayer, a seventeen-year-old immigrant from Mexico, was in high school when he founded Voters of Tomorrow, a group aimed at engaging and turning out young voters, in 2019. During the 2020 election cycle, Voters of Tomorrow launched the "Prom at the Polls" campaign, in which high school seniors—deprived of the traditional prom experience due to the pandemic—showed up to vote wearing full prom attire.

Black Lives Matter and Gen-Z for Change are politically left of center, but the defense of American democracy was a bipartisan effort. It included right-of-center groups like R Street, Stand Up Republic, Republican Voters Against Trump, and Republicans for the Rule of Law. It also included grassroots conservatives. Sharlee Mullins Glenn grew up in a small Mormon farming community in northeastern Utah. Her community was deeply conservative; her family even belonged to the far-right John Birch Society. Glenn was a lifelong Republican, but in 2016 she grew "concerned . . . when a man who built his candidacy on a platform of fear—of immigrants, Muslims, refugees and others—inexplicably became not only the nominee of the party I had belonged to my entire life, but also president."

So in January 2017, shortly after Trump's inauguration, Glenn created a nonpartisan Facebook group called Mormon Women for Ethical Government (MWEG). By 2018, the group had six thousand members and chapters in nearly every state. The group registered tens of thousands of voters, worked to defend voting and immigrant rights, went to court to oppose gerrymandering in Utah, and lobbied their representatives—particularly the Utah senators, Mike Lee and Mitt Romney—to impeach and convict Donald Trump for his "abuse of power" and pass legislation to protect voting rights and shore up America's electoral guardrails. According to the Idaho member Cindy Wilson, MWEG members seek to be "loud advocates against extremism." As Glenn wrote in 2020, "We believe that Jesus really meant it when he said that we should love our neighbors—meaning everyone, as the parable of the good Samaritan makes clear." Although MWEG members hold conservative views on issues like abortion and same-sex marriage, they are united in their commitment to multiracial democracy.

If there is one thing we've learned from democracy movements, past and present, it's this: Democratic reform doesn't just happen. It is made.

Reforming American democracy requires a reckoning with our not-so-democratic past. If we are truly committed to our democracy, we must face up not only to its achievements but also to its failures. Reformers throughout U.S. history have admired our Constitution while recognizing its flaws and working to correct them. They have simultaneously loved their country and worked to make it better, fairer, and more democratic. To say we cannot both admire America and confront its past is based on a false choice. The German president, Frank-Walter Steinmeier, poignantly captured the necessity of such clear-eyed patriotism when talking about his own country's tragic history in a 2020 speech:

> Rabbi Nachman once said: "*No heart is as whole as a broken heart.*" [Our country's] past is a fractured past—with re-

sponsibility for the murdering of millions and the suffering of millions. That breaks our hearts to this day. And that is why I say that this country can only be loved with a broken heart.

Loving America with a broken heart means recognizing our own country's failure to live up to its stated democratic ideals—its failure, for too long, to provide liberty and justice for all. It means committing ourselves to achieving those ideals, by building an inclusive, multiracial democracy that all Americans can embrace.

We ended our book *How Democracies Die*—written in the early days of the Trump presidency—by placing that current moment in the context of American history. We reminded readers that this was not the first time that history had called upon Americans to stand up for our democratic ideals. During the Civil War, in the showdown against fascism and totalitarianism in the 1930s and 1940s, and in the civil rights movement of the 1950s and 1960s, Americans stood up to preserve and advance our democracy. We know the stories well: during World War II, anxious citizens bought war bonds, grew victory gardens, and sent loved ones into harm's way. In the civil rights era, citizens joined marches, boycotts, and voter registration drives—often in the face of beatings, jail, and even death.

History called again after 2016. And Americans responded. Citizen activist groups met, planned, and marched; reading clubs raised the awareness of fellow citizens; bipartisan groups of activists formed civic associations to resist moves toward authoritarianism; get-out-the-vote campaigns reached new voters; professionals— doctors, scientists, lawyers, journalists, civil servants, and military officers—stood up for public ethics in the face of corruption; citizens volunteered their aid at airports and the southern border to advocate for defenseless refugees. And in the wake of the George Floyd killing, a multiracial cross section of Americans braved the risk of COVID-19 to mount the largest protest movement our country has ever seen.

Americans tapped into a vibrant democratic tradition. And the effects of these democratic victories reverberated beyond our borders, providing a model for activists around the world.

The fact that our constitutional system survived four years of the Trump presidency could be taken as evidence that the threat wasn't really so serious and that claims of democratic decline were—and still are—overblown. This is deeply mistaken. Americans who feared for the survival of their democracy came together to defend it, and because they did, democracy survived.

Americans are understandably worn down by the past seven years. Defending democracy is tiring work. Mobilizing people to vote, despite the obstacles thrown up around them, election after election after election, can exhaust even the most committed activist.

With Trump out of the White House (for now), it is tempting to conclude—or even to *hope*—that we can rest easy, that our democracy has regained its balance.

In 1888, *The Atlantic*'s founding editor, James Russell Lowell, looked back at the Civil War and worried how Americans remembered their own democracy's near-death experience. He wrote,

After our Constitution got fairly into working order it really seemed as if we had invented a machine that would go of itself, and this begot a faith in our luck which even the civil war itself but momentarily disturbed. . . . We are a nation that has struck [oil], but we are also a nation that is sure the well will never run dry. And this confidence in our luck with the absorption in material interests, generated by unparalleled opportunity, has . . . made us neglectful of our political duties.

At the very moment at which Lowell worried about Americans' confidence that our Constitution was "a machine that would go of itself," the Fourteenth and Fifteenth Amendments were being eviscerated. With the Civil War rapidly disappearing in the rearview mirror, white Americans were turning a blind eye to the construction of an apartheid-like system in the South, poisoning our polity for generations and staining our national identity to this day.

Let us not repeat our past mistake of turning away from public life out of exhaustion. Pro-democratic forces achieved important victories in 2020 and 2022, but the factors responsible for America's recent backsliding—a radicalized partisan minority and institutions that protect and empower it—endure. Our democracy remains unmoored. History is calling again.

Defending democracy is not the work of selfless heroes. Standing up for democracy means standing up for ourselves. Think back to the scenes from January 5 and January 6 that opened this book. What kind of society do we want to live in? Think of the millions of Americans—young and old, religious and secular, of every

imaginable skin color—who took to the streets in the name of justice in the summer of 2020. The young people who marched that
summer could have turned away from the system, but they turned
out to vote instead. A new generation of Americans stood up to
defend our imperfect democracy. But they also showed us a vision
of a better democracy—a democracy for all.

As the civil rights generation passes into history, the work of
building a truly multiracial democracy falls upon us. Future generations will hold us to account.

ACKNOWLEDGMENTS

We are very fortunate. In writing this book, we benefited enormously from the generosity, support, and advice of friends, students, and colleagues.

We could not have written the book without the collaboration of a group of extraordinary research assistants. Many thanks to Oliver Adler, Florian Bochert, Joyce Chen, Nourhan Elsayed, Addie Esposito, Daniel Lowery, Dorothy Manevich, Sarah Mohamed, Andrew O'Donohue, Connor Phillips, Emilie Segura, Elizabeth Thom, Aaron Watanabe, and Michael Waxman for their hard work. Special thanks to Ethan Jasny, whose contributions permeate this book, and to Manuel Meléndez, who coordinated the research on comparative institutions and provided invaluable feedback on the full manuscript.

We thank the staff at Harvard University's Center for European Studies and the David Rockefeller Center for Latin American Studies, as well as the Wissenschaftszentrun Berlin, for their generous support (and patience).

We benefited from conversations with numerous colleagues, including Danielle Allen, Ian Bassin, Sheri Berman, Jamelle Bouie, Dan Carpenter, Larry Diamond, Lee Drutman, Peter Hall, Richard Hasen, Gretchen Helmke, Torben Iversen, Michael Klarman, Mary Lewis, Rob Mickey, Paul Pierson, Richard Pildes, Michael Podhorzer, Theda Skocpol, Dan Slater, Todd Washburn, Lucan Ahmad Way, and Daniel's colleagues and friends at the Wissenschaftszentrum Berlin.

We are also grateful to Bernard Fraga, Jennifer Hochschild, Hakeem Jefferson, Evan Lieberman, Jamila Michener, Rob Mickey, and Vesla Weaver for generously devoting half a day teaching us about the concept of multiracial democracy.

Several colleagues took the time to read and comment on parts or all of the manuscript. Feedback from Ian Bassin, Larry Diamond, Lee Drutman, Patrice Higonnet, Michael Klarman, Mary Lewis, James Loxton, Suzanne Mettler, Rob Mickey, Chris Millington, and Ben Radersdorf made this a far better book.

We are grateful, once again, to Amanda Cook, our uncommonly incisive editor at Crown. Amanda always saw the book more clearly than we did, and she somehow managed to drag us most of the way there. Amanda, we appreciate your confidence in us, your patience with us, and your unfailing commitment to this project. We also thank the rest of the team at Crown, including Katie Berry, Mark Birkey, Gillian Blake, Julie Cepler, David Drake, Melissa Esner, Dyana Messina, Annsley Rosner, and Penny Simon.

We are deeply thankful to Katherine Flynn, Sarah Khalil, and the Kneerim & Williams agency, who were always there for us.

We experienced two enormous losses during the writing of this book. Our extraordinary agent, Jill Kneerim, passed away in 2022. The impact of her support, her wisdom, and her writing lessons is impossible to overstate. Neither of our books would have been possible without her. Jill, we miss you terribly.

Finally, Daniel's father, David Ziblatt, passed away in 2022. He was Daniel's first editor. His imprint on Daniel's thinking on the issues in this book is immense, and he is missed every day.

We dedicate this book to Jill and David.

NOTES

INTRODUCTION

3   **That night, he introduced supporters** See Steve Peoples, Bill Barrow, and Russ Bynum, "Warnock Makes History with Senate Win as Dems near Majority," Associated Press, Jan. 5, 2021.

3   **"There's a new South rising"** See Rachel Epstein, "LaTosha Brown Says a New South Is Rising," *Marie Claire,* Nov. 27, 2021.

4   **Few societies have** On how other societies have coped with situations in which ethnic minorities collectively constitute a majority of the population, see Justin Gest, *Majority Minority* (Oxford: Oxford University Press, 2022).

4   **A multiracial democracy** A more accurate term might be "multiethnic democracy," because the concept encompasses not only different races but also ethnic groups (such as Latinos or Jews) that are not based on race. Given the historical centrality of race in the United States, however, and given that the term "multiracial democracy" is more commonly employed in U.S. public debates, we will use the term "multiracial democracy."

5   **Access to the ballot** A study of the 2018 election found that on average Latino and Black voters waited 46 and 45 percent longer to vote, respectively, than white voters. See Hannah Klain et al., "Waiting to Vote: Racial Disparities in Election Day Experiences," Brennan Center for Justice, June 2020. Also Daniel Garisto, "Smartphone Data Show Voters in Black Neighborhoods Wait Longer," *Scientific American,* Oct. 1, 2019.

5   **A 2018 survey** See Vann R. Newkirk II, "Voter Suppression Is Warping Democracy," *Atlantic,* July 17, 2018.

5   **Black men are more than twice** See Lynne Peeples, "What the Data Say About Police Shootings," *Nature,* Sept. 4, 2019.

5   **they are more likely** See Jennifer Hochschild, Vesla Weaver, and Traci Burch, *Creating a New Racial Order: How Immigration, Genomics, and the Young Can Remake Race in America* (Princeton, N.J.: Princeton University Press, 2012), 128, 148. A 2020 study of nearly one hundred million traffic stops found that Black drivers are stopped more frequently than white drivers and that when they are stopped, Black motorists are nearly twice as likely to be searched. See Emma Pierson et al., "A Large-Scale Analysis of Racial Disparities in Police Stops Across the United States," *Nature Human Behaviour* 4 (July 2020): 736–45.

5   **and they are more likely** See "Report to the United Nations on Racial Disparities in the U.S. Criminal Justice System," Sentencing Project, April 19, 2018; Glenn R. Schmitt et al., "Demographic Differences in Sentencing: An Update to the 2012 *Booker* Report," U.S. Sentencing Commission, Nov. 2017; E. Anne Carson and William J. Sabol, "Prisoners in 2011," U.S. Department of Justice Bureau of Justice Statistics, Dec. 2012.

5   **If you have any doubt** Justin Hansford, "The First Amendment Freedom of Assembly as a Racial Project," *Yale Law Journal* 127 (2018).

5   **A massive wave of immigration** William H. Frey, *Diversity Explosion: How New Racial Demographics Are Remaking America* (Washington, D.C.: Brookings Institution Press, 2018).

5   **And at the same time** Hochschild, Weaver, and Burch, *Creating a New Racial Order,* 24.

5   **Public opinion research shows** See Mohamed Younis, "Americans Want More, Not Less, Immigration for First Time," Gallup, July 1; "Voters' Attitudes About Race and Gender Are Even More Divided Than in 2016," Pew Research Center, Sept. 10, 2020; Hannah Fingerhut, "Most Americans Express Positive Views of Country's Growing Racial and Ethnic Diversity," Pew Research Center, June 14, 2018; Juliana Menasce Horowitz, "Americans See Advantages and Challenges in Country's Growing Racial and Ethnic Diversity," Pew Research Center, May 8, 2019; "General Social Survey (GSS)," NORC at the University of Chicago.

6   **But the assault on American democracy** Over the last five years, several important books have been written on the challenges of American democracy, including Theda Skocpol and Caroline Tervo, eds., *Upending American Politics: Polarizing Parties, Ideological Elites, and Citizen Activists from the Tea Party to the Anti-Trump Resistance* (New York: Oxford University Press, 2020); Suzanne Mettler and Robert C. Lieberman, *Four Threats: The Recurring Crises of American Democracy* (New York: St. Martin's Press, 2020); Robert C. Lieberman, Suzanne Mettler, and Kenneth M. Roberts, eds., *Democratic Resilience: Can the United States Withstand Rising Polarization?* (Cambridge, UK: Cambridge University Press, 2022).

7   **In a well-known study** Adam Przeworski and Fernando Limongi, "Modernization: Theories and Facts," *World Politics* 49 (1997): 165.

7   **And the 2015 refugee crisis** Rafaela Dancygier, *Dilemmas of Inclusion: Muslims in Europe* (Cambridge, U.K.: Cambridge University Press, 2017).

8   **Together with the fallout** Dominik Hangartner et al., "Does Exposure to the Refugee Crisis Make Natives More Hostile?," *American Political Science Review* 113, no. 2 (2019): 442–55; Pippa Norris and Ronald Inglehart, *Cultural Backlash: Trump, Brexit, and Authoritarian Populism* (New York: Cambridge University Press, 2019).

8   **In nearly every western European country** Tarik Abou-Chadi and Simon Hix, "Brahmin Left Versus Merchant Right? Education, Class, Multiparty Competition, and Redistribution in Western Europe," *British Journal of Sociology* 72, no. 1 (2021): 79–92; J. Law-

rence Broz, Jeffry Frieden, and Stephen Weymouth, "Populism in Place: The Economic Geography of the Globalization Backlash," *International Organization* 75, no. 2 (2021): 464–94; Larry Bartels, *Democracy Erodes from the Top: Leaders, Citizens, and the Challenge of Populism in Europe* (Princeton, N.J.: Princeton University Press, 2023), 166.

10   **But flaws in our Constitution** For an excellent discussion of some of these flaws, see Sanford Levinson, *Our Undemocratic Constitution: Where the Constitution Goes Wrong (and How We the People Can Correct It)* (Oxford: Oxford University Press, 2008).

CHAPTER 1: FEAR OF LOSING

12   **On the evening of October 30** Gustavo Beliz, *CGT: El otro poder* (Buenos Aires: Planeta, 1988), 74.

12   **"We didn't see it coming"** Mario Wainfeld, interview with Levitsky, Dec. 22, 2021.

14   **"They still haven't counted the votes"** See Redacción LAVOZ, "A 38 años del retorno de la democracia: La asunción de Raúl Alfonsín," *La Voz,* Dec. 10, 2021.

14   **Peronist vice presidential candidate** See Rogelio Alaniz, "Las elecciones del 30 de octubre de 1983," *El Litoral,* Oct. 29, 2014.

14   **Party leaders, licking their wounds** See "Raúl Alfonsín exige a los militares argentinos el traspaso inmediato del poder," *El País,* Nov. 1, 1983.

14   **But none of them considered rejecting** Wainfeld, interview with Levitsky, Dec. 22, 2021.

14   **"All politicians have to live"** Audio of press conference of Italo Luder and Raúl Alfonsín, Nov. 1, 1983, *Radio Universidad Nacional de La Plata,* sedici.unlp.edu.ar/bitstream/handle/10915/34284 /Audio_de_Luder_y_Alfons%C3%ADn__04_19_.mp3?sequence= 1&isAllowed=y.

15   **"Democracy is a system"** Adam Przeworski, *Democracy and the Market* (New York: Cambridge University Press, 1991), 10.

15   **On March 4, 1801** Sean Wilentz, *The Rise of American Democracy: Jefferson to Lincoln* (New York: W. W. Norton, 2005), 94.

15   **This transition was indispensable** Seymour Martin Lipset, *The First New Nation: The United States in Historical and Comparative Perspective* (New York: W. W. Norton, 1979), 44.

15   **But it was neither inevitable** See Joanne B. Freeman, "Corruption and Compromise in the Election of 1800: The Process of Politics on the National Stage," in *The Revolution of 1800: Democracy, Race, and the New Republic,* ed. James Horn, Jan Ellen Lewis, and Peter S. Onuf (Charlottesville: University of Virginia Press, 2002), 87–120.

15   **Politicians, including many of the founders** Richard Hofstadter, *The Idea of a Party System: The Rise of Legitimate Opposition in the United States, 1780–1840* (Berkeley: University of California Press, 1969), 92–96, 106–11.

15   **"plunge into the unknown"** The phrase "plunge into the unknown" is from Adam Przeworski, "Acquiring the Habit of Changing Governments Through Elections," *Comparative Political Studies* 48, no. 1 (2015): 102.

16   **As designers of the Constitution** Lipset, *First New Nation,* 38–39.

16   **The emergence of the Democratic-Republicans** Wilentz, *Rise of American Democracy,* 49–62.

16   **They regarded the Federalists as quasi-monarchists** Hofstadter, *Idea of a Party System,* 123–24.

16   **They suspected them** James MacGregor Burns, *The Vineyard of Liberty* (New York: Knopf, 1982), 125–26.

16   **The Federalists feared** James Sharp, *American Politics in the Early Republic: The New Nation in Crisis* (New Haven, Conn.: Yale University Press, 1993), 322n1.

16   **These fears were reinforced** Ibid., 241–42.

16   **Federalists charged that slave rebellions** Ibid., 242; Douglas Egerton, *Gabriel's Rebellion: The Virginia Slave Conspiracies of 1800 and 1802* (Chapel Hill: University of North Carolina Press, 1993), 114–15. The fact that two Frenchmen were actively involved in Gabriel's Rebellion didn't help (Egerton, *Gabriel's Rebellion,* 45).

17   **Seeing Virginia's behavior** Quoted in Sharp, *American Politics in the Early Republic,* 214.

17   **In response, Virginia's state legislature** John Murrin et al., *Liberty, Equality, Power: A History of the American People* (New York: Harcourt Brace, 1996), 292.

17   **"Federalists and Republicans were willing"** Sharp, *American Politics in the Early Republic,* 250.

17   **"decide which votes to count"** Ibid., 219.

18   **"In times like these"** *The Political Writings of Alexander Hamilton,* ed. Carson Holloway and Bradford Wilson (Cambridge, U.K.: Cambridge University Press, 2017), 2:417.

18   **Some floated the idea** John Ferling, *Adams vs. Jefferson: The Tumultuous Election of 1800* (Oxford: Oxford University Press, 2004), 177.

18   **Others wanted to elect Burr** Sharp, *American Politics in the Early Republic,* 266.

19   **"the spirit of the Constitution"** Susan Dunn, *Jefferson's Second Revolution: The Election Crisis of 1800 and the Triumph of Republicanism* (Boston: Houghton Mifflin, 2004), 196.

19   **"throw the Government"** James E. Lewis, "What Is to Become of Our Government? The Revolutionary Potential of the Election of 1800," in Horn, Lewis, and Onuf, *Revolution of 1800,* 14. Federalists split over the wisdom of such a strategy. Adams viewed it as no more dangerous than a Jefferson or Burr presidency (Dunn, *Jefferson's Second Revolution,* 205). By contrast, Hamilton described "the game of preventing an election" as "most dangerous and unbecoming" (Dunn, *Jefferson's Second Revolution,* 197).

19   **Federalist leaders' consideration** Sharp, *American Politics in the Early Republic,* 257.

19   **"resistance by force"** Ferling, *Adams vs. Jefferson,* 182.

19   **The governors of Pennsylvania and Virginia** Ibid.

20   **Soon Maryland and Vermont** Dunn, *Jefferson's Second Revolution,* 212–13.

20   **"Some of our [Federalist] Gentlem[e]n"** Bayard to Richard Bassett, Feb. 16, 1801, in *Papers of James Bayard, 1796–1815,* ed. Elizabeth Donnan (Washington, D.C.: American Historical Association, 1913), 126–27. Jefferson later also attributed Federalist acquiescence to the likelihood "that a legislative usurpation would be resisted by

arms." Jefferson to Madison, Feb. 18, 1801, as quoted by Lewis, "What Is to Become of Our Government?," 20.

21 **"We are not dead yet"** Dunn, *Jefferson's Second Revolution,* 228.

22 **"should soon stand on high ground"** Ibid., 227–28.

22 **"remain a party"** Hofstadter, *Idea of a Party System,* 142.

22 **Indeed, a New Jersey Federalist** Dunn, *Jefferson's Second Revolution,* 226.

22 **"wade in blood"** Hofstadter, *Idea of a Party System,* 140.

22 **Hamilton and other founding leaders** Ibid., 137.

22 **"I have no notion"** Ibid., 145–46.

22 **Backroom negotiations** Freeman, "Corruption and Compromise in the Election of 1800," 109–10; see also discussion in Ferling, *Adams vs. Jefferson,* 194.

23 **For good measure** Hofstadter, *Idea of a Party System,* 163.

23 **The Federalists thus left power** Ibid., 142–43.

23 **"the new president will not lend"** Dunn, *Jefferson's Second Revolution,* 225.

23 **Research in political psychology** See Henri Tajfel, "Experiments in Intergroup Discrimination," *Scientific American* 223, no. 5 (1970): 96–102; James Sidanius and Felicia Pratto, *Social Dominance: An Intergroup Theory of Social Hierarchy and Oppression* (New York: Cambridge University Press, 1999); Noam Gidron and Peter A. Hall, "The Politics of Social Status: Economic and Cultural Roots of the Populist Right," *British Journal of Sociology* 68, no. S1 (2017): 57–84; Diana C. Mutz, "Status Threat, Not Economic Hardship, Explains the 2016 Presidential Vote," *PNAS* 115, no. 19 (2018).

23 **"fear of falling"** Barbara Ehrenreich, *Fear of Falling: The Inner Life of the Middle Class* (New York: Pantheon, 1989).

25 **"rule by the undifferentiated masses"** Stenographische Berichte, Haus der Abgeordneten 77 Sitzung, 21 Legislative Period, May 20, 1912.

25 **"a terror without end"** Cited by Daniel Ziblatt, *Conservative Parties and the Birth of Democracy* (Cambridge, U.K.: Cambridge University Press, 2017), 40.

25 **Popular protests** Surin Maisrikrod, "Thailand 1992: Repression and Return of Democracy," *Southeast Asian Affairs* (1993): 333–38.

26   **Some observers even surmised** See, for example, James Fallows, *Looking at the Sun: The Rise of the New East Asian Economic and Political System* (New York: Pantheon Books, 1994).

26   **Protesters, drawn mainly from Thailand's** For a careful analysis of the demographic background of this movement done by the Asia Foundation, see Duncan McCargo, "Thailand in 2014: The Trouble with Magic Swords," *Southeast Asian Affairs* (2015): 335–58.

26   **University students and professionals** See Andrew R. C. Marshall, "High Society Hits the Streets as Prominent Thais Join Protests," Reuters, Dec. 13, 2013.

27   **The Democrats** Abhisit Vejjajiva, interview with Ziblatt, Jan. 13, 2022.

27   **two days before the polls opened** See Suttinee Yuvejwattana and Anuchit Nguyen, "Thai Opposition to Petition Court to Annul Weekend Vote," Bloomberg, Feb. 4, 2014.

27   **On Election Day, protesters interfered** See Thomas Fuller, "Protesters Disrupt Thai Voting, Forcing Additional Elections," *New York Times,* Feb. 2, 2014; see also Kocha Olarn, Pamela Boykoff, and Jethro Mullen, "After Disrupting Thailand Election, Protesters Pledge More Demonstrations," CNN, Feb. 3, 2014.

27   **Voting was disrupted** Olarn, Boykoff, and Mullen, "After Disrupting Thailand Election, Protesters Pledge More Demonstrations."

28   **"Moral righteousness comes above democracy!"** Marshall, "High Society Hits the Streets as Prominent Thais Join Protests."

28   **"This is a victory day"** Thomas Fuller, "Thailand's Military Stages Coup, Thwarting Populist Movement," *New York Times,* May 22, 2014.

28   **The Democrats later joined** Kaweewit Kaewjinda, "Thailand's Oldest Party Will Join Coup Leader's Coalition," Associated Press, June 5, 2019.

28   **The millions of voters** Suchit Bunbongkarn, "Thailand's November 1996 Election and Its Impact on Democratic Consolidation," *Democratization* 4, no. 2 (1997).

29   **Thaksin was a controversial prime minister** Duncan McCargo,
      "Thaksin and the Resurgence of Violence in the Thai South: Net-
      work Monarchy Strikes Back?," *Critical Asian Studies* 38, no. 1
      (2006); Dan Rivers, "Ousted Thai PM Thaksin Guilty of Corrup-
      tion," CNN, Oct. 21, 2008.

29   **In 2001, Thaksin campaigned** Kevin Hewison, "Crafting Thai-
      land's New Social Contract," *Pacific Review* 17, no. 4 (2004); Mi-
      chael Montesano, "Thailand in 2001: Learning to Live with
      Thaksin," *Asia Survey* 42, no. 1 (2002): 91.

29   **And he delivered** See Nick Cumming-Bruce, "For Thaksin, How
      Big a Victory?," *New York Times,* Feb. 4, 2005.

29   **His government spent billions of dollars** David Hughes and
      Songkramchai Leethongdee, "Universal Coverage in the Land of
      Smiles: Lessons from Thailand's 30 Baht Health Reforms," *Health
      Affairs* 26, no. 4 (2007): 999–1008.

29   **Poverty rates fell dramatically** See Thomas Fuller, "Thaksin Can
      Rely on Thai Villagers," *New York Times,* March 5, 2006; Thanasak
      Jenmana, "Income Inequality, Political Instability, and the Thai
      Democratic Struggle" (master's thesis, Paris School of Economics,
      2018).

31   **Since 2001, the poor's share** Jenmana, "Income Inequality, Politi-
      cal Instability, and the Thai Democratic Struggle."

31   **Even though Thaksin's reputation** McCargo, "Thaksin and the
      Resurgence of Violence in the Thai South."

31   **"true understanding"** See Thomas Fuller, "Thai Beer Loses Es-
      teem After Heiress's Remarks," CNBC, Jan. 13, 2014.

31   **"I'm not really for democracy"** See Marshall, "High Society Hits
      the Streets as Prominent Thais Join Protests."

31   **In a 2014 survey** Asia Foundation, *Profile of the "Bangkok Shutdown"
      Protestors: A Survey of Anti-Government PDRC Demonstrators in Bang-
      kok,* Jan. 2014; 18.

32   **"found themselves to be the . . . minority"** See Marc Saxer,
      "Middle Class Rage Threatens Democracy," *New Mandala,* Jan. 21,
      2014.

32   **"an imagined pre-Thaksin era"** See Peter Shadbolt, "Thailand
      Elections: Politics of Crisis," CNN, Feb. 2, 2014.

32   **the Democrats, who had once fiercely opposed** See Petra Desa-
       tova, "What Happened to Thailand's Democrat Party?," *Thai Data
       Points,* Dec. 4, 2019; Punchada Sirivunnabood, "Thailand's Demo-
       crat Party: The Gloomy Light at the End of the Tunnel," *Diplomat,*
       May 24, 2022; Joshua Kurlantzick, "Thailand's Coup, One Year
       On," Council on Foreign Relations, May 26, 2015.

CHAPTER 2: **THE BANALITY OF AUTHORITARIANISM**

34   **On the afternoon of February 6** For a comparison between
       the events of February 6, 1934, in France and January 6, 2021, in
       the United States, see John Ganz, "Feb 6 1934/Jan 6 2021: What
       Do the Two Events Really Have in Common?," *Unpopular Front,*
       July 15, 2021, johnganz.substack.com/p/feb-6-1934jan-6-2021; see
       also Baptiste Roger-Lacan, "Le 6 février de Donald Trump," *Le
       Grand Continent,* Jan. 7, 2021.

35   **The Young Patriots** William Irvine, *French Conservatism in Crisis:
       The Republican Federation of France in the 1930s* (Baton Rouge: Louisi-
       ana State University Press, 1979), 105.

35   **A few groups sought** See, for example, Brian Jenkins and Chris
       Millington, *France and Fascism: February 1934 and the Dynamics of Po-
       litical Crisis* (London: Routledge, 2015), 52, 89–90.

35   **Others merely aimed** René Rémond, *The Right Wing in France:
       From 1815 to de Gaulle* (1969; Philadelphia: University of Pennsylva-
       nia Press, 2016), 283.

35   **But all the groups regarded themselves** The right-wing leagues
       often had important financial backers among conservative powerful
       economic interests, such as Ernest Mercier (a tycoon of electrical
       and oil trusts). See William L. Shirer, *The Collapse of the Third Repub-
       lic: An Inquiry into the Fall of France in 1940* (New York: Simon &
       Schuster, 1969), 200, 202–3.

35   **That night events took** The following description relies on the
       firsthand account of William L. Shirer. See ibid., 213–20.

35   **"Hang the Deputies!"** Ibid., 210.

35   **"They are storming the doors"** Ibid., 215.

35   **"Notice to the Demonstrators"** Ibid.

36   **"I am telephoning you"** *Guardian,* Feb. 7, 1934.

36   **One minister attempted to escape** Shirer, *Collapse of the Third Republic*, 216.

36   **He was replaced by Gaston Doumergue** Julian Jackson, *France: The Dark Years, 1940–1944* (Oxford: Oxford University Press, 2001), 72.

36   **"assault against republican institutions"** Shirer, *Collapse of the Third Republic*, 954n16, 226.

37   **Parties of the left** This cooperation paved the way for the formation of a left-leaning Popular Front government (1936–38). Julian Jackson, *The Popular Front in France: Defending Democracy, 1934–1938* (Cambridge, U.K.: Cambridge University Press, 1988).

37   **Founded in 1903** Irvine, *French Conservativism in Crisis*, 100.

37   **At least thirty-five Federation members** Ibid., 107–8.

37   **"shock troops"** Ibid., 123.

38   **Eyewitnesses to the attack** Max Beloff, "The Sixth of February," in *The Decline of the Third Republic*, ed. James Joll (London: Chatto and Windus, 1959), 11; see also Jenkins and Millington, *France and Fascism*, 88.

38   **"a sort of political headquarters"** Quoted in Jenkins and Millington, *France and Fascism*, 88.

38   **"This is a decisive moment"** Ibid., 179.

38   **"meaning of February 6"** Ibid., 126–48.

38   **Some conservative newspapers and politicians** Ibid., 130; see also Kevin Passmore, *The Right in France: From the Third Republic to Vichy* (Oxford: Oxford University Press, 2013), 295–96.

38   **The insurrectionists, they claimed, were heroic** Irvine, *French Conservatism in Crisis*, 117–18; Jenkins and Millington, *France and Fascism*, 132.

38   **It was the police** See details in Jenkins and Millington, *France and Fascism*, 131–33.

39   **"martyrs who can never be sufficiently"** Irvine, *French Conservatism in Crisis*, 118.

39   **"the brains behind February 6"** Jenkins and Millington, *France and Fascism*, 88.

39   **"There are moments when insurrection"** Irvine, *French Conservatism in Crisis*, 116–17.

39   **They sought to include language** *Rapport général: Evénements du 6 février 1934 procès verbaux de la commission,* 2820.

39   **Seeking to forge a consensus** Ibid., 2861–62.

40   **The Republican Federation representatives** Ibid., 2839–40.

40   **Politicians who are committed to democracy** Juan Linz, *The Breakdown of Democratic Regimes* (Baltimore: Johns Hopkins University Press, 1978).

40   **First, they must respect the outcome** For a more elaborate discussion of the importance of losing in democracy, see Jan-Werner Müller, *Democracy Rules* (New York: Farrar, Straus and Giroux, 2021), 58–64.

41   **"semi-loyal" democrats** Linz, *Breakdown of Democratic Regimes.*

41   **But make no mistake** Ibid., 38.

41   **Indeed, throughout history, cooperation** Ibid.

42   **Sweden's largest conservative party** Ziblatt, *Conservative Parties and the Birth of Democracy,* 344.

42   **They may form political alliances** Gabriel Jackson, *The Spanish Republic and the Civil War, 1931–1939* (Princeton, N.J.: Princeton University Press, 1965), 148–69, 184–95; Stanley G. Payne, *Spain's First Democracy: The Second Republic, 1931–1936* (Madison: University of Wisconsin Press, 1993).

44   *loyal democrats join forces* This point draws on Linz, *Breakdown of Democratic Regimes,* 37.

44   **Nevertheless, mainstream center-left politicians** Jackson, *Spanish Republic and the Civil War,* 148–69, 184–95; Payne, *Spain's First Democracy.*

44   **And likewise, when military officials** Ziblatt, *Conservative Parties and the Birth of Democracy,* 347–53.

44   **Early in the transition, economic growth** Javier Tusell, *Spain: From Dictatorship to Democracy* (Oxford: Wiley-Blackwell, 2011), 294–95.

45   **Prime Minister Adolfo Suárez grew unpopular** Ibid., 311.

45   **Suárez had already angered** Javier Cercas, *Anatomía de un instante* (Barcelona: Mondadori, 2009), 276, 337, 371.

45   **Now, it seemed, he had fallen** Ibid., 144–46.

45   **But at 6:23 in the evening** Tusell, *Spain,* 309; Cercas, *Anatomía de un instante,* 324. For a detailed account of the coup, see Cercas, *Anatomía de un instante.*

45   **The coup plotters aimed to prevent** Cercas, *Anatomía de un instante,* 169.

45   **General Armada was a longtime aide** Ibid., 271, 325.

45   **His close ties to Juan Carlos** Ibid., 161, 168–69, 283–84.

45   **Only three men refused to hide** Ibid., 30, 180.

45   **Santiago Carrillo, an old communist** Ibid., 176–77.

46   **each put his body on the line** Ibid., 183.

46   **Tanks rolled through the streets** Ibid., 160.

46   **National radio played** Bill Cemlyn-Jones, "King Orders Army to Crush Coup," *Guardian,* Feb. 23, 1981. For a detailed account of the coup, see Cercas, *Anatomía de un instante.*

46   **Outside the parliament building** Cemlyn-Jones, "King Orders Army to Crush Coup."

46   **"biggest demonstration in Spain's history"** See "La manifestación más grande de la historia de España desfiló ayer por las calles de Madrid," *El País,* Feb. 27, 1981.

46   **At its head, leaders** Ibid.

46   **Politically isolated, the coup leaders** Cercas, *Anatomía de un instante,* 419.

47   **On the day of the assaults** Renaud Meltz, *Pierre Laval: Un mystère français* (Paris: Perrin, 2018), 494.

48   **"winning ticket in the lottery"** Carmen Callil, *Bad Faith: A Forgotten History of Family, Fatherland, and Vichy France* (New York: Vintage Press, 2006), 106–8.

48   **"were a kind of fraternity"** Robert Paxton, *Vichy France: Old Guard and New Order, 1940–1944* (New York: Columbia University Press, 1972), 249. Also Stanley Hoffmann, "The Vichy Circle of French Conservatives," in *Decline or Renewal? France Since the 1930s* (New York: Viking Press, 1960), 3–25.

49   **Radicalized right-wing forces** Sheri Berman, *Democracy and Dictatorship in Europe: From the Ancien Régime to the Present Day* (New York: Oxford University Press, 2019), 181.

49   **"Better Hitler than Blum"** Ibid.

49   **But by 1940** See Philip Nord, *France 1940: Defending the Republic* (New Haven, Conn.: Yale University Press, 2015), 150–51.

50   **"drift off the floor"** Larry Tye, *Demagogue: The Life and Long Shadow of Senator Joe McCarthy* (Boston: Houghton Mifflin Harcourt, 2020), 457–59.

50   **This is the banality** Our phrase borrows from Hannah Arendt, *Eichmann in Jerusalem: A Report on the Banality of Evil* (1963; London: Penguin, 2006).

50   **constitutional hardball** The term "constitutional hardball" was coined by the constitutional scholar Mark Tushnet. See Mark Tushnet, "Constitutional Hardball," *John Marshall Law Review* 37 (2004): 523–54. See also Steven Levitsky and Daniel Ziblatt, *How Democracies Die* (New York: Crown, 2018).

50   **politicians do not openly violate** Scholars have used the term "autocratic legalism" in a similar way. See Javier Corrales, "Autocratic Legalism in Venezuela," *Journal of Democracy* 26, no. 2 (April 2015): 37–51; Kim Lane Scheppele, "Autocratic Legalism," *University of Chicago Law Review* 85, no. 2, art. 2 (2018).

52   **Most qualified nominees were promptly approved** Lee Epstein and Jeffrey Segal, *Advice and Consent: The Politics of Judicial Appointments* (New York: Oxford University Press, 2005).

52   **Indeed, in the 150-year span** Robin Bradley Kar and Jason Mazzone, "The Garland Affair: What History and the Constitution *Really* Say About President Obama's Powers to Appoint a Replacement for Justice Scalia," *New York University Law Review* 91 (May 2016): 53–115.

52   **Every president who attempted to fill** Ibid., 107–14.

53   **Peruvian legislators began** See Abraham García Chávarry, "Tres maneras de conceptualizar la figura de permanente incapacidad moral del presidente de la República como causal de vacancia en el cargo," IDEHPUCP, Nov. 17, 2020.

53   **"presidential hunting season"** See Diego Salazar, "¿Cuántas vidas le quedan al presidente Pedro Castillo?," *Washington Post,* Dec. 8, 2021.

54   **"a question of arithmetic"** See ibid.

54 **He received an honorarium** See Ian MacKinnon, "Court Rules Thai Prime Minister Must Resign over Cookery Show," *Guardian*, Sept. 9, 2008.

54 **But in a polarized country** See "Thai Leader Ordered to Quit over Cooking Show," MSNBC, Sept. 8, 2008.

55 **Jayaprakash Narayan, a widely respected figure** Gyan Prakash, *Emergency Chronicles: Indira Gandhi and Democracy's Turning Point* (Princeton, N.J.: Princeton University Press, 2019), 92–108.

55 **By 1975, Narayan's anticorruption drive** Christophe Jaffrelot and Pratinay Anil, *India's First Dictatorship: The Emergency, 1975–77* (Oxford: Oxford University Press, 2021), 233–64.

55 **In 1971, a political opponent** Granville Austin, *Working a Democratic Constitution: A History of the Indian Experience* (New Delhi: Oxford University Press, 1999), 214; Jaffrelot and Anil, *India's First Dictatorship*, 6–7.

56 **The Supreme Court granted a stay** Prakash, *Emergency Chronicles*, 158–59.

56 **Narayan launched a series** Ibid., 160–61; Jaffrelot and Anil, *India's First Dictatorship*, 4–5.

56 **Gandhi and her aides** Austin, *Working a Democratic Constitution*, 304; Jaffrelot and Anil, *India's First Dictatorship*, 14.

56 **"perusing it with hermeneutical rigor"** Jaffrelot and Anil, *India's First Dictatorship*, 15; Austin, *Working a Democratic Constitution*, 305.

56 **Ray settled on Article 352** Prakash, *Emergency Chronicles*, 9; Jaffrelot and Anil, *India's First Dictatorship*, 15–16.

56 **A legacy of colonial rule** Jaffrelot and Anil, *India's First Dictatorship*, 15.

56 **"pretzeled interpretation of the law"** Ibid., 15–16.

56 **Within hours, police were knocking** Prakash, *Emergency Chronicles*, 166.

56 **By dawn, 676 politicians** Ibid., 166, 307; Jaffrelot and Anil, *India's First Dictatorship*, 2–3.

56 **Dusting off laws** Jaffrelot and Anil, *India's First Dictatorship*, 12, 28–98; Prakash, *Emergency Chronicles*.

56 **It also imposed** Prakash, *Emergency Chronicles*, 180–83.

57   **"cloaked in constitutional dress"** Ibid., 10.

57   **Governments can punish their rivals** Daniel Brinks, Steven Lev-
      itsky, and María Victoria Murillo, *Understanding Institutional Weak-
      ness: Power and Design in Latin American Institutions* (New York:
      Cambridge University Press, 2019).

57   **Bribery, fraud, and tax** Alena V. Ledeneva, *How Russia Really
      Works: The Informal Practices That Shaped Post-Soviet Politics and Busi-
      ness* (Ithaca, N.Y.: Cornell University Press, 2014).

57   **Under President Boris Yeltsin** David E. Hoffman, *The Oligarchs:
      Wealth and Power in the New Russia* (New York: Public Affairs,
      2011).

58   **In July 2000** Marshall I. Goldman, *Petrostate: Putin, Power, and the
      New Russia* (Oxford: Oxford University Press, 2008), 102–3.

58   **When Mikhail Khodorkovsky** Ibid., 113–16.

58   **Berezovsky and Khodorkovsky** Ibid., 105, 116.

58   **This is a form of** This definition is a refinement of a widely used
      term to characterize the use of legal institutions to target political
      opponents.

58   **The longtime autocrat Kenneth Kaunda** See "Zambia: Elections
      and Human Rights in the Third Republic," *Human Rights Watch* 8,
      no. 4 (A), Dec. 1996.

59   **"precisely tailored to disqualify"** See ibid.

59   **As if to vanquish** See Joe Chilaizya, "Zambia-Politics: Kaunda's
      Comeback Finally Over," Inter Press Service News Agency,
      May 16, 1996.

60   **He had always been known** See Paul Lendvai, *Orbán: Europe's
      New Strongman* (Oxford: Oxford University Press, 2017).

60   **"In politics everything is possible"** Ibid., 149.

60   **Orbán used his party's parliamentary supermajority** András
      Bozóki and Eszter Simon, "Two Faces of Hungary: From Democ-
      ratization to Democratic Backsliding," in *Central and Southeast Euro-
      pean Politics Since 1989,* ed. Sabrina P. Ramet and Christine M.
      Hassenstab, 2nd ed. (Cambridge, U.K.: Cambridge University
      Press, 2019), 229.

60   **Prior to 2010** Lendvai, *Orbán,* 103.

61   **The new constitution replaced this** Miklós Bánkuti, Gábor Hal-

mai, and Kim Lane Scheppele, "Hungary's Illiberal Turn: Disabling the Constitution," *Journal of Democracy* 23, no. 3 (July 2012): 139.

61 **Another constitutional amendment** Ibid., 140.

61 **Baka was forced** Paul Lendvai, *Hungary: Between Democracy and Authoritarianism* (New York: Columbia University Press, 2012), 222.

61 **A total of 274 judges** "Wrong Direction on Rights: Assessing the Impact of Hungary's New Constitution and Laws," Human Rights Watch, May 16, 2013. Also Lendvai, *Orbán,* 104.

61 **Although the law was later repealed** "Wrong Direction on Rights."

61 **"puppet of the government"** Bozóki and Simon, "Two Faces of Hungary," 231.

61 **"an unconstitutional coup"** Quoted in Lendvai, *Orbán,* 110.

61 **This was the spirit of the law** Bozóki and Simon, "Two Faces of Hungary," 231.

61 **Under Orbán, however, public television** Lendvai, *Hungary,* 220; Bozóki and Simon, "Two Faces of Hungary," 231.

62 **As part of a "restructuring" process** Lendvai, *Hungary,* 219–20.

62 **The new Orbán-friendly ownership** Lendvai, *Orbán,* 158–63.

62 **In 2016, the newspaper *Népszabadság*** Ibid., 161–62; Bozóki and Simon, "Two Faces of Hungary," 231.

62 **A 2010 law prohibited reporting** "Hungary: Media Law Endangers Press Freedom: Problematic Legislation Part of Wider Concern About Country's Rights Record," Human Rights Watch, Jan. 7, 2011. Also Lendvai, *Hungary,* 218; U.S. Department of State, "Hungary 2013 Human Rights Report."

62 **A Media Council** Bánkuti, Halmai, and Scheppele, "Hungary's Illiberal Turn," 140; Lendvai, *Orbán,* 115; U.S. Department of State, "Hungary 2013 Human Rights Report," 25; "Hungary: Media Law Endangers Press Freedom."

62 **Dozens of media organizations** U.S. Department of State, "Hungary 2011 Human Rights Report"; U.S. Department of State, "Hungary 2012 Human Rights Report"; U.S. Department of State, "Hungary 2013 Human Rights Report."

62 **In 2020, for example, it declined** See Attila Mong, "Hungary's Klubrádió Owner András Arató on How the Station Is Responding

to the Loss of Its Broadcast License," Committee to Protect Journalists, Nov. 9, 2021.

62 **According to Klubrádió's director, András Arató** See ibid.

63 **One study found that 90 percent** Zack Beauchamp, "It Happened There: How Democracy Died in Hungary," *Vox,* Sept. 13, 2018.

63 **Some 80 percent of Hungarian television** Lendvai, *Orbán,* 119.

63 **This ensured that no single party** Bánkuti, Halmai, and Scheppele, "Hungary's Illiberal Turn," 140.

63 **Fidesz abandoned this practice** Ibid.; Bozóki and Simon, "Two Faces of Hungary," 229.

63 **The politicized Electoral Commission** Lendvai, *Orbán,* 129–30; see also Dylan Difford, "How Do Elections Work in Hungary?," Electoral Reform Society, April 1, 2022.

63 **One think tank calculated** Lendvai, *Orbán,* 129.

63 **"a good 30-yard advantage"** Quoted in Lendvai, *Hungary,* 226.

63 **In another act of lawfare** Bozóki and Simon, "Two Faces of Hungary," 230.

64 **"neither fair nor free"** Ibid.

64 **In the 2014 election** Lendvai, *Orbán,* 128.

64 **Fidesz repeated the trick in 2018** Bozóki and Simon, "Two Faces of Hungary," 230.

64 **"cannot be defeated under 'normal' circumstances"** Lendvai, *Orbán,* 91.

64 **"the spine of Hungarian democracy"** Quoted in Lendvai, *Hungary,* 221.

CHAPTER 3: **IT HAS HAPPENED HERE**

65 **Founded on the coastal edge** On the transformation of the cotton industry during this period, see Sven Beckert, *Empire of Cotton: A New History of Global Capitalism* (London: Penguin, 2014), 312–39.

65 **New railroad lines** Ronald Hartzer, "To Great and Useful Purpose: A History of the Wilmington, North Carolina District, U.S. Army Corps of Engineers (United States)" (PhD diss., Indiana University, 1987), 37.

65 **The city's largest employer** John R. Killick, "The Transformation

of Cotton Marketing in the Late Nineteenth Century: Alexander
Sprunt and Son of Wilmington, NC, 1884–1956," *Business History
Review* 55, no. 2 (1981): 155.

65   **And in its warehouses** Ibid., 145.

65   **And as its post–Civil War economy** 1898 Wilmington Race Riot
Commission, *1898 Wilmington Race Riot Report* (Raleigh: North
Carolina Department of Cultural Resources, 2006), 228–29.

66   **Black Wilmington became wealthier** Ibid., 30.

66   **At the center of the community** Ibid., 31.

66   **The catalyst was the emergence** Elizabeth Sanders, *Roots of Reform: Farmers, Workers, and the American State, 1877–1917* (Chicago:
University of Chicago Press, 1999).

66   **The Fusion** Steven Hahn, *A Nation Under Our Feet: Black Political
Struggles in the Rural South from Slavery to the Great Migration* (Cambridge, Mass.: Harvard University Press, 2003), 436–38; Helen Edmonds, *The Negro and Fusion Politics in North Carolina, 1894–1901*
(Chapel Hill: University of North Carolina Press, 1951).

67   **"probably the fairest and most democratic"** J. Morgan Kousser,
*The Shaping of Southern Politics: Suffrage Restriction and the Establishment
of the One-Party South, 1880–1910* (New Haven, Conn.: Yale University Press, 1974), 187.

67   **As a result, Black Republicans** David Zucchino, *Wilmington's Lie:
The Murderous Coup of 1898 and the Rise of White Supremacy* (New
York: Grove Press, 2021), xv–xvii, 68, 91–92, 156.

67   **For a moment, one could** See account in Suzanne Mettler and
Robert C. Lieberman, *Four Threats: The Recurring Crises of American
Democracy* (New York: St. Martin's Press, 2020), 92–101.

67   **And the Democratic Party establishment** Zucchino, *Wilmington's
Lie,* 80, 65–82.

68   **"the white people who settled"** Ibid., 146.

68   **Backed by the Democratic Party** 1898 Wilmington Race Riot
Commission, *Report,* 66–67.

68   **Because more than 56 percent** Ibid., 33.

68   **"We cannot outnumber"** Zucchino, *Wilmington's Lie,* 137.

68   **"preparing for a siege"** Ibid., 148.

68   **Whites formed militias** Ibid., 125–37.

68   **The militias were backed** Ibid., 147, 149–50.

69   **"Shall we surrender"** 1898 Wilmington Race Riot Commission, *Report,* 79–80.

69   **As Election Day approached** Mettler and Lieberman, *Four Threats,* 93–95.

69   **Red Shirts terrorized** Zucchino, *Wilmington's Lie,* 119–20.

69   **"You must do your duty"** 1898 Wilmington Race Riot Commission, *Report,* 92.

69   **On Election Day, White Government Unions** Zucchino, *Wilmington's Lie,* 160–63.

70   **In predominantly Black precincts** 1898 Wilmington Race Riot Commission, *Report,* 107–9.

70   **On November 10** Zucchino, *Wilmington's Lie,* 189–219.

70   **At least twenty-two** Ibid., 341–42.

70   **The mob entered Wilmington's city hall** Mettler and Lieberman, *Four Threats,* 94.

70   **They, along with other Fusionist politicians** Zucchino, *Wilmington's Lie,* 228–56.

70   **Waddell, the coup's leader** Mettler and Lieberman, *Four Threats,* 121.

70   **Days earlier, North Carolina's African American** Richard M. Valelly, *The Two Reconstructions: The Struggle for Black Enfranchisement* (Chicago: University of Chicago Press, 2004), 132; Zucchino, *Wilmington's Lie,* 159–60.

71   **After reclaiming statewide power** Kousser, *Shaping of Southern Politics,* 190–92, 239.

71   **The number of registered Black voters** Zucchino, *Wilmington's Lie,* 330; Kent Redding, *Making Race, Making Power: North Carolina's Road to Disfranchisement* (Urbana: University of Illinois Press, 2003), 37.

71   **In Wilmington, after three Black aldermen** Zucchino, *Wilmington's Lie,* 330.

71   **The conclusion of the Civil War** See Eric Foner, *Reconstruction: America's Unfinished Revolution, 1863–1877* (New York: Harper & Row, 1988); W.E.B. Du Bois, *Black Reconstruction in America: An Essay Toward a History of the Part Which Black Folk Played in the Attempt*

to Reconstruct Democracy in America, 1860–1880 (1935; New York: Free Press, 1998).

71 **"Second Founding"** Eric Foner, *The Second Founding: How the Civil War and Reconstruction Remade the Constitution* (New York: Norton, 2019), 7; Foner, *Reconstruction*, 278.

72 **The Fourteenth Amendment** Foner, *Second Founding*, 68–78.

72 **"Never was a revolution"** Quoted in ibid., 112.

72 **The Reconstruction Amendments** Xi Wang, *The Trial of Democracy: Black Suffrage and Northern Republicans, 1860–1910* (Athens: University of Georgia Press, 2012), 36–37.

72 **"the equality of all men"** Rayford W. Logan, *The Betrayal of the Negro, from Rutherford B. Hayes to Woodrow Wilson* (New York: Hachette Books, 1965), 107.

72 **"Give up our right"** Quoted in Foner, *Second Founding*, 33.

73 **"made for white men"** Ibid., 86.

73 **And they opposed the Fifteenth Amendment** Ibid., 107.

73 **In the U.S. Congress, no Democrat** J. Morgan Kousser, *Colorblind Injustice: Minority Voting Rights and the Undoing of the Second Reconstruction* (Chapel Hill: University of North Carolina Press, 1999), 39.

73 **Although nearly the entire Republican Party** Kenneth Stampp, *The Era of Reconstruction, 1865–1877* (New York: Vintage Books, 1965), 83.

73 **The two leading Radicals** Others included Senators Henry Wilson of Massachusetts, Benjamin Wade of Ohio, and Zachariah Chandler of Michigan as well as Representatives George Boutwell of Massachusetts and George Julian of Indiana. See ibid., 83–84.

73 **Stevens and Sumner** Foner, *Reconstruction*, 230–31.

73 **Their vision of democracy** James Morone, *Hellfire Nation: The Politics of Sin in American History* (New Haven, Conn.: Yale University Press, 2003), 123–44; Daniel Carpenter, *Democracy by Petition: Popular Politics in Transformation, 1790–1870* (Cambridge, Mass.: Harvard University Press, 2021), 75–76.

73 **"Show me a creature"** *Congressional Globe,* Feb. 6, 1866, 687.

74 **"Caucasian, Mongolian, Malay, African, and American"** Ibid.

74 **"prophetic rhetoric"** Sandra Gustafson, *Imagining Deliberative De-*

mocracy in the Early American Republic (Chicago: University of Chicago Press, 2011), 125.

74   **Among the leaders of this movement** Marilyn Richardson, *Maria W. Stewart: America's First Black Woman Political Writer* (Bloomington: Indiana University Press, 1987), xiii; Valerie C. Cooper, *Word, Like Fire: Maria Stewart, the Bible, and the Rights of African Americans* (Charlottesville: University of Virginia Press, 2011), 1.

74   **"colored citizen"** Stephen Kantrowitz, *More Than Freedom: Fighting for Black Citizenship in a White Republic, 1829–1889* (New York: Penguin, 2012), 28.

75   **"the most sacred of all"** Pauline Maier, *American Scripture: Making the Declaration of Independence* (New York: Vintage, 1997), 129.

75   **And in the 1840s** Kantrowitz, *More Than Freedom,* 52, 109, 130–31.

75   **a proposal guaranteeing the right** Foner, *Second Founding,* 98.

75   **"blessed" by the "Great Ruler"** Ibid., 101.

76   **Within one year** Valelly, *Two Reconstructions,* 3.

76   **By 1867, at least 85 percent** Ibid., 33.

76   **African Americans were a majority** Ibid., 122; Foner, *Reconstruction,* 294.

76   **By 1867, registered Black voters** Du Bois, *Black Reconstruction in America,* 371.

76   **A majority of delegates** Ibid., 372; Foner, *Reconstruction,* 318.

76   **African Americans won a majority** Du Bois, *Black Reconstruction in America,* 404, 444; Foner, *Reconstruction,* 354; Valelly, *Two Reconstructions,* 3.

76   **There were Black lieutenant governors** Du Bois, *Black Reconstruction in America,* 469–70; Foner, *Reconstruction,* 354.

76   **Across the Deep South** Foner, *Reconstruction,* 356–63.

77   **More than thirteen hundred Black Americans** Trevon D. Logan, "Do Black Politicians Matter? Evidence from Reconstruction," *Journal of Economic History* 80, no. 1 (2020): 2; Eric Foner, *Freedom's Lawmakers: A Directory of Black Officeholders During Reconstruction* (Baton Rouge: Louisiana State University Press, 1996).

77   **Sixteen Black Americans** Robert Mickey, *Paths Out of Dixie: The*

*Democratization of Authoritarian Enclaves in America's Deep South,
1944–1972* (Princeton, N.J.: Princeton University Press, 2015), 38;
Foner, *Reconstruction,* 355.

77   **"The body is almost literally"** Quoted in Hahn, *Nation Under Our
Feet,* 243.

77   **"was just as bad"** Zucchino, *Wilmington's Lie,* 307.

78   **Many whites came to harbor** Hahn, *Nation Under Our Feet,* 237.

78   **These fears were fanned** See Michael Perman, *Struggle for Mastery:
Disenfranchisement in the South, 1888–1908* (Chapel Hill: University
of North Carolina Press, 2001), 22–27; Zucchino, *Wilmington's Lie.*

78   **the prospect of democratized *social relations*** Glenda Elizabeth
Gilmore, *Gender and Jim Crow* (Chapel Hill: University of North
Carolina Press, 2019); Jane Dailey, *White Fright: The Sexual Panic at
the Heart of America's Racist History* (New York: Basic Books, 2020).

78   **the widespread diffusion** Gilmore, *Gender and Jim Crow,* 83.

78   **"We felt the very foundations"** Quoted in Earl Black and Merle
Black, *The Rise of Southern Republicans* (Cambridge, Mass.: Harvard
University Press, 2002), 44.

78   **"the offensive theory of majority rule"** Quoted in Perman,
Struggle for Mastery, 23.

78   **White reactionaries responded** Allen W. Trelease, *White Terror:
The Ku Klux Klan Conspiracy and Southern Reconstruction* (Baton
Rouge: Louisiana State University Press, 1971).

79   **"brute force"** Cited in Jamelle Bouie, "Why I Keep Coming Back
to Reconstruction," *New York Times,* Oct. 25, 2022.

79   **Backed by the Democratic Party** Logan, *Betrayal of the Negro,* 10.

79   **The Klan carried out** Equal Justice Initiative, "Reconstruction in
America" (Montgomery, Ala., 2020); Foner, *Reconstruction,* 425–28.

79   **Republican politicians** Foner, *Reconstruction,* 427, 440–42.

79   **Klan terror crippled Republican organizations** Du Bois, *Black
Reconstruction in America;* Wang, *Trial of Democracy,* 79–83; Foner,
Reconstruction, 342–43.

79   **"civil war of secret assassination"** Du Bois, *Black Reconstruction in
America,* 474; Equal Justice Initiative, "Reconstruction in America";
Foner, *Reconstruction,* 342.

79   **In Georgia, Klan terror** Foner, *Reconstruction,* 343.

79   **In 1871, Klan pressure** Richard Abbott, "The Republican Party Press in Reconstruction Georgia, 1867–1874," *Journal of Southern History* 61, no. 4 (Nov. 1995): 758.

79   **In North Carolina, Klan violence** Foner, *Reconstruction,* 440–41.

80   **In response to this wave** Wang, *Trial of Democracy,* 78–92; Foner, *Reconstruction,* 454–59.

80   **These included an 1870 law** Foner, *Reconstruction,* 454–55.

80   **With the help of federal troops** Wang, *Trial of Democracy,* 93–102.

80   **"broken the Klan's back"** Foner, *Reconstruction,* 458–59.

80   **"the fairest and most democratic election"** James M. McPherson, "War and Peace in the Post–Civil War South," in *The Making of Peace: Rulers, States, and the Aftermath of War,* ed. Williamson Murray and Jim Lacey (Cambridge, U.K.: Cambridge University Press, 2009), 168.

80   **Prioritizing issues such as free trade** Wang, *Trial of Democracy,* 102–5; Foner, *Reconstruction,* 497–99.

80   **The multiracial democratic coalition** Foner, *Reconstruction,* 523–31.

81   **"era of moral politics"** "The Era of Moral Politics," *New York Times,* Dec. 30, 1874; Foner, *Reconstruction,* 525–27.

81   **"committed in broad daylight"** Foner, *Reconstruction,* 559.

81   **They then impeached** Foner, *Reconstruction,* 562.

81   **In South Carolina, the 1876 election** Ibid., 574–75; Du Bois, *Black Reconstruction in America,* 687–89.

81   **"one of the grandest farces"** Foner, *Reconstruction,* 574–75.

81   **By the time Grant's successor** Mickey, *Paths Out of Dixie,* 39.

81   **Democrats had seized power** Logan, *Betrayal of the Negro,* 10; Valelly, *Two Reconstructions,* 47.

81   **Overall, nearly two thousand Black Americans** Equal Justice Initiative, "Reconstruction in America."

81   **The prospects for multiracial democracy** For a discussion of this point and problems with the so-called fait accompli thesis, see Valelly, *Two Reconstructions,* 186n14.

82   **much of the legal foundation** Du Bois, *Black Reconstruction in America,* 597–98.

82   **According to one estimate** Kousser, *Colorblind Injustice,* 20;
      Valelly, *Two Reconstructions,* 52.

82   **Amid the agrarian depression** C. Vann Woodward, *The Strange
      Career of Jim Crow* (Oxford: Oxford University Press, 2002), 57–65,
      77; Kousser, *Shaping of Southern Politics.*

82   **Populist or Fusion tickets** Kousser, *Shaping of Southern Politics,*
      27–28.

82   **a populist-Republican Fusion ticket** Ibid., 36–42.

82   **These biracial coalitions** Woodward, *Strange Career of Jim Crow,*
      61–64, 79; Kousser, *Shaping of Southern Politics.*

82   **"Negro domination"** Perman, *Struggle for Mastery,* 22–27; Wood-
      ward, *Strange Career of Jim Crow,* 79.

82   **"Africanization of the state"** Kousser, *Shaping of Southern Poli-
      tics,* 37.

83   **"We now have the rule"** Quoted in ibid., 145.

83   **And Democratic leaders were concerned** Perman, *Struggle for
      Mastery;* Kousser, *Shaping of Southern Politics.*

83   **Between 1888 and 1908** See Kousser, *Shaping of Southern Politics;*
      Perman, *Struggle for Mastery.*

83   **"We intend"** Quoted in Foner, *Reconstruction,* 590.

83   **"legal machinery"** Perman, *Struggle for Mastery,* 12.

84   **"carefully avoided open contravention"** Michael J. Klarman,
      *From Jim Crow to Civil Rights: The Supreme Court and the Struggle for
      Racial Equality* (Oxford: Oxford University Press, 2004), 33.

84   **"ingenious contrivances"** V. O. Key, *Southern Politics in State and
      Nation* (New York: Vintage Books, 1949), 531.

84   **Australian (or secret) ballot** The secret ballot was first used in
      Australia in the 1850s.

84   **Though these ballots were justified** Kousser, *Shaping of Southern
      Politics,* 110–14, 239; Perman, *Struggle for Mastery,* 54.

84   **"works smoothly, quietly, satisfactorily"** Quoted in Perman,
      Struggle for Mastery, 20.

85   **As Democrats in southern state legislatures** Alexander Keyssar,
      *The Right to Vote: The Contested History of Democracy in the United
      States* (New York: Basic Books, 2000), chap. 5.

85 **Mississippi served as an early model** Kousser, *Shaping of Southern Politics*, 139–45; Perman, *Struggle for Mastery*, 70–90.

85 **Over the next decade** Kousser, *Shaping of Southern Politics*, 239.

85 **"eliminate the Negro from politics"** Ibid., 134.

85 **The laws were designed** Keyssar, *Right to Vote*, 89–90; 111–13.

85 **"grandfather clauses"** Kousser, *Shaping of Southern Politics*, 239.

86 **By 1908, all states** Ibid.

86 **"practical, constitutional, and happy solution"** Quoted in Perman, *Struggle for Mastery*, 58.

86 **In one of history's rare cases** David Bateman, *Disenfranchising Democracy: Constructing the Electorate in the United States, the United Kingdom, and France* (Cambridge, U.K.: Cambridge University Press, 2018), 25.

86 **The U.S. Supreme Court** Klarman, *From Jim Crow to Civil Rights*, 34; Valelly, *Two Reconstructions*, 104–5.

86 **In the 1890s, civil rights groups** R. Volney Riser, *Defying Disfranchisement: Black Voting Rights Activism in the Jim Crow South, 1890–1908* (Baton Rouge: Louisiana State University Press, 2010).

86 **"one of the most momentous decisions"** Richard Pildes, "Democracy, Anti-democracy, and the Canon," *Constitutional Commentary* 17 (2000): 297.

86 *Giles* **was a voting rights lawsuit** See Brian Lyman, "The Journey of Jackson Giles," *Montgomery Advertiser*, Feb. 7, 2022.

87 **After passage of the constitution** John Hope Franklin and Evelyn Brooks Higginbotham, *From Slavery to Freedom: A History of African Americans*, 9th ed. (New York: McGraw-Hill, 2011), 268.

87 **"What is it that we want"** Quoted by Pildes, "Democracy, Anti-democracy, and the Canon," 302.

87 **But the horrors of Holmes's** Louis Menand, *The Metaphysical Club: A Story of Ideas in America* (New York: Farrar, Straus and Giroux, 2001), 4.

87 **This skepticism** Klarman, *From Jim Crow to Civil Rights*, 38.

87 **"the most disingenuous analysis"** Pildes, "Democracy, Anti-democracy, and the Canon," 306. On the 1883 *Civil Rights Cases*, see Wang, *Trial of Democracy*, 212–13.

87 **Holmes argued that since the complaint** Samuel Brenner,

"Airbrushed out of the Constitutional Canon: The Evolving
Understanding of *Giles v. Harris,* 1903–1925," *Michigan Law Review* 107, no. 5 (2009): 862; see also Valelly, *Two Reconstructions,* 112–20.

88 **After Democrats won the presidency** Valelly, *Two Reconstructions,* 131; Wang, *Trial of Democracy,* 254.

88 **"principles which we all thought"** David W. Blight, *Frederick Douglass: The Prophet of Freedom* (New York: Simon & Schuster, 2018), 743.

88 **Moreover, Black suffrage and federal enforcement** Wang, *Trial of Democracy,* 224.

89 **"effective legislation to secure the integrity"** Quoted in Richard Valelly, "Partisan Entrepreneurship and Policy Windows: George Frisbie Hoar and the 1890 Federal Elections Bill," in *Formative Acts: American Politics in the Making,* ed. Stephen Skowronek and Matthew Glassman (Philadelphia: University of Pennsylvania Press, 2007), 126.

89 **"abolitionist and radical sentiments"** Keyssar, *Right to Vote,* 109.

89 **The legislators drafted a seventy-five-page bill** Kousser, *Shaping of Southern Politics,* 29–30.

89 **The bill empowered** Wang, *Trial of Democracy,* 236–37.

89 **In the summer of 1890** Gregory Wawro and Eric Schickler, *Filibuster: Obstruction and Lawmaking in the U.S. Senate* (Princeton, N.J.: Princeton University Press, 2013), 76–78.

90 **"[McMillin] asked me"** *Reminiscences of Senator William M. Stewart,* ed. George Rothwell Brown (New York: Neale, 1908), 297–98.

90 **Suspicion began to emerge** Wawro and Schickler, *Filibuster,* 82–83.

90 **Indeed eight "silver" Republicans** Wang, *Trial of Democracy,* 248.

90 **When the Lodge bill** Ibid.

91 **In a final desperate attempt** Wawro and Schickler, *Filibuster,* 76–87.

91 **But the measure was blocked** Wang, *Trial of Democracy,* 249.

91 **Black turnout plummeted** Kent Redding and David James, "Estimating Levels and Modeling Determinants of Black and White Voter Turnout in the South, 1880–1912," *Historical Methods* 34, no. 4 (2001): 148.

91   **In Louisiana, Mississippi, and South Carolina** Valelly, *Two Re-constructions,* 128.

91   **"Give us a convention"** Quoted by Kousser, *Shaping of Southern Politics,* 209.

91   **The South succumbed** Mickey, *Paths Out of Dixie,* 35–61.

91   **Black disenfranchisement** Ibid.

91   **"Democracy died save in the hearts"** Du Bois, *Black Reconstruction in America,* 30.

CHAPTER 4: WHY THE REPUBLICAN PARTY ABANDONED DEMOCRACY

92   **"We have talked long enough"** See Lyndon B. Johnson, "Address Before a Joint Session of the Congress," Nov. 27, 1963, American Presidency Project, UC Santa Barbara.

93   **Under his leadership** Geoffrey M. Kabaservice, *Rule and Ruin: The Downfall of Moderation and the Destruction of the Republican Party, from Eisenhower to the Tea Party* (Oxford: Oxford University Press, 2012), 100.

93   **more than 80 percent** Julian Zelizer, *The Fierce Urgency of Now: Lyndon Johnson, Congress, and the Battle for the Great Society* (New York: Penguin Press, 2015), 128.

93   **According to his biographer** Byron C. Hulsey, *Everett Dirksen and His Presidents: How a Senate Giant Shaped American Politics* (Lawrence: University Press of Kansas, 2000), 201.

93   **The same party that was pivotal** Conservatives in the Republican Party had tried to weaken the Voting Rights Act before. In 1970, for example, the Nixon administration attempted—unsuccessfully—to dismantle Section 5, a key pillar of the Voting Rights Act. See Ari Berman, *Give Us the Ballot: The Modern Struggle for Voting Rights in America* (New York: Farrar, Straus and Giroux, 2015).

93   **"walked away from democracy"** "Walking Away: The Republican Party and Democracy," *Economist,* Jan. 1, 2022.

94   **"Democracy isn't the objective"** Glenn Thrush, " 'We're Not a Democracy,' Says Mike Lee, a Republican Senator. That's a Good Thing, He Adds," *New York Times,* Oct. 8, 2020.

94   **The V-Dem (Varieties of Democracy) Institute** Anna Luhrmann
      et al., "New Global Data on Political Parties: V-Party," V-Dem In-
      stitute Briefing Paper No. 9, Oct. 26, 2020, 1–2.

94   **"more similar to autocratic ruling parties"** Ibid., 1.

94   **Why has the Republican Party** Some important works on this
      question include Daniel Schlozman, *When Movements Anchor Parties:
      Electoral Alignments in American History* (Princeton, N.J.: Princeton
      University Press, 2015); E. J. Dionne, *Why the Right Went Wrong:
      Conservatism—from Goldwater to Trump and Beyond* (New York:
      Simon & Schuster, 2016); Theda Skocpol and Vanessa Williamson,
      The Tea Party and the Remaking of Republican Conservativism (New
      York: Oxford University Press, 2016); Sam Rosenfeld, *The Polariz-
      ers: Postwar Architects of Our Partisan Era* (Princeton, N.J.: Princeton
      University Press, 2017); Jacob Hacker and Paul Pierson, *Let Them
      Eat Tweets: How the Right Rules in an Age of Extreme Inequality* (New
      York: W. W. Norton, 2020).

94   **In the first half** See Lewis L. Gould, *The Republicans: A History of the
      Grand Old Party* (Oxford: Oxford University Press, 2014); Heather
      Cox Richardson, *To Make Men Free: A History of the Republican Party*
      (New York: Basic Books, 2014).

95   **Millions of urban working-class voters** James L. Sundquist, *Dy-
      namics of the Party System: Alignment and Realignment of Political Parties
      in the United States,* rev. ed. (Washington, D.C.: Brookings Institu-
      tion, 1983), 214–26.

95   **"permanent minority"** Black and Black, *Rise of Southern Republi-
      cans,* 15.

95   **"conservative dilemma"** Ziblatt, *Conservative Parties and the Birth of
      Democracy,* 33–37; Hacker and Pierson, *Let Them Eat Tweets,* 21.

95   **After World War II** Eric Schickler, *Racial Realignment: The
      Transformation of American Liberalism, 1932–1965* (Princeton, N.J.:
      Princeton University Press, 2016), 252–53; Boris Heersink and Jef-
      frey A. Jenkins, *Republican Party Politics and the American South,
      1865–1968* (Cambridge, U.K.: Cambridge University Press, 2020),
      163–76; Sam Rosenfeld, *The Polarizers: Postwar Architects of Our Par-
      tisan Era* (Chicago: University of Chicago Press, 2017), 70–89.

95   **"Republican" was still used** Black and Black, *Rise of Southern Republicans,* 57.

95   **In the late 1930s** Schickler, *Racial Realignment,* 104–18; Tali Mendelberg, *The Race Card: Campaign Strategy, Implicit Messages, and the Norm of Equality* (Princeton, N.J.: Princeton University Press, 2001), 67–70.

96   **Gradually, the civil rights coalition** Schickler, *Racial Realignment,* 81–97; Philip A. Klinkner, *The Unsteady March: The Rise and Decline of Racial Equality in America,* with Rogers M. Smith (Chicago: University of Chicago Press, 1999), 207–34.

96   **The change did not sit well** Black and Black, *Rise of Southern Republicans,* 45–46.

96   **"we resented it"** Quoted in ibid., 32.

96   **Cracks in the Democratic coalition** Schickler, *Racial Realignment,* 213–18.

96   **"great hunting ground"** Ibid., 248–49.

97   **Whereas conservatives like Gabrielson** Joseph Lowndes, *From the New Deal to the New Right: Race and the Southern Origins of Modern Conservatism* (New Haven, Conn.: Yale University Press, 2008), 48–49, 60–64; Schickler, *Racial Realignment,* 248–53.

97   **High-profile events** Schickler, *Racial Realignment,* 253–70; Heersink and Jenkins, *Republican Party Politics and the American South,* 177–78; Lowndes, *From the New Deal to the New Right,* 52–61; Mickey, *Paths Out of Dixie,* 180–89.

97   **"envisioned substantial political gold"** Robert Novak, *The Agony of the G.O.P. 1964* (New York: Macmillan, 1965), 179.

97   **"Long Southern Strategy"** Angie Maxwell and Todd G. Shields, *The Long Southern Strategy: How Chasing White Voters in the South Changed American Politics* (New York: Oxford University Press, 2019), 8.

97   **Although most congressional Republicans** Schickler, *Racial Realignment,* 237–38.

97   **"hunting where the ducks are"** Sundquist, *Dynamics of the Party System,* 290.

97   **He voted against** Ibid.; Kabaservice, *Rule and Ruin,* 98–113; Heersink and Jenkins, *Republican Party Politics and the American South,*

182; John H. Kessel, *The Goldwater Coalition: Republican Strategies in 1964* (New York: The Bobbs-Merrill Company, 1968), 195–96.

98   **The civil rights revolution** Edward G. Carmines and James A. Stimson, *Issue Evolution: Race and the Transformation of American Politics* (Princeton, N.J.: Princeton University Press, 1989), 38–39, 164–66; Donald R. Kinder and Lynn M. Sanders, *Divided by Color: Racial Politics and Democratic Ideals* (Chicago: University of Chicago Press, 1996), 206–7.

98   **"de facto White Party"** Stuart Stevens, *It Was All a Lie: How the Republican Party Became Donald Trump* (New York: Alfred A. Knopf, 2020), 12.

98   **And public opinion polls** Klinkner, *Unsteady March*, 275.

98   **Although support for formal segregation** Kinder and Sanders, *Divided by Color*, 20–23, 33.

98   **White backlash was reinforced** Ibid., 101–3; Klinkner, *Unsteady March*, 280–81.

98   **"social disorder"** Kinder and Sanders, *Divided by Color*, 101–3; Sundquist, *Dynamics of the Party System*, 382–87; Klinkner, *Unsteady March*, 280.

98   **Mounting white resentment** Black and Black, *Rise of Southern Republicans*, 205; Kevin Phillips, *The Emerging Republican Majority* (New Rochelle, N.Y.: Arlington House, 1969).

98   **"if the Democrats could be labeled"** Sundquist, *Dynamics of the Party System*, 364–65.

99   **"desert their party in droves"** Quoted in Kabaservice, *Rule and Ruin*, 274.

99   **Although openly racist appeals** Mendelberg, *Race Card*, 95–98.

99   **four-fifths of southern whites** Phillips, *Emerging Republican Majority*, 227.

99   **Four years later, Nixon won three-quarters** Lowndes, *From the New Deal to the New Right*, 137.

99   **He had opposed** Carmines and Stimson, *Issue Evolution*, 54; Black and Black, *Rise of Southern Republicans*, 215–16.

99   **In an act marked by unmistakable symbolism** Rick Perlstein, *Reaganland: America's Right Turn, 1976–1980* (New York: Simon & Schuster, 2020), 830.

99   **But Reagan added a new prong** Robert P. Jones, *The End of White
      Christian America* (New York: Simon & Schuster, 2016), 88; see also
      Maxwell and Shields, *Long Southern Strategy,* chaps. 7–9.

99   **White evangelical Christians** See Daniel K. Williams, *God's Own
      Party: The Making of the Christian Right* (Oxford: Oxford University
      Press, 2010); Frances Fitzgerald, *The Evangelicals: The Struggle to
      Shape America* (New York: Simon & Schuster, 2017).

99   **In the late 1970s** Daniel Schlozman, *When Movements Anchor Par-
      ties: Electoral Alignments in American History* (Princeton, N.J.: Prince-
      ton University Press, 2015), 77–107; Williams, *God's Own Party,*
      171–79.

99   **Multiple issues triggered evangelical leaders' entry** Schlozman,
      When Movements Anchor Parties, 87–88.

99   **But as the Christian right activist** Ibid., 90–101; Jones, *End of
      White Christian America,* 171; Fitzgerald, *Evangelicals,* 303–5.

100   **Under Falwell's leadership** Williams, *God's Own Party,* 188–94.

100   **Reagan, in turn, championed** Williams, *God's Own Party,*
      189–90; Kabaservice, *Rule and Ruin,* 361; Maxwell and Shields,
      Long Southern Strategy, 291–92.

100   **Reagan succeeded in bringing southern white** Black and Black,
      Rise of Southern Republicans, 205–40.

100   **And he was reelected** Ibid., 217–19; Williams, *God's Own Party,*
      206.

100   **"Great White Switch"** Black and Black, *Rise of Southern Republi-
      cans,* 206; also Sundquist, *Dynamics of the Party System,* 417.

100   **In 1994, the Republicans captured the House** Black and Black,
      Rise of Southern Republicans, 268–368; David Lublin, *The Republican
      South: Democratization and Partisan Change* (Princeton, N.J.: Prince-
      ton University Press, 2004), 33–41.

100   **"racial resentment"** Alan Abramowitz, *The Great Alignment: Race,
      Party Transformation, and the Rise of Donald Trump* (New Haven,
      Conn.: Yale University Press, 2018), 130–31.

100   **Racial resentment scores** Taken from Kinder and Sanders, *Divided
      by Color,* 106.

101   **it left the GOP vulnerable** Ziblatt, *Conservative Parties and the Birth
      of Democracy,* 174–75.

101 **American society grew** See William H. Frey, *The Diversity Explosion: How New Racial Demographics Are Remaking America* (Washington, D.C.: Brookings Institution Press, 2018).

101 **The percentage of Americans** Data from 2020 U.S. census.

101 **African Americans** Frey, *Diversity Explosion,* 247.

101 **Among Americans under the age of eighteen** Tara Bahrampour and Ted Mellnik, "Census Data Shows Widening Diversity: Number of White People Falls for First Time," *Washington Post,* Aug. 12, 2021.

101 **Across America** Frey, *Diversity Explosion,* 168–77, 184–89.

101 **According to the U.S. census** See Ted Mellnik and Andrew Van Dam, "How Mixed-Race Neighborhoods Quietly Became the Norm in the U.S.," *Washington Post,* Nov. 4, 2022.

102 **Rates of intermarriage rose dramatically** Frey, *Diversity Explosion,* 193–211.

102 **Whereas more than 80 percent** Robert P. Jones and Daniel Cox, "America's Changing Religious Identity: Findings from the 2016 American Values Atlas," Public Religion Research Institute, Washington, D.C., Sept. 2017, 18.

102 **Over the last four decades** See Katherine Schaeffer, "Racial, Ethnic Diversity Increases Yet Again with the 117th Congress," Pew Research Center, Jan. 28, 2021.

102 **The number of African Americans** See ibid.

102 **"racial order"** Hochschild, Weaver, and Burch, *Creating a New Racial Order.*

103 **Public support for immigration and diversity** Younis, "Americans Want More, Not Less, Immigration for First Time."

103 **According to the Pew Research Center** See ibid.; "Voters' Attitudes About Race and Gender Are Even More Divided Than in 2016"; Fingerhut, "Most Americans Express Positive Views of Country's Growing Racial and Ethnic Diversity"; Horowitz, "Americans See Advantages and Challenges in Country's Growing Racial and Ethnic Diversity."

103 **In 1973, only 35 percent** Emily Badger, "28 Percent of Whites Say They Favor a Law Allowing Homeowners to Discriminate," *Washington Post,* July 9, 2015; "General Social Survey (GSS)," NORC at the University of Chicago.

103 **And according to Gallup** "Race Relations," Gallup.

103 **In a 2014 PRRI survey** See John Sides, "White Christian America Is Dying," *Washington Post,* Aug. 15, 2016; Public Religion Research Institute, American Values Atlas (2014).

103 **Younger generations** Frey, *Diversity Explosion,* 31–32, 254. In 2018, Pew found that 52 percent of millennials agreed that discrimination is the "main reason why many black people can't get ahead these days," compared with 36 percent of baby boomers and 28 percent of the so-called Silent Generation. Nearly 80 percent of millennials believed immigrants strengthen the country, compared with 47 percent of the Silent Generation. See "The Generation Gap in American Politics," Pew Research Center, March 1, 2018.

103 **In 2018, Pew found** See "Generation Gap in American Politics."

104 **But rights violations** Hochschild, Weaver, and Burch, *Creating a New Racial Order,* 173.

104 **Due to shifting public opinion** See "Voting Rights Restoration," Brennan Center for Justice.

104 **In 2012, four out of five** Jones, *End of White Christian America,* 107–8.

104 **But white Christians** Ibid., 106; Jones and Cox, "America's Changing Religious Identity," 18.

104 **Barack Obama's election** Stevens, *It Was All a Lie,* 32.

105 **The recent wave of immigration** Manuel Pastor, *State of Resistance: What California's Dizzying Descent and Remarkable Resurgence Mean for America's Future* (New York: New Press, 2018), 37; Soraya Sarhaddi Nelson and Richard O'Reilly, "Minorities Become Majority in State, Census Officials Say," *Los Angeles Times,* Aug. 30, 2000.

105 **Because whites still constituted 80 percent** "A Summary Analysis of the 1994 General Election," *California Opinion Index* (Jan. 1995); Daniel Martinez HoSang, *Racial Propositions: Ballot Initiatives and the Making of Postwar California* (Berkeley: University of California Press, 2010), 197.

105 **He embraced Proposition 187** HoSang, *Racial Propositions,* 161; 173–77.

105 **Wilson was reelected** "Summary Analysis of the 1994 General Election."

105 **Proposition 187 also sailed to victory** HoSang, *Racial Propositions*, 196–97; "Summary Analysis of the 1994 General Election."

105 **Republicans also supported ballot initiatives** HoSang, *Racial Propositions*, 212–28; 231–41.

106 **By 2000, a majority of Californians** Nelson and O'Reilly, "Minorities Become Majority in State, Census Officials Say"; Jill Cowan, "Census Confirms Hispanic Residents Are Now the Biggest Ethnic Group in California," *New York Times,* Aug. 12, 2021; "California Voter and Party Profiles," Public Policy Institute of California Fact Sheet, Sept. 2021. Also Pastor, *State of Resistance,* 3, 7.

106 **GOP membership declined** Pastor, *State of Resistance,* 129.

106 **Reince Priebus** Jeremy W. Peters, *Insurgency: How Republicans Lost Their Party and Got Everything They Ever Wanted* (New York: Crown, 2022), 140.

106 **"The conclusion seemed undeniable"** Ibid.

107 **"We're not generating enough"** See Rosalind S. Helderman and Jon Cohen, "As Republican Convention Emphasizes Diversity, Racial Incidents Intrude," *Washington Post,* Aug. 29, 2012.

107 **"I am here today"** Stevens, *It Was All a Lie,* 174.

107 **"coalitions department"** Elyse Siegel, "Michael Steele: For Decades GOP Pursued 'Southern Strategy' That Alienated Minorities," *HuffPost,* May 25, 2011; Steele, interview with authors, Dec. 13, 2021.

107 **"the most comprehensive election review"** Shushannah Walshe, "RNC Completes 'Autopsy' on 2012 Loss, Calls for Inclusion Not Policy Change," ABC News, March 18, 2013.

107 **"marginalizing itself"** Republican National Committee, "Growth and Opportunity Project," March 2013, 4.

107 **"looks different"** Ibid., 7–8.

107 **"does not want them"** Ibid., 8.

107 **"talking to itself"** Ibid., 5.

108 **Among the report's principal recommendations** Ibid., 5–8.

108 **Indeed, at the same time** Tova Wang, *The Politics of Voter Suppres-*

sion: Defending and Expanding Americans' Right to Vote (Ithaca, N.Y.: Cornell University Press, 2012); Berman, *Give Us the Ballot;* Carol Anderson, *One Person, No Vote: How Voter Suppression Is Destroying Our Democracy* (New York: Bloomsbury, 2018).

108   **"coalition of the ascendant"** See "Dissecting the 2008 Electorate: Most Diverse in U.S. History: Overview," Pew Research Center, April 30, 2009; "Dissecting the 2008 Electorate: Most Diverse in U.S. History: Voter Turnout Rates," Pew Research Center, April 30, 2009. On the "coalition of the ascendant," see Ronald Brownstein and National Journal, "Analysis: Obama Gambles with Whites," *Atlantic,* June 29, 2012.

108   **In 2012, Black turnout** Berman, *Give Us the Ballot,* 22.

108   **Following the Republicans' victory** Anderson, *One Person, No Vote,* 62–63; Berman, *Give Us the Ballot,* 10, 260; Wendy R. Weiser, "Voter Suppression: How Bad? (Pretty Bad)," Brennan Center for Justice, Oct. 1, 2014.

109   **Prior to 2005** Benjamin Highton, "Voter Identification Laws and Turnout in the United States," *Annual Review of Political Science* 20 (2017): 151–58.

109   **But between 2011 and 2016** Ibid., 153.

109   **First, election fraud** Lorraine C. Minnite, *The Myth of Voter Fraud* (Ithaca, N.Y.: Cornell University Press, 2011); Richard L. Hasen, *The Voting Wars: From Florida 2020 to the Next Election Meltdown* (New Haven, Conn.: Yale University Press, 2012), 52–62; Justin Levitt, "The Truth About Voter Fraud," Brennan Center for Justice, 2007.

109   **Under President George W. Bush** Hasen, *Voting Wars,* 52–53; Minnite, *Myth of Voter Fraud,* 86–128.

109   **According to a study** Keesha Gaskins and Sundeep Iyer, "The Challenge of Obtaining Voter Identification," Brennan Center for Justice, July 2012.

109   **The problem was most severe** Ibid.

109   **For example, when Texas passed** Weiser, "Voter Suppression," 5; Berman, *Give Us the Ballot,* 266.

110   **In Florida, for example** Wang, *Politics of Voter Suppression,* 3.

110   **The move hit Black voters** Anderson, *One Person, No Vote,* 118.

110   **The new legislation placed onerous** Wang, *Politics of Voter Suppression,* 2; Anderson, *One Person, No Vote,* 119.

110   **The law was so extreme** See Michael Cooper and Jo Craven McGinty, "Florida's New Election Law Blunts Voter Drives," *New York Times,* March 27, 2012.

110   **Finally, in 2011** See Abby Goodnough, "In a Break from the Past, Florida Will Let Felons Vote," *New York Times,* April 6, 2007; *Give Us the Ballot,* 263.

110   **a stunning 21 percent** Anderson, *One Person, No Vote,* 94, 118.

110   **the state went from thirty-seventh** Berman, *Give Us the Ballot,* 291.

110   **Black turnout increased by 65 percent** Ibid.; Anderson, *One Person, No Vote,* 68.

110   **But after winning control** Berman, *Give Us the Ballot,* 295; Weiser, "Voter Suppression," 4.

111   **"gathered . . . data"** Anderson, *One Person, No Vote,* 68.

111   **"are not where the country is"** Stevens, interview with authors, April 29, 2022.

111   **"were giddy about the ramifications"** See Michael Wines, "Some Republicans Acknowledge Leveraging Voter ID Laws for Political Gain," *New York Times,* Sept. 16, 2016.

111   **Of the eleven states** Wendy R. Weiser and Erik Opsal, "The State of Voting in 2014," Brennan Center for Justice, June 17, 2014.

111   **Studies have found** See Jason D. Mycoff, Michael W. Wager, and David C. Wilson, "The Empirical Effects of Voter ID Laws: Present or Absent?," *PS: Political Science and Politics* 42, no. 1 (Jan. 2009): 121–26; Highton, "Voter Identification Laws and Turnout in the United States," 149–67; Nicholas A. Valentino and Fabian G. Neuner, "Why the Sky Didn't Fall: Mobilizing Anger in Reaction to Voter ID Laws," *Political Psychology* 38, no. 2 (2017): 331–50; Justin Grimmer et al., "Obstacles to Estimating Voter ID Laws' Effects on Turnout," *Journal of Politics* 80, no. 3 (2018), 1045–51; Justin Grimmer and Jesse Yoder, "The Durable Differential Deterrent Effects of Strict Photo Identification Laws," *Political Science Research and Methods* 10, no. 3 (2022): 453–69.

111   **When the welterweight boxing champion** See "Margarito Banned for One Year over 'Loaded' Gloves," *Guardian*, Feb. 11, 2009.

112   **Republican politicians might have feared** See Ashley Jardina, *White Identity Politics* (New York: Cambridge University Press, 2019); Jones, *End of White Christian America*.

112   **Throughout American history** Lawrence D. Bobo, "Inequalities That Endure? Racial Ideology, American Politics, and the Peculiar Role of the Social Sciences," in *The Changing Terrain of Race and Ethnicity*, ed. Maria Krysan and Amanda E. Lewis (New York: Russell Sage Foundation, 2004); Hochschild, Weaver, and Burch, *Creating a New Racial Order*.

112   **every single American president** Jardina, *White Identity Politics*, 22, 35–36.

112   **"glass floor"** Joel Olson, "Whiteness and the Polarization of American Politics," *Political Research Quarterly* 61, no. 4 (Dec. 2008): 708.

112   **"psychological wage"** Du Bois, *Black Reconstruction in America*, 700.

113   **Not only was America no longer** Hochschild, Weaver, and Burch, *Creating a New Racial Order*; Jardina, *White Identity Politics*.

113   **Challenges to white Americans'** Olson, "Whiteness and the Polarization of American Politics," 704–18; Justin Gest, *The New Minority: White Working Class Politics in an Age of Immigration and Inequality* (New York: Oxford University Press, 2016); Arlie Russell Hochschild, *Strangers in Their Own Land: Anger and Mourning on the American Right* (New York: New Press, 2018); Jardina, *White Identity Politics*.

113   **A 2015 PRRI survey** Jones, *End of White Christian America*, 86.

113   **The leveling of long-standing social hierarchies** Gest, *New Minority*, 16; Hochschild, *Strangers in Their Own Land*, 137–39; Jardina, *White Identity Politics*, 153.

113   **When one grows up** Olson, "Whiteness and the Polarization of American Politics"; Jardina, *White Identity Politics*, 153.

113   **Indeed, many white Americans** Gest, *New Minority*, 16; Hochschild, *Strangers in Their Own Land*, 137–39; Rogers M. Smith and

Desmond King, "White Protectionism in America," *Perspectives on Politics* 19, no. 2 (June 2021): 460–78.

113   **Surveys showed** Michael I. Norton and Samuel R. Sommers, "Whites See Racism as a Zero-Sum Game That They Are Now Losing," *Perspectives on Psychological Science* 6, no. 3 (2011): 215–18; Alex Samuels and Neil Lewis Jr., "How White Victimhood Fuels Republican Politics," FiveThirtyEight, March 21, 2022.

113   **These feelings were turbocharged** Michael Tesler, *Post-racial or Most Racial? Race and Politics in the Obama Era* (Chicago: University of Chicago Press, 2016).

113   **Although President Obama** Ibid., 47–63.

113   **The mere presence** Ibid.

114   **Much of the resistance** See Philip S. Gorski and Samuel L. Perry, *The Flag and the Cross: White Christian Nationalism and the Threat to American Democracy* (New York: Oxford University Press, 2022); Andrew L. Whitehead and Samuel L. Perry, *Taking America Back for God: Christian Nationalism in the United States* (New York: Oxford University Press, 2020).

114   **"the United States was founded"** See Philip Gorski, "Christianity and Democracy After Trump," Political Theology Network, July 18, 2018.

114   **"White Christians"** Whitehead and Perry, *Taking America Back for God,* 10; Gorski, "Christianity and Democracy After Trump."

114   **Although white evangelical Christians** Gorski and Perry, *The Flag and the Cross,* 10, 84–85. Indeed, among evangelical Christians, less frequent churchgoers were more likely to support Donald Trump in 2016 than more frequent churchgoers. See Gorski, "Christianity and Democracy After Trump."

114   **"mak[e] white Christianity culturally dominant"** See Gorski, "Christianity and Democracy After Trump."

114   **White Christian nationalism helped fuel** On the roots of the Tea Party, see Theda Skocpol and Vanessa Williamson, *The Tea Party and the Remaking of Republican Conservatism* (New York: Oxford University Press, 2012); Christopher Parker and Matt A. Barreto, *Change They Can't Believe In: The Tea Party and Reactionary Politics in America* (Princeton, N.J.: Princeton University Press, 2013).

114 **Following nationwide protests** For estimates, see Skocpol and Williamson, *Tea Party and the Remaking of American Conservatism,* 22; Parker and Barreto, *Change They Can't Believe In,* 242.

114 **The Tea Party** Skocpol and Williamson, *Tea Party and the Remaking of American Conservatism,* 76–82; Parker and Barreto, *Change They Can't Believe In;* Rachel M. Blum, *How the Tea Party Captured the GOP: Insurgent Factions in American Politics* (Chicago: University of Chicago Press, 2020), 95–97.

114 **Surveys showed Tea Party members** Skocpol and Williamson, *Tea Party and the Remaking of American Conservatism,* 57–58, 69–72; Parker and Barreto, *Change They Can't Believe In,* 165–72; Blum, *How the Tea Party Captured the GOP,* 64–95.

115 **"losing their country"** Parker and Barreto, *Change They Can't Believe In,* 249. Also 3, 245, 257.

115 **"the white establishment"** Quoted in Jardina, *White Identity Politics,* 219.

115 **"I went to bed . . . thinking"** Quoted in ibid.

115 **But Republican politicians** Maxwell and Shields, *Long Southern Strategy;* Abramowitz, *Great Alignment.*

115 **According to the political scientist** Abramowitz, *Great Alignment,* 130-1.

116 **Republicans' radicalizing voters** Lawrence R. Jacobs, *Democracy Under Fire: Donald Trump and the Breaking of American History* (Oxford: Oxford University Press, 2022), 163–88.

116 **The rise of well-funded outside groups** Sam Rosenfeld and Daniel Schlozman, "The Hollow Parties," in *Can America Govern Itself?,* ed. Frances Lee and Nolan McCarty (Cambridge, U.K.: Cambridge University Press, 2019), 120–51; Hacker and Pierson, *Let Them Eat Tweets.*

116 **"angry about everything"** Tony Fabrizio, quoted in Peters, *Insurgency,* 18.

116 **Republicans in Congress** Ibid., 143–44.

116 **"cut him off immediately"** Ibid.

116 **Indeed, surveys showed** See Jon Cohen and Dan Balz, "Poll: Immigration a Quandary for Republicans," *Washington Post,* July 23, 2013.

117 **"encourage the party to shift"** Quoted in Peters, *Insurgency,* 223.

117 **"I'm not a grievance candidate"** Quoted in ibid., 224.

117 **"The audience tells you"** Ibid., 180–81.

117 **Trump quickly learned** Ibid., 256–57.

117 **"maintain the racial hierarchy"** Jardina, *White Identity Politics,* 45.

117 **Indeed, studies show** Ibid., 230–45; Tahema Lopez Bunyasi, "The Role of Whiteness in the 2016 Presidential Primaries," *Perspectives on Politics* 17, no. 3 (Sept. 2019); Brenda Major, Alison Blodorn, and Gregory Major Blascovich, "The Threat of Increasing Diversity: Why Many White Americans Support Trump in the 2016 Presidential Election," *Group Processes and Intergroup Relations* 21, no. 6 (2018): 931–40; Mutz, "Status Threat, Not Economic Hardship, Explains the 2016 Presidential Vote"; Michael Tesler and John Sides, "How Political Science Helps Explain the Rise of Trump: The Role of White Identity and Grievances," *Washington Post,* March 3, 2016.

117 **"Trump didn't hijack the Republican Party"** Matthew Continetti on *The Ezra Klein Show,* "Donald Trump Didn't Hijack the G.O.P. He Understood It," *New York Times,* May 6, 2022.

117 **At the same time, many Republicans** See Nathaniel Rakich, "Congressional Republicans Left Office in Droves Under Trump. Just How Conservative Are Their Replacements?," FiveThirtyEight, April 27, 2021.

118 **A 2021 survey** See Larry Schack and Mick McWilliams, "Project Home Fire/Center for Politics Research Reveals Outsized Role Immigration Plays in Fueling Our National Divide," *Sabato's Crystal Ball,* UVA Center for Politics, Oct. 7, 2021.

118 **During the 2017 Unite the Right** See Hawes Spencer and Sheryl Gay Stolberg, "White Nationalists March on University of Virginia," *New York Times,* Aug. 11, 2017.

118 **The white supremacists** See Tim Arango, Nicholas Bogel-Burroughs, and Katie Benner, "Minutes Before El Paso Killing, Hate-Filled Manifesto Appears Online," *New York Times,* Aug. 3, 2019; Alan Feuer, "How Buffalo Suspect's Racist Writings Reveal Links to Other Attacks," *New York Times,* May 16, 2022.

118   **"Democrats . . . want to replace you"** See Ian Schwartz, "Laura
      Ingraham: Democrats Want to Replace American Voters with
      Newly Amnestied Citizens," RealClearPolitics, Oct. 17, 2018.

118   **According to an investigation** See *The New York Times*'s *Tucker
      Carlson Tonight* interactive.

119   **"change the racial mix of the country"** Quoted in Jonathan
      Chair, "Yes, Tucker Carlson Shares Blame for the Buffalo Super-
      market Attack. The White Nationalist's Allies Mount an Uncon-
      vincing Defense," *Intelligencer,* May 16, 2022.

119   **A 2021 survey** See Daniel A. Cox, "After the Ballots Are Counted:
      Conspiracies, Political Violence, and American Exceptionalism:
      Findings from the January 2021 American Perspectives Survey,"
      Survey Center on American Life, American Enterprise Institute,
      Feb. 11, 2021.

120   **During the 2016 presidential race** See Alan Yuhas, "Trump Says
      He May Not Accept Result if Clinton Wins, in Reversal from De-
      bate," *Guardian,* Oct. 1, 2016; Jeremy Diamond, "Donald Trump:
      'I Will Totally Accept' Election Results 'if I Win,'" CNN, Oct. 20,
      2016.

120   **"I won the popular vote"** "Trump Claims Millions Voted Illegally
      in Presidential Poll," BBC, Nov. 28, 2016.

120   **He also claimed fraud** Mark Bowden and Matthew Teague, *The
      Steal* (New York: Atlantic Monthly Press, 2022), 2–3.

120   **"The only way they can take"** Bob Woodward and Robert Costa,
      Peril (New York: Simon & Schuster, 2021), 131.

120   **He repeated that claim** Bowden and Teague, *Steal,* 3; Kevin Lip-
      tak, "A List of the Times Trump Has Said He Won't Accept the
      Election Results or Leave Office if He Loses," CNN, Sept. 24,
      2020.

120   **"fraud on the American public"** Quoted in Bowden and Teague,
      Steal, 82.

120   **Despite pleas from his advisers** Woodward and Costa, *Peril,* 144,
      153, 288.

120   **Instead, he waged** For detailed accounts of these efforts, see
      Bowden and Teague, *Steal;* Woodward and Costa, *Peril;* and Jona-

than Karl, *Betrayal: The Final Act of the Trump Show* (New York: Dutton, 2021).

120   **"I just want to find"** Bowden and Teague, *Steal,* 202–3.

121   **"We are on the way"** Quoted in Woodward and Costa, *Peril,* 151–52. See Betsy Woodruff Swan, "Read the Never-Issued Trump Order That Would Have Seized Voting Machines," *Politico,* Jan. 25, 2022; and Alan Feuer et al., "Trump Had Role in Weighing Proposals to Seize Voting Machines," *New York Times,* Jan. 31, 2022.

121   **Finally, Trump's inner circle** Karl, *Betrayal,* 258, 266, 271; Woodward and Costa, *Peril,* 230, 238–39.

121   **As part of this plan** See Katie Benner, "Justice Dept. Is Reviewing Role of Fake Trump Electors, Top Official Says," *New York Times,* Jan. 25, 2022.

121   **Trump then (unsuccessfully) lobbied** Jamie Gangel and Jeremy Herb, "Memo Shows Trump Lawyer's Six-Step Plan for Pence to Overturn the Election," CNN, Sept. 21, 2021; Karl, *Betrayal,* 259–60; Woodward and Costa, *Peril,* 209–12; Richard L. Hasen, "Identifying and Minimizing the Risk of Election Subversion and Stolen Elections in the Contemporary United States," *Harvard Law Review Forum* 135 (2022): 273–74.

121   **As of December 16, 2021** Andrew Solender, "Just 25 Republicans in Congress Have Acknowledged Biden's Win Since Electoral College Vote," *Forbes,* Dec. 17, 2020.

121   **The Republican Accountability Project** See "GOP Democracy Report Card," Republican Accountability, accountability.gop /report-card/.

121   **And on January 6** See Karen Yourish, Larry Buchanan, and Denise Lu, "The 147 Republicans Who Voted to Overturn Election Results," *New York Times,* Jan. 7, 2021.

121   **South Carolina's senator Lindsey Graham** See Matthew Choi, "Georgia Elections Official Says Lindsey Graham Looked for Way to Exclude Some Legal Ballots," *Politico,* Nov. 16, 2020.

121   **"if a very small handful"** Aaron Blake, "The Big Disconnect Between Mike Lee's Words and His Actions," *Washington Post,* April 18, 2022.

122 **Texas's senator Ted Cruz** See Michael Kranish, "Inside Ted Cruz's Last-Ditch Battle to Keep Trump in Power," *Washington Post,* March 28, 2022.

122 **In a study of Republican** See Nick Corasaniti, Karen Yourish, and Keith Collins, "How Trump's 2020 Election Lies Have Gripped State Legislatures," *New York Times,* May 22, 2022.

122 **In Arizona, Pennsylvania, and Wisconsin** See ibid.

122 **"The Big Lie"** Zack Beauchamp, "The Big Lie Is the GOP's One and Only Truth," *Vox,* May 21, 2021; Ashley Parker and Marianna Sotomayor, "For Republicans, Fealty to Trump's Election Falsehood Becomes Defining Loyalty Test," *Washington Post,* May 2, 2021.

122 **After 2016, but especially after 2020** See Michael Gerson, "The Threat of Violence Now Infuses GOP Politics. We Should All Be Afraid," *Washington Post,* May 20, 2021.

122 **A few Republican congresspeople** See Luke Broadwater and Matthew Rosenberg, "Republican Ties to Extremist Groups Are Under Scrutiny," *New York Times,* June 10, 2021; Catie Edmondson, "Marjorie Taylor Greene's Controversies Are Piling Up. Republicans Are Quiet," *New York Times,* May 25, 2021; Felicia Sonmez, "Rep. Paul Gosar Tweets Altered Anime Video Showing Him Killing Rep. Ocasio-Cortez and Attacking President Biden," *Washington Post,* Nov. 8, 2021.

123 **In April 2020, armed protesters** Craig Mauger and Beth Leblanc, "Trump Tweets 'Liberate' Michigan, Two Other States with Dem Governors," *Detroit News,* April 17, 2020; Lois Beckett, "Armed Protesters Demonstrate Against COVID-19 Lockdown at Michigan Capitol," *Guardian,* April 30, 2020; Kathleen Gray, "In Michigan, a Dress Rehearsal for the Chaos at the Capitol on Wednesday," *New York Times,* Jan. 9, 2021.

123 **"Liberate Michigan!"** See Mauger and Leblanc, "Trump Tweets 'Liberate' Michigan, Two Other States with Dem Governors."

123 **Two weeks later** Katelyn Burns, "Armed Protesters Entered Michigan's State Capitol During Rally Against Stay-at-Home Order," *Vox,* April 30, 2020; Beckett, "Armed Protesters Demonstrate Against COVID-19 Lockdown at Michigan Capitol."

123 **During the summer of 2020** See Emily Singer, "Republicans Encourage Violence Against Protesters amid Anti-racism Demonstrations," *American Independent,* Sept. 4, 2020.

123 **"Now that we clearly see Antifa"** Doha Madani, "Matt Gaetz Tweet on Hunting Antifa Hit with Warning from Twitter for Glorifying Violence," MSNBC, June 2, 2020.

123 **Republican leaders embraced Kyle Rittenhouse** See David Smith, "Why Republicans Are Embracing Kyle Rittenhouse as Their Mascot," *Guardian,* Nov. 27, 2021; John Fritze, Kevin Johnson, and David Jackson, "Trump Defends Kyle Rittenhouse on Eve of Visit to Kenosha," *USA Today,* Aug. 31, 2020.

123 **Trump received Rittenhouse** See Smith, "Why Republicans Are Embracing Kyle Rittenhouse as Their Mascot."

123 **The Republicans also championed** Joan E. Greve, "St. Louis Couple Who Threatened Black Lives Matter Protesters Speak at RNC," *Guardian,* Aug. 25, 2020.

123 **Election officials** See Michael Wines, "Here Are the Threats Terrorizing Election Workers," *New York Times,* Dec. 3, 2020; Linda So and Jason Szep, "U.S. Election Workers Get Little Help from Law Enforcement as Terror Threats Mount," Reuters, Sept. 8, 2021. See also Bowden and Teague, *Steal.*

123 **A 2022 poll of election officials** "Local Election Officials Survey," Brennan Center for Justice, March 2022, 6, 19.

123 **"prepare for war"** See Rich Kremer, "County Republican Parties Facing Scrutiny over Online Rhetoric in Wake of Insurrection," Wisconsin Public Radio, Jan. 12, 2021.

124 **Instead, he *aided* the insurrection** See Alana Wise, "DOD Took Hours to Approve National Guard Request During Capitol Riot, Commander Says," NPR, March 3, 2021.

124 **"remember this day forever"** Woodward and Costa, *Peril,* 256.

124 **"Some people were saying it's 1776"** Karl, *Betrayal,* 339.

124 **"the greatest movement"** Libby Cathey, "Trump's Attempts to Discredit Jan. 6 Committee Being Put to Test Thursday," ABC News, June 9, 2022.

124 **"normal tourist visit"** See Cristina Marcos, "GOP Efforts to Downplay Danger of Capitol Riot Increase," *Hill,* May 21, 2021.

124   **"never really felt threatened"** See Allison Pecorin, "GOP Sen.
       Ron Johnson Says He Didn't Feel 'Threatened' by Capitol Marchers
       but May Have if BLM or Antifa Were Involved," ABC News,
       March 13, 2021.

124   **"would have been armed"** See Eugene Scott, "White House Con-
       demns Greene over Claim She Would Have 'Won' Jan. 6 Insurrec-
       tion," *Washington Post,* Dec. 12, 2022.

124   **"ordinary citizens"** See Jonathan Weisman and Reid J. Epstein,
       "G.O.P. Declares Jan. 6 Attack 'Legitimate Political Discourse,'"
       New York Times, Feb. 4, 2022.

124   **The Republican flirtation with violence** Paul Waldman, "Elite
       Republicans Are Now Openly Encouraging Political Violence,"
       Washington Post, June 20, 2022.

125   **During the 2022 primary season** See Katie Glueck, Azi Paybarah,
       and Leah Askarinam, "In More Than 100 G.O.P. Midterm Ads
       This Year: Guns, Guns, Guns," *New York Times,* May 27, 2022.

125   **"crusade to undermine our democracy"** Cristina Marcos,
       "Cheney in Defiant Floor Speech: Trump on 'Crusade to Under-
       mine Our Democracy,'" *Hill,* May 11, 2021.

125   **"The President of the United States"** See John Eligon and
       Thomas Kaplan, "These Are the Republicans Who Supported Im-
       peaching Trump," *New York Times,* Sept. 17, 2021.

126   **After voting to impeach Trump** Jonathan Martin and Alexander
       Burns, *This Will Not Pass: Trump, Biden, and the Battle for America's
       Future* (New York: Simon & Schuster, 2022), 432–33; "Wyoming
       GOP Votes to Stop Recognizing Cheney as a Republican," Associ-
       ated Press, Nov. 15, 2021.

126   **They engaged in appeasement** Martin and Burns, *This Will Not
       Pass,* 338–41, 217–18.

126   **Both McConnell and McCarthy knew** Karl, *Betrayal,* 240–41;
       Martin and Burns, *This Will Not Pass,* 127.

126   **Both men were appalled** See Alexander Burns and Jonathan Mar-
       tin, "'I've Had It with This Guy': G.O.P. Leaders Privately Blasted
       Trump After Jan. 6," *New York Times,* April 21, 2022; Martin and
       Burns, *This Will Not Pass,* 222–23, 230–32.

126   **an act of "terrorism"** Woodward and Costa, *Peril,* 342.

126   **McCarthy held Trump responsible** See Burns and Martin, " 'I've Had It with This Guy' "; Martin and Burns, *This Will Not Pass,* 222–23.

127   **"If this isn't impeachable"** See Burns and Martin, " 'I've Had It with This Guy' "; Martin and Burns, *This Will Not Pass,* 218, 230–31.

127   **"head-snapping reversal"** Martin and Burns, *This Will Not Pass,* 245–46.

127   **But the RNC** Karl, *Betrayal,* 331–33.

127   **And most leading Republicans** See Paul LeBlanc, "McConnell Says He'll 'Absolutely' Support Trump in 2024 if He's the GOP Nominee," CNN, Feb. 25, 2021; and Carly Roman, "Kevin McCarthy: Trump Wants Me to Be Speaker," *Washington Examiner,* June 19, 2021.

127   **McConnell believed** Martin and Burns, *This Will Not Pass,* 361.

128   **Had McCarthy backed impeachment** Ibid., 226, 244.

128   **"Who knows"** Karl, *Betrayal,* 243–44.

128   **In 1987, Argentina** Deborah L. Norden, *Military Rebellion in Argentina: Between Coups and Consolidation* (Lincoln: University of Nebraska Press, 1996), 117–19.

129   **Their hostility toward Alfonsín** Ibid.

129   **The *Carapintadas*** Ibid., 136–37.

129   **Some right-wing Peronists** José Luis Manzano (former Peronist leader), interview with Levitsky, Jan. 19, 2022.

129   **"heroes from the Malvinas"** Ibid.

129   **"Why should we help this guy?"** Mario Wainfeld (journalist and former Peronist activist), interview with Levitsky, Dec. 21, 2021.

129   **He considered** Ibid.; Manzano, interview with Levitsky, Jan. 19, 2022.

130   **Menem was in no hurry** Ibid.

130   **"didn't want to complicate"** Manzano, interview with Levitsky, Jan. 19, 2022.

130   **an "albatross"** Wainfeld, interview with Levitsky, Dec. 21, 2021.

130   **"embraced a president who was failing"** Ibid.

130   **"didn't want to be president"** Manzano, interview with Levitsky, Jan. 19, 2022.

130   **"what we got in return"** Ibid.

130   **The Republican Accountability Project** See "GOP Democracy Report Card."

131   **More than 60 percent** See ibid.

CHAPTER 5: FETTERED MAJORITIES

133   **As a young civil rights leader** Zelizer, *Fierce Urgency of Now,* 209.

133   **The VRA helped** Whether a jurisdiction required preclearance was determined by a formula specified in Section 4 of the Voting Rights Act (1965).

134   **In 1982, the Senate renewed it** Steven V. Roberts, "Voting Rights Act Renewed in Senate by Margin of 85–8," *New York Times,* June 19, 1982.

134   **In 2006, the VRA was renewed** Carl Hulse, "By a Vote of 98–0, Senate Approves 25-Year Extension of Voting Rights Act," *New York Times,* July 21, 2006.

134   **"landmark for all Americans"** Drosenfeld, "July 20, 2006: Mitch McConnell Votes to Re-authorize the Voting Rights Act," C-SPAN, July 28, 2020.

134   **as well as polls** "Public Opinion on the Voting Rights Act," Roper Center for Public Opinion Research, Aug. 6, 2015.

134   **"A statute's 'current burdens' "** Vann R. Newkirk II, "How *Shelby County v. Holder* Broke America," *Atlantic,* July 10, 2018.

134   **"throwing out preclearance"** Linda Greenhouse, *Justice on the Brink: A Requiem for the Supreme Court* (New York: Random House, 2021), 13.

134   **In the wake of the decision** See Caterina Feder and Michael G. Miller, "Voter Purges After *Shelby,*" *American Politics Research* 46, no. 6 (2020): 687–92; Matt Vasilogambros, "Polling Places Remain a Target Ahead of November Elections," Pew Charitable Trusts, Sept. 4, 2018.

135   **And in the eight years** Ari Berman, "Eight Years Ago, the Supreme Court Gutted the Voting Rights Act. Widespread Voter Suppression Resulted," *Mother Jones,* June 25, 2021.

135   **"dagger in the heart"** John Lewis et al., "John Lewis and Others
      React to the Supreme Court's Voting Rights Act Ruling," *Washing-
      ton Post,* June 25, 2013.

135   **"To say thank you"** Caitlin Oprysko, "House Passes Voting
      Rights Package Aimed at Restoring Protections," *Politico,* Dec. 6,
      2019.

135   **Republicans controlled the Senate** Marianne Levine, "McCon-
      nell Won't Allow Vote on Election Reform Bill," *Politico,* March 6,
      2019.

135   **"monumental figure"** Luke Broadwater, "After Death of John
      Lewis, Democrats Renew Push for Voting Rights Law," *New York
      Times,* July 21, 2020.

135   **"founding father"** "Read the Full Transcript of Obama's Eulogy
      for John Lewis," *New York Times,* July 30, 2020.

136   **Although the bill had majority support** Mike DeBonis, "Senate
      Republicans Block Debate on a Third Major Voting Rights Bill,"
      Washington Post, Nov. 3, 2021.

136   **The legislation standardized voting laws** Grace Panetta, "What's
      in the Major Voting Rights Bill That Senate Republicans Voted to
      Block," *Insider,* Jan. 20, 2022.

136   **A January 2022 survey** Adam Eichen and Kevin Rissmiller, "A
      Majority of Americans Support Fixing the Filibuster to Pass the
      Freedom to Vote: John R. Lewis Act," Data for Progress, Jan. 19,
      2022.

136   **Another poll found** "National Tracking Poll 2201029," Morning
      Consult and Politico, Jan. 2022.

136   **Again, however, the Democratic majority** Nicholas Reimann,
      "Sinema Won't Support Eliminating Filibuster—Effectively Killing
      Democrats' Voting Rights Bill," *Forbes,* Jan. 13, 2022.

137   **not made for democracy** This phrase "not made for democracy" is
      taken from Jamelle Bouie, "American Power, Prosperity, and De-
      mocracy" (public lecture, LaFollette Forum, University of Wiscon-
      sin, Madison, May 4, 2022).

137   **In 2019, when efforts to restore** Nate Silver, "The Senate's Rural
      Skew Makes It Very Hard for Democrats to Win the Supreme
      Court," FiveThirtyEight, Sept. 20, 2020.

137   **Although liberal democracy** Paul Starr, *Entrenchment: Wealth, Power, and the Constitution of Democratic Societies* (New Haven, Conn.: Yale University Press, 2019), 118.

138   **"beyond the reach of majorities"** *West Virginia State Board of Education v. Barnette,* 319 U.S. 624, 638 (1943).

138   **"may not be submitted to vote"** Ibid.

139   **"The teacher tried to force"** Noah Feldman, *Scorpions: The Battles and Triumphs of FDR's Great Supreme Court Justices* (New York: Hachette, 2010), 179.

139   **"Miss Shofstal, I can't salute"** Ibid.

139   **In one incident, a mob** Ibid., 185.

139   **"village tyrants"** *Barnette,* 319 U.S. at 638.

139   **So constitutional safeguards** Akhil Reed Amar, *The Bill of Rights: Creation and Reconstruction* (New Haven, Conn.: Yale University Press, 2008); Ronald Dworkin, *Freedom's Law: The Moral Reading of the American Constitution* (Cambridge, Mass.: Harvard University Press, 1996); Richard Fallon, "The Core of an Uneasy Case for Judicial Review," *Harvard Law Review* 121, no. 7 (May 2008): 1700.

141   **Democracies must create mechanisms** John Hart Ely, *Democracy and Distrust: A Theory of Judicial Review* (Cambridge, Mass.: Harvard University Press, 1980); Robert Post and Reva Siegel, "Popular Constitutionalism, Departmentalism, and Judicial Supremacy," *California Law Review* 92 (2004).

141   **The process of constitutional amendment** Starr, *Entrenchment,* 106.

141   **Most democracies require supermajorities** Donald Lutz, "Toward a Theory of Constitutional Amendment," *American Political Science Review* 88, no. 2 (June 1994): 363. Also Melissa Schwartzberg, *Counting the Many: The Origins and Limits of Supermajority Rule* (New York: Cambridge University Press, 2014), 187–88.

141   **One proposed law** Isabel Kershner, "A Proposal to Overhaul the Judiciary Is Roiling Israel. What Is the Plan?," *New York Times,* Feb. 14, 2023.

142   **"imminent danger of collapse"** Patrick Kingsley, "Netanyahu Surges Ahead with Judicial Overhaul, Prompting Fury in Israel," *New York Times,* Jan. 12, 2023.

142 **All democracies must therefore** One of the most prominent analysts of how different democracies balance majority and minority rights is Arend Lijphart, *Patterns of Democracy: Government Forms and Performance in Thirty-six Countries* (New Haven, Conn.: Yale University Press, 1999).

142 **This is the danger of counter-majoritarianism** See Robert A. Dahl, *Democracy and Its Critics* (New Haven, Conn.: Yale University Press, 1989), 155–56.

142 **"tyranny of the majority"** See ibid.

142 **First, those with more votes** In presidential systems, this means that candidates who win electoral pluralities or majorities should win; in parliamentary democracies, governments should have the (explicit or implicit) support of parties that represent an electoral majority.

143 **From a democratic standpoint** See Schwartzberg, *Counting the Many.*

143 **The political theorist Melissa Schwartzberg** Ibid., 142–44.

143 **For example, Thailand's military leaders** See Duncan McCargo, "Democratic Demolition in Thailand," *Journal of Democracy* 30, no. 4 (Oct. 2019): 119–33.

144 **Similarly, when Chile democratized in 1989** Pamela Constable and Arturo Valenzuela, *A Nation of Enemies: Chile Under Pinochet* (New York: W. W. Norton, 1991), 313–16.

145 **the problem of the dead hand** Andrew Coan, "The Dead Hand Revisited," *Emory Law Journal* 7 (2020).

145 **Do parents ever have the right** John Locke as cited by Stephen Holmes, *Passions and Constraint: On the Theory of Liberal Democracy* (Chicago: University of Chicago Press, 1995), 140.

145 **"whether one generation of men"** Holmes, *Passions and Constraint,* 140.

145 **"The dead"** Jefferson to Madison, Sept. 6, 1789, quoted in Zachary Elkins, Tom Ginsburg, and James Melton, *The Endurance of National Constitutions* (New York: Cambridge University Press, 2009), 1.

145 **an "expiration date"** Elkins, Ginsburg, and Melton, *Endurance of National Constitutions,* 1.

145   **"A people always have the right"** Quoted in ibid., 13.

145   **Madison and others recognized** Starr, *Entrenchment,* 106.

146   **"consummate arrogance"** Michael Klarman, *The Framers' Coup: The Making of the United States Constitution* (New York: Oxford University Press, 2016), 628.

146   **"will certainly be defective"** Ibid.

146   **"iron cage"** Levinson, *Our Undemocratic Constitution,* 165.

147   **It was this problem that provoked** James MacGregor Burns, *Packing the Court: The Rise of Judicial Power and the Coming Crisis of the Supreme Court* (New York: Penguin Press, 2009), 145–52.

148   **Extensive judicial review power** Robert Dahl, *How Democratic Is the American Constitution?* (New Haven, Conn.: Yale University Press, 2002), 18–19.

148   **Federalism is often viewed** Mickey, *Paths Out of Dixie;* Edward Gibson, *Boundary Control: Subnational Authoritarianism in Federal Democracies* (New York: Cambridge University Press, 2013).

149   **comparative research suggests** Elkins, Ginsburg, and Melton, *Endurance of National Constitutions,* 141–42; Steven L. Taylor et al., *A Different Democracy: American Government in a Thirty-One-Country Perspective* (New Haven, Conn.: Yale University Press, 2014), 79–81.

149   **The founders' ideas** Gordon Wood, *The Radicalism of the American Revolution* (New York: Vintage Books, 1991).

149   **Still, the founders did not aspire** Woody Holton, *Unruly Americans and the Origins of the Constitution* (New York: Farrar, Straus and Giroux, 2007).

150   **"the worst . . . of all political evils"** Klarman, *Framers' Coup,* 228, 244–45; Dahl, *How Democratic Is the American Constitution?,* 68.

150   **And guided by an outsized fear** Klarman, *Framers' Coup,* 243–44.

150   **The founders might have been inspired** David Brian Robertson, *The Constitution and America's Destiny* (New York: Cambridge University Press, 2005), 101–2.

150   **America's first constitution** Klarman, *Framers' Coup,* 126–27.

150   **Not only would the country's emerging** Linda Colley, *The Gun, the Ship, and the Pen: Warfare, Constitutions, and the Making of the Modern World* (New York: Liveright, 2021); Klarman, *Framers' Coup.*

151   **"kick over the board"** Guillermo O'Donnell and Philippe C.
      Schmitter, *Transitions from Authoritarian Rule: Tentative Conclusions
      About Uncertain Democracies* (Baltimore: Johns Hopkins University
      Press, 1986).

151   **The Chilean dictator Augusto Pinochet** Constable and Valen-
      zuela, *Nation of Enemies,* 311–13.

151   **In South Africa** Timothy Sisk, *Democratization in South Africa: The
      Elusive Social Contract* (Princeton, N.J.: Princeton University Press,
      1997).

152   **The demands of the five southern** David Waldstreicher, *Slavery's
      Constitution: From Revolution to Ratification* (New York: Hill and
      Wang, 2009), 57–104; Klarman, *Framers' Coup.*

152   **Southern delegates resisted** Klarman, *Framers' Coup,* 264.

152   **But southern slaveholders** Of the fifty-five delegates to the con-
      vention, twenty-five owned slaves. Ibid., 263.

152   **However, since 40 percent** Klarman, *Framers' Coup,* 264.

152   **"as close to ironclad"** Sean Wilentz, *No Property in Man: Slavery
      and Antislavery at the Nation's Founding* (Cambridge, Mass.: Harvard
      University Press, 2019), 2, 5; Klarman, *Framers' Coup,* 272.

152   **Seven weeks into the convention** Wilentz, *No Property in
      Man,* 58.

153   **"keep slavery completely outside"** Ibid., 2.

153   **If this demand were not met** Klarman, *Framers' Coup,* 287.

153   **Although many northern delegates** See Wilentz, *No Property in
      Man,* 97–98.

153   **few (if any) of them** Klarman, *Framers' Coup,* 264; Wilentz, *No
      Property in Man,* 3.

153   **"strengthened the slaveholders' hand"** Wilentz, *No Property in
      Man,* 4, 22.

153   **Protections included a twenty-year congressional ban** Waldst-
      reicher, *Slavery's Constitution,* 6, 8–9.

153   **"something like an equality"** Quoted in Wilentz, *No Property in
      Man,* 64.

153   **For example, in 1790** Jill Lepore, *These Truths: A History of the
      United States* (New York: W. W. Norton, 2018), 125.

154 **Overall, the three-fifths clause** David A. Bateman, Ira Katznelson, and John S. Lapinski, *Southern Nation: Congress and White Supremacy After Reconstruction* (Princeton, N.J.: Princeton University Press, 2018), 8.

154 **"thwart any national lawmaking"** Wilentz, *No Property in Man,* 113.

154 **The word "slavery" didn't appear** Waldstreicher, *Slavery's Constitution,* 3.

154 **Many of the founders** See Hamilton, "Federalist No. 22," in Alexander Hamilton, James Madison, and John Jay, *The Federalist, with Letters of "Brutus,"* ed. Terence Ball (Cambridge, U.K.: Cambridge University Press, 2003), 100–1; Greg Weiner, *Madison's Metronome: The Constitution, Majority Rule, and the Tempo of American Politics* (Lawrence: University Press of Kansas, 2012), 13–14.

154 **"As states are a collection"** Hamilton, quoted in Dahl, *How Democratic Is the American Constitution?,* 13–14.

155 **"contradicts that fundamental maxim"** Hamilton, "Federalist No. 22," 100.

155 **"It may happen"** Ibid., 101.

155 **"evidently unjust"** Weiner, *Madison's Metronome,* 14; Klarman, *Framers' Coup,* 185.

155 **"Can we forget"** Klarman, *Framers' Coup,* 185.

155 **Wilson backed Madison's** Robertson, *Constitution and America's Destiny,* 83–99.

155 **But the smaller states** Klarman, *Framers' Coup,* 191–93.

155 **"the small [states] will find"** Ibid., 193.

155 **Benjamin Franklin** Ibid., 194.

156 **Madison himself opposed** We thank Michael Klarman (personal communication) for reminding us of this point.

156 **Rather, it was adopted by default** Dahl, *How Democratic Is the American Constitution?,* 67, 74–76; Wegman, *Let the People Pick the President,* 58.

156 **"most difficult"** Keyssar, *Why Do We Still Have an Electoral College?,* 17.

156 **"from scratch"** Ibid., 18; Dahl, *How Democratic Is the American Constitution?*, 70–71.

156 **The initial draft proposal** Klarman, *Framers' Coup*, 227.

156 **Parliamentarism eventually became** Keyssar, *Why Do We Still Have an Electoral College?*, 19–21.

157 **James Wilson argued for popular election** Ibid., 19.

157 **But at the time** Klarman, *Framers' Coup*, 228, 244–45; Dahl, *How Democratic Is the American Constitution?*, 68.

157 **Southern delegates were particularly opposed** Klarman, *Framers' Coup*, 228; Wegman, *Let the People Pick the President*, 70–75.

157 **As Madison recognized** Keyssar, *Why Do We Still Have an Electoral College?*, 21; Klarman, *Framers' Coup*, 228.

157 **"dealbreaker"** Akhil Reed Amar, "Actually the Electoral College Was a Pro-Slavery Play," *New York Times*, April 6, 2019.

157 **The delegates debated the issue** Wegman, *Let the People Pick the President*, 57–58.

157 **Every proposed alternative was voted down** Dahl, *How Democratic Is the American Constitution?*, 74–75.

157 **Finally, as the convention was drawing** Klarman, *Framers' Coup*, 230–31.

157 **When the emperor died** Peter H. Wilson, *The Heart of Europe: A History of the Holy Roman Empire* (Cambridge, Mass.: Harvard University Press, 2016), 305–7.

158 **"elect a successor"** Josep M. Colomer and Iain McLean, "Electing Popes: Approval Balloting and Qualified-Majority Rule," *Journal of Interdisciplinary History* 29, no. 1 (1998): 1–22.

158 **"medieval relic"** Josep M. Colomer, "The Electoral College Is a Medieval Relic. Only the U.S. Still Has One," *Washington Post*, Dec. 11, 2016.

158 **"consensus second choice"** Keyssar, *Why Do We Still Have an Electoral College?*, 24.

158 **"fittest" method** Klarman, *Framers' Coup*, 228; Wegman, *Let the People Pick the President*, 69–70.

158 **This arrangement satisfied the southern states** Klarman, *Framers' Coup*, 231.

158   **The Electoral College never did** See Dahl, *How Democratic Is the American Constitution?*, 77–79.

158   **Hamilton expected it to be composed** Alexander Hamilton, Federalist No. 68, 331.

159   **The Constitution also explicitly stated** Burns, *Packing the Court*, 11–12. See also Edgar B. Herwick III, "Why Did the Framers Give Lifetime Tenure to Supreme Court Justices?," WGBH, Oct. 2, 2018.

159   **The court didn't even have** Burns, *Packing the Court*, 7–8.

159   **The first chief justice, John Jay** Ibid., 8.

159   **Indeed, the six justices** Tom Ginsburg, "Term Limits and Turnover on the U.S. Supreme Court: A Comparative View," Testimony for the Presidential Commission on the Supreme Court, July 20, 2021, 5.

159   **The framers clearly aimed to establish** Klarman, *Framers' Coup*, 160–61.

160   **Ultimately, it appears, the framers** Burns, *Packing the Court*, 13–14.

160   **On the eve of Thomas Jefferson's** Burns, *Vineyard of Liberty*, 188.

160   **Like judicial review, the Senate filibuster** For detailed discussions of the origins and evolution of the filibuster, see Sarah A. Binder and Steven S. Smith, *Politics or Principle? Filibustering in the United States Senate* (Washington, D.C.: Brookings Institution, 1997); Wawro and Schickler, *Filibuster;* and Gregory Koger, *Filibustering: A Political History of Obstruction in the House and Senate* (Chicago: University of Chicago Press, 2010).

160   **The filibuster is often viewed** See Binder and Smith, *Politics or Principle?*

160   **"the fountainhead of all our freedoms"** Quoted in Wawro and Schickler, *Filibuster*, 8.

161   **"part of the fabric"** Binder and Smith, *Politics or Principle?*, 11.

161   **Many of the framers of the Constitution** Koger, *Filibustering*, 40.

161   **In the wake of its failure** One example of Madison's explicit embrace of majority rule as the defining feature of "republicanism" is in his letter reprinted in *The Mind of the Founder: Sources of the Political Thought of James Madison,* ed. Marvin Meyers (Indianapolis: Bobbs-Merrill, 1973), 520–30. See also Weiner, *Madison's Metronome*.

161   **"the vital principle of republican government"** Quoted in Meyers, *Mind of the Founder,* 530.

161   **"the fundamental principle of free government"** Madison, quoted in Weiner, *Madison's Metronome,* 16.

161   **"subject the sense of the greater"** Hamilton, "Federalist No. 22," 101.

161   **"we are apt to rest satisfied"** Ibid., 102.

161   **With the exception of treaty ratification** Binder and Smith, *Politics or Principle?,* 5, 20, 29–33; Adam Jentleson, *Kill Switch: The Rise of the Modern Senate and the Crippling of American Democracy* (New York: Liveright, 2021), 27.

161   **Rather, it adopted the so-called** Binder and Smith, *Politics or Principle?,* 35.

162   **The rule was little used** Ibid., 35–37.

162   **Burr's rationale seems to have been** Ibid., 38.

162   **There is no evidence that Burr** Ibid.; Wawro and Schickler, *Filibuster,* 14.

162   **"by mistake"** Quoted in Jentleson, *Kill Switch,* 47.

162   **There were no organized filibusters** Binder and Smith, *Politics or Principle?,* 39; Koger, *Filibustering,* 62–63; Jentleson, *Kill Switch,* 50.

162   **In the 1840s and 1850s** Binder and Smith, *Politics or Principle?,* 55–58.

162   **There were only twenty successful filibusters** Ibid., 60; Wawro and Schickler, *Filibuster,* 42–54.

162   **Filibuster use picked up** Binder and Smith, *Politics or Principle?,* 79; Jentleson, *Kill Switch,* 64–65.

162   **Although many senators supported** Binder and Smith, *Politics or Principle?,* 79.

163   **This minority veto power** Jentleson, *Kill Switch,* 67.

163   **Senators had to physically hold** Koger, *Filibustering,* 54–58.

163   **After reforms in the 1970s** Ibid., 179–80; Jentleson, *Kill Switch,* 212.

163   **As filibustering became costless** Koger, *Filibustering,* 179–87; Wawro and Schickler, *Filibuster,* 180; Jentleson, *Kill Switch,* 212.

163   **"widely accepted that legislation"** Wawro and Schickler, *Filibuster,* 259.

163   **"quiet revolution"** Koger, *Filibustering,* 3.

164   **"The American majority"** Louis Hartz, *The Liberal Tradition in America* (1952; New York: Harcourt, 1991), 129.

CHAPTER 6: **MINORITY RULE**

165   **In February 1909, rural landowners** "Die Junker gegen das Volk," *Vorwärts,* Feb. 23, 1909, 1.

165   **"Gentlemen, I know"** "Stenographischer Bericht über die 16 General-Versammlung des Bund der Landwirte," *Korrespondenz des Bundes der Landwirte,* Feb. 22, 1909, 70.

168   **"creeping counter-majoritarianism"** Hacker and Pierson, *Let Them Eat Tweets,* 172–73.

168   **By 1912** Stanley Suval, *Electoral Politics in Wilhelmine Germany* (Chapel Hill: University of North Carolina Press, 1985), 229.

168   **in 1907, Social Democrats** George D. Crothers, *The German Elections of 1907* (New York: Columbia University Press, 1941), 175.

169   **In 1790, a voter in Delaware** Dylan Matthews, "You Can't Understand What's Happened to the Senate Without These Two Graphs," *Washington Post,* April 18, 2013.

170   **In 1920, the U.S. Census Bureau** Margo Anderson, *The American Census: A Social History* (New Haven, Conn.: Yale University Press, 2015), 133–55.

170   **This meant that rural jurisdictions** From 1920 until the 1960s, rural interests also gained disproportionate influence in the U.S. House of Representatives. This ended with two U.S. Supreme Court decisions (*Baker v. Carr* in 1962 and *Reynolds v. Sims* in 1964).

170   **Rural voters in the Northeast and the Midwest** Stephen Ansolabehere and James M. Snyder, *The End of Inequality: One Person, One Vote and the Transformation of American Politics* (New York: Norton, 2008), 81–82.

171   **With the rise** See Jonathan Rodden, *Why Cities Lose* (New York: Basic Books, 2019).

171   **At the same time** Ibid.

171   **Left-of-center parties** Ibid.

171   **Today, then, Republicans are predominantly** Suzanne Mettler and Trevor Brown, "The Growing Rural-Urban Political Divide

and Democratic Vulnerability," *Annals of the American Academy of Political and Social Science* 699, no. 1 (2022): 130–42; Rodden, *Why Cities Lose*.

173 **"dictatorial power"** James MacGregor Burns, *The Deadlock of Democracy: Four-Party Politics in America* (Englewood Cliffs, N.J.: Prentice-Hall, 1963), 295–96.

174 **Because the U.S. Senate heavily overrepresents** Nate Cohn, "The Electoral College's Real Problem: It's Biased Toward the Big Battlegrounds," *New York Times,* March 22, 2019.

174 **In 2000, for example** Ibid.

174 **One way in which analysts measure** Laura Bronner and Nathaniel Rakich, "Advantage, GOP," FiveThirtyEight, April 29, 2021.

175 **Sparsely populated states** Frances E. Lee and Bruce I. Oppenheimer, *Sizing Up the Senate: The Unequal Consequences of Equal Representation* (Chicago: University of Chicago Press, 1999), 10–11.

175 **And states representing 11 percent** Matthews, "You Can't Understand What's Happened to the Senate Without These Two Graphs."

175 **Although the Republicans have won** See Stephen Wolf, "How Minority Rule Plagues Senate: Republicans Last Won More Support Than Democrats Two Decades Ago," *Daily Kos,* Feb. 23, 2021.

175 **And yet the Republicans controlled** The years are between 1996 and 2001, 2003 and 2007, and 2015 and 2020. The Republicans briefly lost control of the Senate in 2001 when the Vermont senator James Jeffords left the party, but they regained control in 2002.

175 **Drawing on the tipping state logic** Bronner and Rakich, "Advantage, GOP."

176 **Over the past few decades** Ibid.

176 **Based on states' populations** In states with one senator from each party, each senator is assigned half the state's population.

176 **But their senators represented** Wolf, "How Minority Rule Plagues Senate."

176 **After the 2020 election** Ian Millhiser, "America's Anti-democratic Senate, in One Number," *Vox,* Jan. 6, 2021.

176 **The pattern continued in 2022** Data from Stephen Wolf, based on preliminary 2022 election results.

176   **"The makeup of the Republican coalition"** Alexander Burns,
       "Making the Senate Work for Democrats," *New York Review of
       Books,* Jan. 19, 2023.

177   **Four of nine current Supreme Court** Philip Bump, "The Minori-
       tarian Third of the Supreme Court," *Washington Post,* Dec. 2, 2021.

177   **And three of them** Ibid.

177   **Historically, scholars of the Supreme Court** Christopher J.
       Casillas, Peter K. Enns, and Patrick C. Wohlfarth, "How Public
       Opinion Constrains the U.S. Supreme Court," *American Journal of
       Political Science* 55, no. 1 (January 2011): 74–88.

177   **Recent research has found** Stephen Jessee, Neil Malhotra, and
       Maya Sen, "A Decade-Long Longitudinal Survey Shows That the
       Supreme Court Is Now Much More Conservative Than the Pub-
       lic," *Proceedings of the National Academy of Sciences* 119, no. 24 (2022):
       e2120284119.

177   **A fourth pillar of minority rule** Miriam Seifter, "Countermajori-
       tarian Legislatures," *Columbia Law Review* 121, no. 6 (2021): 1733–
       800; David Pepper, *Laboratories of Autocracy: A Wake-Up Call from
       Behind the Lines* (Cincinnati: St. Helena Press, 2021); Jacob Grum-
       bach, *Laboratories Against Democracy: How National Parties Transformed
       State Politics* (Princeton, N.J.: Princeton University Press, 2022).
       Also Christian R. Grose et al., "The Worst Partisan Gerrymanders
       in U.S. State Legislatures," University of Southern California
       Schwarzenegger Institute for State and Global Policy, Sept. 4,
       2019, 2.

178   **Recall that in the twenty-first century** Rodden, *Why Cities Lose.*

178   **"the fountainhead of representative government"** Seifter,
       "Countermajoritarian Legislatures," 1744–45.

178   **America's state legislatures** Ibid.

178   **To see how this works** See Rodden, *Why Cities Lose,* 131–48.

179   **This pattern occurred across Pennsylvania** Ibid.

179   **Although geographic sorting** Richard H. Pildes et al., "Brief of
       Political Geography Scholars as Amici Curiae in Support of Appel-
       lees," Counsel for Amici Curiae, Sept. 5, 2017.

180   **"head start"** Rodden, *Why Cities Lose.*

180   **And second, polarization and Republican radicalization** David

Daley, *Ratf**ked: Why Your Vote Doesn't Count* (New York: Liveright, 2017).

180 **Indeed, in 2010, the Republican Party** Ibid.

180 **Financed by wealthy Republican donors** Ibid.; Grose et al., "Worst Partisan Gerrymanders in U.S. State Legislatures," 1.

181 **"a corrupt way of taking power"** Daley, *Ratf**ked,* 139.

181 **In 2018, the Democrats** Grose et al., "Worst Partisan Gerrymanders in U.S. State Legislatures," 3; Pepper, *Laboratories of Autocracy,* 104.

181 **"manufactured majorities"** Seifter, "Countermajoritarian Legislatures," 1762–63.

181 **Between 1968 and 2016** Ibid., 1764–65.

181 **Whereas in the past both parties** Grose et al., "Worst Partisan Gerrymanders in U.S. State Legislatures."

182 **Scholars and pundits alike** Frances Lee, *Insecure Majorities: Congress and the Perpetual Campaign* (Chicago: University of Chicago Press, 2016); John Sides, Chris Tausanovich, and Lynn Vavreck, *The Bitter End: The 2020 Presidential Campaign and the Challenge to American Democracy* (Princeton, N.J.: Princeton University Press, 2022). Also "The Great Mystery of American Politics," *Economist,* Jan. 5, 2023; and Ezra Klein, "Three Theories That Explain This Strange Moment," *New York Times,* Nov. 12, 2022.

183 **Citizens tend to be inconsistent** See Larry Bartels and Christopher Achen, *Democracy for Realists* (Princeton, N.J.: Princeton University Press, 2017).

183 **In addition, organized (and often well-financed)** Benjamin I. Page and Martin Gilens, *Democracy in America? What Has Gone Wrong and What We Can Do About It* (Chicago: University of Chicago Press, 2020); Jacob S. Hacker and Paul Pierson, *Winner-Take-All Politics: How Washington Made the Rich Richer—and Turned Its Back on the Middle Class* (New York: Simon & Schuster, 2010).

183 **"heed the Constitution"** Wendy Brown, "Alito's Dobbs Decision Will Further Degrade Democracy," *Washington Post,* June 27, 2022.

183 **"the people's authority"** Jonathan Weisman and Jazmine Ulloa, "Supreme Court Throws Abortion to an Unlevel State Playing Field," *New York Times,* June 25, 2022.

184 **a May 2022 Gallup poll** "Abortion," Gallup, 2022.

184 **According to the Pew Research Center** "Public Opinion on Abortion," Pew Research Center, 2022.

184 **The Women's Health Protection Act** Alexandra Hutzler, "House Passes Bills to Codify Roe, Protect Interstate Travel for Abortion," ABC News, July 15, 2022; "Bill to Protect Abortion Rights Fails to Pass Senate," *Axios,* May 11, 2022.

184 **Thirteen U.S. states** Elizabeth Nash and Lauren Cross, "26 States Are Certain or Likely to Ban Abortion Without Roe: Here's Which Ones and Why," Guttmacher Institute, Oct. 28, 2021.

184 **The political scientists** See Jacob Grumbach and Christopher Warshaw, "In Many States with Antiabortion Laws, Majorities Favor Abortion Rights," *Washington Post,* June 25, 2022.

184 **"This imbalance only runs one direction"** Ibid.

185 **Grumbach and Warshaw found** Jacob M. Grumbach, "The Supreme Court Just Rolled Democracy Back. You Can Measure How Much," *Politico,* June 30, 2022.

185 **The state's so-called heartbeat bill** Laura Hancock, "Federal Judge Allows Blocked 'Heartbeat Bill' to Take Effect, Banning Abortion Around Six Weeks in Ohio," Cleveland.com, June 24, 2022.

185 **According to a 2019 poll** Jane Mayer, "State Legislatures Are Torching Democracy," *New Yorker,* Aug. 6, 2022.

185 **"after [*Dobbs*]"** Grumbach, "Supreme Court Just Rolled Democracy Back."

185 **According to polling conducted** Eli Yokley, "After Texas Shooting, Republican and Independent Voters Drive Increase in Support for Gun Control," Morning Consult, May 26, 2022.

185 **Surveys by Gallup and Pew** Katherine Schaeffer, "Key Facts About Americans and Guns," Pew Research Center, Sept. 13, 2021; Frank Newport, "Analyzing Surveys on Banning Assault Weapons," Gallup, Nov. 14, 2019; "Guns," Gallup, 2022.

186 **the twenty states** Ronald Brownstein, "The Real Reason America Doesn't Have Gun Control," *Atlantic,* May 25, 2022.

186 **In the aftermath** Jentleson, *Kill Switch,* 18–19.

186 **The forty-five senators** Ibid., 19.

186   **The House passed** Gabby Birenbaum, "The House Just Passed
      Universal Background Checks for Gun Sales—Again," *Vox,*
      March 11, 2021.

186   **A Fox News poll** Mychael Schnell, "House Passes Bill to Ban As-
      sault Weapons," *Hill,* July 29, 2022.

186   **But because the bill's supporters** Brianna Herlihy, "Key GOP
      Senator Says Schumer's Assault Weapons Ban 'No Longer on the
      Table,'" Fox News, Dec. 7, 2022.

186   **In Ohio, 2018 polling** Shawn Salamone, "Baldwin Wallace CRI
      Poll Finds Broad Support for New Gun Laws in Ohio," Baldwin
      Wallace University, March 22, 2018.

187   **Instead of passing gun control legislation** Mayer, "State Legisla-
      tures Are Torching Democracy."

187   **"Few Americans want"** Jamelle Bouie, "It's Not Looking Too
      Good for Government of the People, by the People, and for the
      People," *New York Times,* May 27, 2022.

187   **America's counter-majoritarian institutions** Mads Andreas
      Elkjær and Torben Iversen, "The Democratic State and Redistribu-
      tion: Whose Interests Are Served?," *American Political Science Review*
      117, no. 2 (2022): 14.

187   **A federally mandated minimum wage** Larry M. Bartels, *Unequal
      Democracy: The Political Economy of the New Gilded Age* (New York:
      Russell Sage Foundation, 2008), 224.

187   **It increased steadily for three decades** Martha J. Bailey, John
      DiNardo, and Bryan A. Stuart, "The Economic Impact of a High
      National Minimum Wage: Evidence from the 1966 Fair Labor
      Standards Act," *Journal of Labor Economics* 39, no. S2 (2021): S330.

187   **During the 1960s and 1970s** Ralph E. Smith and Bruce
      Vavrichek, "The Minimum Wage: Its Relation to Incomes and Pov-
      erty," *Monthly Labor Review* (June 1987): 26–27.

187   **Between 1968 and 2006** Bartels, *Unequal Democracy,* 226.

188   **In 2020, workers earning** David Cooper, Elise Gould, and Ben
      Zipperer, "Low-Wage Workers Are Suffering from a Decline in the
      Real Value of the Federal Minimum Wage," *Economic Policy Institute,*
      Aug. 27, 2019, Figure A.

188   **Today, a three-person household** Scott A. Wolla, "Would In-

creasing the Minimum Wage Reduce Poverty?," *Page One Economics,*
March 2014.

188   **For decades, Americans** Bartels, *Unequal Democracy,* 230–31; also
Martin Gilens, *Affluence and Influence: Economic Inequality and Political
Power in America* (Princeton, N.J.: Princeton University Press,
2012), 114.

188   **In 2014, a bill** Wesley Lowery, "Senate Republicans Block Minimum Wage Increase Bill," *Washington Post,* April 30, 2014.

188   **The Congressional Budget Office** See Alexa Fernández Campbell, "The $15 Minimum Wage Bill Has All but Died in the Sen-
ate," *Vox,* Aug. 16, 2019.

188   **In a Hill-HarrisX poll** See "Poll: Majority of Voters Support $15
Minimum Wage," *The Hill,* Jan. 24, 2019.

188   **According to a Pew survey** Amina Dunn, "Most Americans Support a $15 Federal Minimum Wage," *Pew Research Center,* April 22,
2021.

188   **A CBS News poll** Jennifer De Pinto. "Most Americans Favor a
Higher Federal Minimum Wage—CBS News Poll," CBS News,
Sept. 5, 2021.

189   **it was clear that** Emily Cochrane, "Top Senate Official Disqualifies
Minimum Wage from Stimulus Plan," *New York Times,* Feb. 25,
2021.

189   **The failure to deal** See Matthew Desmond, *Poverty, by America*
(New York: Crown, 2023); David Brady, *Rich Democracies, Poor People: How Politics Explains Poverty* (Oxford, U.K.: Oxford University
Press, 2009); Jacob Hacker et al., eds., *The American Political Economy: Politics, Markets, and Power* (Cambridge, U.K.: Cambridge University Press, 2021).

189   **Only the United States** Lane Kenworthy and Jonas Pontusson,
"Rising Inequality and the Politics of Redistribution in Affluent
Countries," *Perspectives on Politics* 3, no. 3 (2005): 449–71.

189   **Scholars have linked** For an overview, see Sheri Berman, "The
Causes of Populism in the West," *Annual Review of Political Science* 24 (2021): 71–88.

189   **Counter-majoritarian institutions are not** Gilens, *Affluence and
Influence;* Brady, *Rich Democracies;* Hacker and Pierson, *Winner-*

Take-All Politics; Jonas Pontusson, "Unionization, Inequality and Redistribution," *British Journal of Industrial Relations* 51, no. 4 (2013): 797–825.

189 **There is a risk today** Starr, *Entrenchment.*

190 **A day after the January 6** Jonathan Martin, "In Capital, a G.O.P. Crisis. At the R.N.C. Meeting, a Trump Celebration," *New York Times,* Jan. 8, 2021.

191 **"operating in a parallel universe"** Ibid.

191 **As Trump headed** Ibid.

191 **In her speech** Ibid.

191 **"You don't have to throw out"** Ibid.

192 **"especially thank President Trump"** Brittany Bernstein, "Kevin McCarthy Thanks Trump After Speakership Win: 'I Don't Think Anybody Should Doubt His Influence,'" *National Review,* Jan. 7, 2023.

192 **Representatives Marjorie Taylor Greene** Leigh Ann Caldwell and Amy B. Wang, "Greene, Gosar Lost Committee Seats over Comments. Now, They're Back," *Washington Post,* Jan. 17, 2023.

193 **"collision of adverse opinions"** John Stuart Mill, *On Liberty* (Boston: Ticknor and Fields, 1863), 102.

193 **"if a faction consists"** Hamilton, Madison, and Jay, *The Federalist,* 43.

194 **In politics, power begets power** Paul Pierson, "Power and Path Dependence," in *Advances in Comparative-Historical Analysis,* ed. James Mahoney and Kathleen Thelen (New York: Cambridge University Press, 2015), 124–46.

195 **Wisconsin's egregiously drawn election maps** Bridgit Bowden and Shawn Johnson, "Wisconsin Republicans' Map Still Stands, but a Supreme Court Case Could Have Changed Everything," Wisconsin Public Radio, Oct. 20, 2021.

195 **"Partisan gerrymandering claims"** Laurel White, "US Supreme Court Ruling Effectively Ends Wisconsin Gerrymandering Challenge," Wisconsin Public Radio, June 27, 2019.

195 **Traditionally, this clause** Ethan Herenstein and Thomas Wolf, "The 'Independent State Legislature Theory,' Explained," Brennan Center for Justice, June 6, 2022.

196 **"virtually unlimited powers"** Hasen, "Identifying and Minimizing the Risk of Election Subversion and Stolen Elections in the Contemporary United States," 287; J. Michael Luttig, "Opinion: The Republican Blueprint to Steal the 2024 Election," CNN, April 27, 2022.

196 **But variants of it** Luttig, "Republican Blueprint to Steal the 2024 Election"; Hasen, "Identifying and Minimizing the Risk of Election Subversion and Stolen Elections in the Contemporary United States," 286.

197 **Many Western societies** See Cas Mudde, *The Far Right Today* (New York: Polity Press, 2019).

CHAPTER 7: AMERICA THE OUTLIER

198 **Norway had been part of Denmark** Håvard Friis Nilsen, "Republican Monarchy: The Neo-Roman Concept of Liberty and the Norwegian Constitution of 1814," *Modern Intellectual History* 16, no. 1 (2019): 29–56.

198 **"like a herd of cattle"** Ruth Hemstad, *"Like a Herd of Cattle": Parliamentary and Public Debates Regarding the Cession of Norway, 1813–1814* (Oslo: Akademisk Publisering, 2014).

199 **Inspired by the ideals** Nilsen, "Republican Monarchy."

199 **The Norwegian press** Ola Mestad, "The Impact of the US Constitution on the Norwegian Constitution and on Emigration to America," in *Norwegian-American Essays 2017,* ed. Terje Mikael Hasle Joranger (Oslo: Novus Press, 2017).

199 **it described the American president** Ibid., 3.

199 **many of the men gathered** Nilsen, "Republican Monarchy," 39.

199 **Christian Magnus Falsen** George Athan Billias, *American Constitutionalism Heard Around the World, 1776–1989* (New York: New York University Press, 2009), 144.

199 **"nearly exclusively"** Mestad, "The Impact of the U.S. Constitution on the Norwegian Constitution and on Emigration to America," 36.

199 **After the constitution was approved** Nilsen, "Republican Monarchy."

200 **Norway remained a hereditary monarchy** Tom Ginsburg and James Melton, "Norway's Enduring Constitution: Implications for Countries in Transition" (Stockholm: International IDEA, 2014).

200 **Members of parliament** Bernt Aardal, "Electoral Systems in Norway," in *The Evolution of Electoral and Party Systems in the Nordic Countries,* ed. Bernard Grofman and Arend Lijphart (New York: Agathon Press, 2002), 174.

200 **Norway was overwhelmingly rural in 1814** Ibid., 178.

200 **"potential time bomb"** Ibid., 175.

200 **So the constitution established** Ibid., 178.

200 **Majority rule was further diluted** Eivind Smith, "The Rise and Fall of the Quasi-bicameral System of Norway (1814–2007)," in *Reforming Senates: Upper Legislative Houses in North Atlantic Small Powers, 1800–Present,* ed. Nikolaj Bijleveld et al. (London: Routledge, 2021).

200 **"Evangelical-Lutheran religion"** "Norway's Constitution of 1814 with Amendments Through 2004," *Comparative Constitutions Project.*

200 **Parliamentary sovereignty was established** Ginsburg and Melton, "Norway's Enduring Constitution," 13–14.

201 **Unlike in the United States** Aardal, "Electoral Systems in Norway," 193.

201 **Norway took additional steps** Smith, "Rise and Fall of the Quasi-bicameral System of Norway."

201 **Indigenous minorities** Ginsburg and Melton, "Norway's Enduring Constitution," 9.

201 **In the late 1970s** Oystein Steinlien, "The Sami Law: A Change of Norwegian Government Policy Toward the Sami Minority?," *Canadian Journal of Native Studies* 9, no. 1 (1989): 1–14.

201 **In 1981, fourteen Sami women** Rauna Kuokkanen, *Restructuring Relations: Indigenous Self-Determination, Governance, and Gender* (Oxford: Oxford University Press, 2019), 80.

202 **A 1988 constitutional amendment** Ginsburg and Melton, "Norway's Enduring Constitution," 9.

202 **A 1992 constitutional amendment** Ibid.

202   **"all religious and philosophical communities"** "Norway's Constitution of 1814 with Amendments Through 2004."

202   **And in 2014** Anine Kierulf, "Norway: Human Rights and Judicial
Review Constitutionalized," *Blog of the International Journal of Constitutional Law,* June 15, 2015.

202   **In total, Norway's constitution was amended** Ginsburg and
Melton, "Norway's Enduring Constitution," 7.

203   **And in Latin America** José A. Cheibub, Fernando Limongi, and
Adam Przeworski, "Electing Presidents: A Hidden Facet of Democratization," SSRN Electronic Journal, 2022.

203   **Most nineteenth-century European political systems** J.A.R.
Marriott, *Second Chambers: An Inductive Study in Political Science* (Oxford: Clarendon Press, 1910), 1, 240.

204   **"tyranny of the minority of one"** Richard Albert, "The Modern
Liberum Veto," *Blog of the International Journal of Constitutional Law,*
Feb. 21, 2013.

204   **Between 1720 and 1764** Nicholas·C. Wheeler, "The Noble Enterprise of State Building: Reconsidering the Rise and Fall of the
Modern State in Prussia and Poland," *Comparative Politics* 44, no. 1
(2011): 31.

204   **"poison" of "giv[ing] a minority"** Hamilton, "Federalist
No. 22," 101–2.

204   **"parliamentary obstruction"** Georg Jellinek, "Parliamentary Obstruction," *Political Science Quarterly* 19, no. 4 (1904): 579.

205   **Indirect elections also disappeared** See Cheibub, Limongi, and
Przeworski, "Electing Presidents."

205   **By the late nineteenth century** Daniele Caramani, *The Societies of
Europe* (London: Macmillan, 2000), 58; France's Senate, the less
prominent of France's two parliamentary bodies, continues to be
elected indirectly via electoral panels.

205   **France experimented** Julian Jackson, *De Gaulle* (Cambridge,
Mass.: Harvard University Press, 2018), 505.

205   **Electoral colleges gradually disappeared** Cheibub, Limongi, and
Przeworski, "Electing Presidents," 6.

206   **Beginning in Belgium in 1899** This description draws on Starr,

Entrenchment, 109. See Jonathan Rodden, "Why Did Western Europe Adopt Proportional Representation? A Political Geography Explanation" (unpublished manuscript, 2010), Stanford University; Patrick Emmenegger and André Walter, "Disproportional Threat: Redistricting as an Alternative to Proportional Representation," *Journal of Politics* 83, no. 3 (2021): 917–33; Lucas Leemann and Isabela Mares, "The Adoption of Proportional Representation," *Journal of Politics* 76, no. 2 (2014): 461–78.

206 **Under these new rules** Arend Lijphart, *Thinking About Democracy: Power Sharing and Majority Rule in Theory and Practice* (London: Routledge, 2008), 125–37.

206 **By World War II** Starr, *Entrenchment,* 109.

206 **Britain suffered a political earthquake** Electoral numbers from F.W.S. Craig, *Electoral Facts: 1885–1975* (London: Macmillan, 1976), 32.

207 **By convention, the House of Lords** Ziblatt, *Conservative Parties and the Birth of Democracy,* 146; Iain McLean, *What's Wrong with the British Constitution?* (Oxford: Oxford University Press, 2010), 9.

207 **"watchdog of the constitution"** Corinne Comstock Weston, *The House of Lords and Ideological Politics: Lord Salisbury's Referendal Theory and the Conservative Party, 1846–1922* (Philadelphia: American Philosophical Society, 1995).

207 **"not a watchdog"** Roy Jenkins, *Mr. Balfour's Poodle: An Account of the Struggle Between the House of Lords and the Government of Mr. Asquith* (London: Heinemann, 1954).

207 **"five hundred ordinary men"** Iain McLean and Jennifer Nou, "Why Should We Be Beggars with the Ballot in Our Hand? Veto Players and the Failure of Land Value Taxation in the United Kingdom, 1909–14," *British Journal of Political Science* 36, no. 4 (2006): 583.

207 **Facing a constitutional crisis** Ziblatt, *Conservative Parties and the Birth of Democracy,* 147.

207 **"measures inflicting irreparable injury"** *The Parliamentary Debates* (Official Report), House of Lords, July 4, 1911, 101.

208 **One of Britain's most powerful** The next big reform came nearly a century later under the government of Prime Minister Tony Blair.

On this later reform, see Meg Russell, *The Contemporary House of Lords: Westminster Bicameralism Revived* (Oxford: Oxford University Press, 2013), 34.

208 **Several other emerging democracies** Louis Massicotte, "Legislative Unicameralism: A Global Survey and a Few Case Studies," *Journal of Legislative Studies* 7, no. 1 (2002): 151.

209 **In August 1948** Peter Bucher, ed., *Der Verfassungskonvent auf Herrenchiemsee* (Boppard: Boldt, 1981).

209 **One of the constitutional designers'** On the origins of the Bundesrat in imperial Germany, see Daniel Ziblatt, *Structuring the State: The Formation of Italy and Germany and the Puzzle of Federalism* (Princeton, N.J.: Princeton University Press, 2006), 137.

209 **When party leaders gathered** Michael F. Feldkamp, *Der Parlamentarische Rat 1948–1949: Die Entstehung des Grundgesetzes* (Göttingen: Vandenhoeck & Ruprecht, 2019).

209 **Despite the outsized role** Ibid., 80–81.

210 **The term "cloture" originated** Jon C. Morgan, "Cloture: Its Inception and Usage in the Alabama Senate," *Journal of the American Society of Legislative Clerks and Secretaries* 17, no. 1 (2011): 15–34.

210 **In Canada, opposition minorities in Parliament** Robert Laird Borden, *Robert Laird Borden, His Memoirs* (Toronto: McClelland and Stewart, 1969), 195.

210 **"the most strenuous and remarkable"** Ibid., 194–95.

211 **For much of the twentieth century** Mikko Mattila, "From Qualified Majority to Simple Majority: The Effects of the 1992 Change in the Finnish Constitution," *Scandinavian Political Studies* 20, no. 4 (1997): 332.

211 **Denmark still has a rule** Matt Qvortrup, *A Comparative Study of Referendums: Government by the People,* 2nd ed. (Manchester: Manchester University Press, 2005), 123.

211 **"deeply rooted in the Icelandic"** Helgi Bernódusson, "Filibustering in the Althingi," Communication from the General Secretary of the Althingi, Association of Secretaries-General of Parliaments, March 2016.

211 **"regarded as an honor"** Ibid.

211 **"freedom of speech"** Ibid.

211 **"There are no indications at present"** Ibid.

211 **Three years later** Gréta Sigríður Einarsdóttir, "Parliament Operations Changed to Eliminate Filibusters," *Iceland Review,* Sept. 11,
2019.

212 **One recent study** Taylor et al., *Different Democracy,* 296–97.

212 **For example, Canada adopted** James G. Snell and Frederick
Vaughan, *The Supreme Court of Canada: History of the Institution* (Toronto: Osgoode Society, 1985), 126.

212 **Similarly, Australia established a retirement age** Michael Kirby,
"Sir Edward McTiernan: A Centenary Reflection," *Federal Law Review* 20, no. 2 (1991): 180.

212 **In an apparent effort** Ibid.

212 **"virtually non-existent"** George Williams and David Hume, *People Power: The History and Future of the Referendum in Australia* (Syd-
ney: University of New South Wales Press, 2010), 158.

213 **"contemporize the courts"** Alysia Blackham, "Judges and Retirement Ages," *Melbourne University Law Review* 39 (2016): 752–53.
See John F. Kowal and Wilfred U. Codrington III, *The People's Constitution: 200 Years, 27 Amendments, and the Promise of a More Perfect
Union* (New York: New Press, 2021).

214 **"an American House of Lords"** Elaine K. Smith, "The Making
of an American House of Lords: The U.S. Senate in the Constitutional Convention of 1787," *Studies in American Political Development* 7, no. 2 (Fall 1993): 177–224; Kowal and Codrington, *People's
Constitution,* 135–40.

214 **For example, Alabama's** Wegman, *Let the People Pick the President,*
132.

214 **The result was massive rural overrepresentation** See Ansolabehere and Snyder, *End of Inequality.*

214 **In 1960, rural counties** Ibid., 70.

214 **In state legislative** Ibid., 32.

214 **In 1956, when the Virginia** Wegman, *Let the People Pick the President,* 132.

214 **This rural bias tipped** Ansolabehere and Snyder, *End of Inequality,*
80, 30–31.

215 **"immediate, complete, and stunning"** Ibid., 9.

215 **Almost overnight, artificial rural majorities** Ibid., 188. See Kowal and Codrington, *People's Constitution,* 183–215.

215 **There were hundreds of attempts** Keyssar, *Why Do We Still Have an Electoral College?;* Wegman, *Let the People Pick the President,* 20.

216 **And as in Canada** Binder and Smith, *Politics or Principle?,* 79; Jentleson, *Kill Switch,* 64–65.

216 **"sixty-vote Senate"** Koger, *Filibustering,* 5.

217 **"elected against the majority"** Cheibub, Limongi, and Przeworski, "Electing Presidents," 23.

217 **"equal representation of unequal states"** Taylor et al., *Different Democracy,* 99–114.

217 **Most important, it is the world's** Ibid., 225.

217 **Among democracies, the U.S. Constitution** Ibid., 79–80; Lutz, "Toward a Theory of Constitutional Amendment," 355–70.

218 **"update the formal text"** Ginsburg and Melton, "Norway's Enduring Constitution," 16–17.

218 **As noted earlier** Lutz, "Toward a Theory of Constitutional Amendment," 369.

218 **Among the thirty-one democracies** Ibid.

218 **For this reason, the United States** Ibid.

218 **there have been 11,848 attempts** "Measures Proposed to Amend the Constitution," U.S. Senate, 2023.

219 **By one count** Wegman, *Let the People Pick the President,* 20.

219 **"game of Russian roulette"** Keyssar, *Why Do We Still Have the Electoral College?,* 207.

219 **"a graveyard"** Wegman, *Let the People Pick the President,* 129.

219 **Bayh was initially skeptical** Ibid., 144–45.

220 **A 1966 Gallup poll** Keyssar, *Why Do We Still Have the Electoral College?,* 211.

220 **That year, the U.S. Chamber** Wegman, *Let the People Pick the President,* 147.

220 **"archaic, undemocratic, complex, ambiguous, indirect"** Ibid., 148.

220 **Bayh's reform proposal** Keyssar, *Why Do We Still Have the Electoral College?,* 216–7.

220   **"seemed unstoppable"** Wegman, *Let the People Pick the President*, 152.

220   **The newly elected president** Keyssar, *Why Do We Still Have the Electoral College?*, 214–28, 240–41; Wegman, *Let the People Pick the President*, 150–52.

220   **"It has become a condition"** Quoted in Keyssar, *Why Do We Still Have the Electoral College?*, 217.

221   **As the proposal moved** Ibid., 227.

221   **A *New York Times* survey** Wegman, *Let the People Pick the President*, 154.

221   **But like so many times** Keyssar, *Why Do We Still Have the Electoral College?*, 246–60.

221   **"The Electoral College"** Quoted in ibid., 259.

221   **"slow-walked it through the Judiciary Committee"** Wegman, *Let the People Pick the President*, 155–59.

221   **When a cloture vote** Quoted in Keyssar, *Why Do We Still Have the Electoral College?*, 244–45.

221   **When a second cloture vote** Quoted in ibid., 248–49.

221   **He reintroduced his Electoral College** Wegman, *Let the People Pick the President*, 160.

221   **In 1977, following yet another** Keyssar, *Why Do We Still Have the Electoral College?*, 267–70.

222   **When a cloture vote** Ibid., 298–302.

222   **"conceded privately"** Quoted in ibid., 307.

222   **Another serious but ultimately unsuccessful** On the failure of the ERA, see Jane Mansbridge, *Why We Lost the ERA* (Chicago: University of Chicago Press, 1986); Julie Suk, *We the Women: The Unstoppable Mothers of the Equal Rights Amendment* (New York: Simon & Schuster, 2020).

222   **It was introduced into Congress** Mansbridge, *Why We Lost the ERA*, 9–10.

222   **In October 1971** Ibid., 10–12.

222   **Hawaii ratified the ERA** Ibid.

222   **Presidents Nixon, Ford, and Carter** Mark R. Daniels, Robert Darcy, and Joseph W. Westphal, "The ERA Won—at Least in the Opinion Polls," *PS* 15, no. 4 (Autumn 1982): 578.

223 **A 1974 Gallup poll** Ibid., 579.

223 **Four decades later** "Three in Four Americans Support Equal Rights Amendment, Poll Shows," *Guardian,* Feb. 24, 2020. On the current status of the ERA, see Suk, *We the Women.*

CHAPTER 8: DEMOCRATIZING OUR DEMOCRACY

224 **"The institutions of the United States"** James Bryce, *The American Commonwealth* (1888; New York: Macmillan, 1896), 1:1.

226 **In Finland in the early 1930s** Giovanni Capoccia, *Defending Democracy: Reactions to Extremism in Interwar Europe* (Baltimore: Johns Hopkins University Press, 2005), 138–78.

226 **In Belgium** Ibid., 108–37.

227 **In Pennsylvania, an alliance** Campbell Robertson, "Surprise in Pennsylvania: Republicans Back a (Former?) Democrat for Speaker," *New York Times,* Jan. 4, 2023.

227 **in Ohio, they elected a mainstream** Morgan Trau, "Statehouse 'Coup'—Ohio GOP Bitterly Divided by Deal with Democrats to Elect House Speaker," *Ohio Capital Journal,* Jan. 9, 2023.

227 **"grand coalitions"** David Fortunato, *The Cycle of Coalition* (Cambridge, U.K.: Cambridge University Press, 2021).

227 **Excessive mainstream party cooperation** Wolfgang Münchau, "Europe's Grand Coalitions Allow Extremes to Prosper," *Financial Times,* May 1, 2016.

227 **A second strategy** This strategy (*wehrhafte Demokratie*) was originally translated as "militant democracy." See Karl Loewenstein, "Militant Democracy and Fundamental Rights, II," *American Political Science Review* 31, no. 4 (1937): 638–58.

228 **Haunted by the experience** In the German constitution, along with other provisions (art. 18), see especially art. 21 (2).

228 **The model has spread** Jan-Werner Müller, "Militant Democracy," in *The Oxford Handbook of Comparative Constitutional Law,* ed. Michel Rosenfeld and András Sajó (Oxford: Oxford University Press, 2012), 1119.

228 **Militant democracy may at first glance seem at odds** Tom Ginsburg, Aziz Z. Huq, and David Landau, "The Law of Democratic Disqualification," *California Law Review* 111 (2023).

228 **A 2021 Pew survey** "Large Majority of the Public Views Prosecution of Capitol Rioters as 'Very Important,'" Pew Research Center, March 18, 2021.

229 **Ideas of militant democracy** Udi Greenberg, *The Weimar Century* (Princeton, N.J.: Princeton University Press, 2015).

230 **"The cure for the ills"** Jane Addams, *Democracy and Social Ethics* (London: Macmillan, 1905), 11–12.

230 **consider three broad areas of reform** The following institutional proposals are broadly similar to others' recommendations. See in particular Page and Gilens, *Democracy in America?*, 210–35; Levinson, *Our Undemocratic Constitution*, 167–80.

231 **In the United States** For an excellent discussion of this problem, see Guy-Uriel E. Charles and Luis E. Fuentes-Rohwer, *Divided by Race: Voting Rights, Political Power, and Saving American Democracy* (New York: Cambridge University Press, forthcoming). H.R. 4959, which was introduced in the House of Representatives in 2021 (but did not pass), was designed to establish a statutory right to vote. See "H.R. 4959—117th Congress 2021–2022: Right to Vote Act," U.S. Congress, 2022.

232 **Even today** See Jennifer S. Rosenberg, "Expanding Democracy: Voter Registration Around the World," with Margaret Chen, Brennan Center for Justice (2009), 2.

232 **Pass a constitutional amendment** See Charles and Fuentes-Rohwer, *Divided by Race*.

233 **"giv[e] the powers of government"** John Stuart Mill, *On Liberty and Other Essays* (Oxford: Oxford University Press, 1998), 304.

234 **Replace "first-past-the-post"** See Grant Tudor and Beau Tremitiere, "Towards Proportional Representation for the U.S. House: Amending the Uniform Congressional Districts Act," Protect Democracy, Feb. 2023.

234 **By ensuring that the distribution of seats** It should be noted that proportional representation systems often give rise to more parties, and some scholars have argued that the combination of presidential and multiparty systems can be destabilizing. In recent years, however, countries like Brazil, Chile, Costa Rica, and Uruguay have shown that multiparty presidentialism can work. See Scott Main-

waring, "Presidentialism, Multipartism, and Democracy: The Difficult Combination," *Comparative Political Studies* 26, no. 2 (July 1993): 198–228.

234 **"treats all voters equally"** Lee Drutman, *Breaking the Two-Party Doom Loop: The Case for Multiparty Democracy in America* (New York: Oxford University Press, 2020), 246.

234 **At present, the ratio of voters** Lee Drutman et al., *The Case for Enlarging the House of Representatives* (Cambridge, Mass.: American Academy of Arts and Sciences, 2021), 26; see also Danielle Allen, "The House Was Supposed to Grow with Population. It Didn't. Let's Fix That.," *Washington Post*, Feb. 28, 2023.

238 **In 2020, the prestigious** *Our Common Purpose: Reinventing American Democracy for the 21st Century* (Cambridge, Mass.: American Academy of Arts and Sciences, 2020).

238 **Organizations such as the Brennan Center** On the Center for American Progress, see "Democracy Policy," Center for American Progress, n.d. On Protect Democracy's proposals, see "Shaping the Democracy of Tomorrow," Protect Democracy, n.d.

238 **And in 2021, the White House** "Presidential Commission on the Supreme Court of the United States," White House, 2021.

238 **Talk and ideas aren't empty** See Daniel Carpenter, "Agenda Democracy," *Annual Review of Political Science* 26 (2023).

239 **"If you go back and look"** Harry Kreisler, "Conversation with Sir Ralf Dahrendorf," Institute of International Studies, UC Berkeley, n.d.

239 **Democratic reform will remain impossible** For one important example of the effort to broaden the historical imagination vis-à-vis constitutional change in America, see Jill Lepore's NEH-funded Amend Project.

239 **"almost religious devotion"** Aziz Rana, "Why Americans Worship the Constitution," *Public Seminar,* Oct. 11, 2021; Aziz Rana, *The Constitutional Bind: Why a Broken Document Rules America* (Chicago: University of Chicago Press, 2023).

240 **"basically perfect"** Levinson, *Our Undemocratic Constitution,* 20.

240 **"The framers adopted life tenure"** John G. Roberts, "Memorandum for Fred F. Fielding," White House, Oct. 3, 1983.

241   **The idea that certain institutions** Douglass C. North, *Institutions, Institutional Change, and Economic Performance* (New York: Cambridge University Press, 1990); Paul Pierson and Eric Schickler, "Polarization and the Fragility of the American Democratic Order" (unpublished manuscript, 2023).

241   **"The warmest friends and best supporters"** George Washington to Bushrod Washington, Nov. 10, 1787.

242   **"look at constitutions with sanctimonious reverence"** Quoted in Elkins, Ginsburg, and Melton, *Endurance of National Constitutions,* 1.

242   **"laws and institutions"** Quoted in ibid., 16.

242   **That figure has increased dramatically** Yascha Mounk and Roberto Stefan Foa, "This Is How Democracy Dies," *Atlantic,* Jan. 29, 2020.

242   **According to the Pew Research Center** Katherine Schaeffer, "On July Fourth, How Americans See Their Country and Their Democracy," Pew Research Center, June 30, 2022. See Kowal and Codrington, *People's Constitution.*

244   **in fact, Wilson opposed women's suffrage** Christine A. Lunardini and Thomas J. Knock, "Woodrow Wilson and Woman Suffrage: A New Look," *Political Science Quarterly* 95, no. 4 (1980): 655–71.

245   **In the 1930s** Schickler, *Racial Realignment.*

245   *The CIO News* Ibid., 59.

245   **"Never before had the proponents"** Harvard Sitkoff, *A New Deal for Blacks: The Emergence of Civil Rights as a National Issue* (1978; New York: Oxford University Press, 2009), 187, cited by Schickler, *Racial Realignment,* 59.

245   **Meaningful change is usually driven** Another account that emphasizes the importance of social movements for constitutional change is Page and Gilens, *Democracy in America?,* 239–63.

245   **In the case of the civil** Thomas J. Sugrue, *Sweet Land of Liberty: The Forgotten Struggle for Civil Rights in the North* (New York: Random House, 2008).

246   **Wilson "converted" to the cause** Lunardini and Knock, "Woodrow Wilson and Woman Suffrage," 660.

247 **"To the unimaginative man"** See Dawn Langan Teele, *Forging the Franchise: The Political Origins of the Women's Vote* (Princeton, N.J.: Princeton University Press, 2018), 100–1. For the fuller quotation, see Carrie Chapman Catt and Nettie Rogers Shuler, *Woman Suffrage and Politics: The Inner Story of the Suffrage Movement* (New York: Scribner's Sons, 1923), 3.

247 **"To get the word male"** Catt and Shuler, *Woman Suffrage and Politics,* 107–8.

247 **The women's suffrage movement** For broad context, see Corrine M. McConnaughy, *The Woman Suffrage Movement in America: A Reassessment* (Cambridge, U.K.: Cambridge University Press, 2013), 170–71.

248 **Leaders like Elizabeth Cady Stanton** Lisa Tetrault, *The Myth of Seneca Falls: Memory and the Women's Suffrage Movement, 1848–1898* (Chapel Hill: University of North Carolina Press, 2014), 16.

248 **Their influential multivolume** Ibid.

248 **But beginning around 1900** Suzanne M. Marilley, *Woman Suffrage and the Origins of Liberal Feminism in the United States, 1820–1920* (Cambridge, Mass.: Harvard University Press, 2013), 188–89.

248 **"willingness to tailor the suffrage message"** JoEllen Lind, "Dominance and Democracy: The Legacy of Woman Suffrage for the Voting Right," *U.C.L.A. Women's Law Journal* 5 (1994): 188–89.

248 **Following the merger** Teele, *Forging the Franchise,* 102–3; data from Lee Ann Banaszak, *Why Movements Succeed or Fail: Opportunity, Culture, and the Struggle for Woman Suffrage* (Princeton, N.J.: Princeton University Press, 1996), 45.

248 **Borrowing strategies used by** Marilley, *Woman Suffrage and the Origins of Liberal Feminism in the United States,* 189.

249 **The Seventeenth Amendment** See Kowal and Codrington, *People's Constitution,* 135–40.

249 **The campaign for direct elections** Herman Vandenburg Ames, *The Proposed Amendments to the Constitution of the United States During the First Century of Its History* (Washington, D.C.: U.S. Government Printing Office, 1897), 2:61.

249 **The House of Representatives** Kowal and Codrington, *People's Constitution,* 137.

249 **In 1906, William Randolph Hearst** James Landers, *The Improbable
First Century of "Cosmopolitan" Magazine* (Columbia: University of
Missouri Press, 2010), 131–46; Kowal and Codrington, *People's
Constitution,* 135–36.

249 **By 1912** Kowal and Codrington, *People's Constitution,* 137.

249 **Finally, in 1913** "Landmark Legislation: The Seventeenth Amendment to the Constitution," U.S. Senate, n.d.

250 **The May 2020 police killing** Larry Buchanan, Quoctrung Bui,
and Jugal K. Patel, "Black Lives Matter May Be the Largest Movement in U.S. History," *New York Times,* July 3, 2020.

250 **Between fifteen million and twenty-six million** Ibid.

250 **There were at least 5,000 protests** Ibid.; Lara Putnam, Jeremy
Pressman, and Erica Chenoweth, "Black Lives Matter Beyond
America's Big Cities," *Washington Post,* July 8, 2020.

250 **The protests reached every U.S. state** Putnam, Pressman, and
Chenoweth, "Black Lives Matter Beyond America's Big Cities."

250 **They were led overwhelmingly** Christopher Sebastian Parker,
"An American Paradox: Progress or Regress? BLM, Race, and
Black Politics," *Perspectives on Politics* 20, no. 4 (Dec. 2022): 1167.

250 **And unlike the 1960s** Ibid.

250 **Nearly three-quarters** Scott Clement and Dan Balz, "Big Majorities Support Protests over Floyd Killing and Say Police Need to
Change, Poll Finds," *Washington Post,* June 9, 2020.

250 **Although this support subsequently waned** Juliana Menasce
Horowitz, "Support for Black Lives Matter Declined After George
Floyd Protests, but Has Remained Unchanged Since," Pew Re-
search Center, Sept. 27, 2021.

250 **The Trump presidency spawned** David S. Meyer and Sidney Tar-
row, eds., *The Resistance: The Dawn of the Anti-Trump Opposition
Movement* (New York: Oxford University Press, 2018); Skocpol and
Tervo, *Upending American Politics.*

251 **Dozens of new national organizations** These include the Center
for Secure and Modern Elections, American Oversight, the Institute
for Constitutional Advocacy and Protection, Voting Rights Lab,
Protect Democracy, Unite America, Renew Democracy Initiative,
Democracy Forward, States United Democracy Center, Keep Our

Republic, Election Reformers Network, Democracy Docket, We
the Action, Stand Up Republic, and Stand Up America.

251 **"prevent our democracy from declining"** "Our Democracy Is in
Danger," Protect Democracy, n.d.

251 **Protect Democracy filed lawsuits** Ian Bassin (executive director,
Protect Democracy), interview with authors, Jan. 3, 2023.

251 **"I didn't know what voting was"** Leah Asmelash, "Why This Bus
Tours the South to Get Disenfranchised Voters to the Polls," CNN,
Nov. 2, 2020.

251 **In 2016, Brown and Cliff Albright** Andrea González-Ramírez,
"LaTosha Brown Is Only Getting Started," Medium, Dec. 4, 2020.

251 **The group organized bus caravans** Asmelash, "Why This Bus
Tours the South to Get Disenfranchised Voters to the Polls."

252 **The 2020 "We Got Power" tour** Epstein, "LaTosha Brown Says a
New South Is Rising."

252 **According to a 2022 survey** "Harvard Youth Poll," Harvard Kennedy School Institute of Politics, Oct. 27, 2022.

252 **Similarly, Pew surveys found that two-thirds** Horowitz, "Support for Black Lives Matter Declined After George Floyd Protests,
but Has Remained Unchanged Since."

252 **Younger Americans** "Shifting Public Views on Legal Immigration
into the U.S.," Pew Research Center, June 28, 2018; Horowitz,
"Americans See Advantages and Challenges in Country's Growing
Racial and Ethnic Diversity."

252 **Only 39 percent of voters** Jen McAndrew and Robin Smyton,
"Half of Young People Voted in 2020, Major Increase from 2016,"
Tufts Now, April 29, 2021.

252 **More than two million people** Ryan Sit, "More Than 2 Million
in 90 Percent of Voting Districts Joined March for Our Lives Protests," *Newsweek,* March 26, 2018.

252 **Although the March for Our Lives** John Della Volpe, *Fight: How
Gen Z Is Channeling Their Fear and Passion to Save America* (New
York: St. Martin's Press, 2021).

253 **Santiago Mayer** "Learn More About Us," Voters of Tomorrow, n.d.

253 **During the 2020 election cycle** Kayla Steinberg, "Prom at the

Polls Encourages Younger Voters to Dress Up and Show Up," *Pittsburgh Jewish Chronicle,* Nov. 3, 2020.

253   **Sharlee Mullins Glenn** Sharlee Mullins Glenn, "Why I Became an Activist Against Fear," *New York Times,* Feb. 19, 2020.

253   **Her community was deeply conservative** Ibid.

253   **"concerned . . . when a man"** Ibid.

253   **By 2018, the group had six thousand** Jenna Alton, "Mormon Women Worldwide Lobby for Ethical Government," *Daily Universe,* April 17, 2018.

253   **The group registered** Audrey Dutton, "They're Women. They're LDS. And They're Speaking Their Minds on Politics," *Idaho Press,* Oct. 2, 2022; Bryan Schott, "State Lawyers Ask Utah Supreme Court to Step In After Judge Declines to Dismiss Gerrymandering Lawsuit," *Salt Lake Tribune,* Nov. 26, 2022; Wendy Dennehy and Erin Young, "Is the Filibuster the Best Tool to Protect Against Extremes? No. Do These Things Instead," *Salt Lake Tribune,* Nov. 8, 2021.

254   **"loud advocates against extremism"** Dutton, "They're Women."

254   **"We believe that Jesus"** Glenn, "Why I Became an Activist Against Fear."

254   **Although MWEG members hold conservative views** Dutton, "They're Women."

254   **"Rabbi Nachman once said"** Der Bundespräsident, "75th Anniversary of the End of the 2nd World War," May 8, 2020.

257   **"After our Constitution got fairly"** James Russell Lowell, *Literary and Political Addresses* (Boston: Houghton, Mifflin and Company, 1890), 207.

INDEX

ABOUT THE AUTHORS

STEVEN LEVITSKY and DANIEL ZIBLATT are professors of government at Harvard University and the authors of the *New York Times* bestseller *How Democracies Die,* which won the Goldsmith Book Prize, was shortlisted for the Lionel Gelber Prize, and was named one of the best books of the year by *The Washington Post, Time,* and *Foreign Affairs.*

ABOUT THE TYPE

This book was set in Bembo, a typeface based on an old-style Roman face that was used for Cardinal Pietro Bembo's tract *De Aetna* in 1495. Bembo was cut by Francesco Griffo (1450–1518) in the early sixteenth century for Italian Renaissance printer and publisher Aldus Manutius (1449–1515). The Lanston Monotype Company of Philadelphia brought the well-proportioned letterforms of Bembo to the United States in the 1930s.